CW00549128

Fiona Gallagher

with Robert Armitage, Robert Hastings and Rawdon W

ELEMENTARY

S I M P L Y
E N G L I S H
Edinburgh

Total English

Teacher's Resource Book

CAPITAL SCHOOL OF ENGLISH
EDINBURGH

Longman

Contents

Syllabus outline

	UNIT	LESSON 1	LESSON 2	LESSON 3	COMMUNICATION
1	**Your life** page 5	**Grammar:** subject pronouns + positive forms of *to be* **Vocabulary:** countries and nationalities **Can do:** talk about where you are from **Skills:** **pronunciation:** stressed syllables in nationality words	**Grammar:** possessive 's; possessive adjectives; *yes/no* questions with *to be* **Vocabulary:** families **Can do:** exchange information about your family **Skills:** **pronunciation:** /ʌ/ **listening:** listen to a dialogue about a photograph	**Grammar:** *a/an*; negative forms of *to be* **Vocabulary:** jobs **Can do:** understand and complete a simple form **Skills:** **reading:** read application forms **listening:** listen to people giving information about themselves **speaking:** ask and answer questions to complete a form	**Can do:** start and finish a basic conversation
		Film bank: Meeting people (page 131) **Photocopiable materials:** Vocabulary, Grammar and Communication (Teacher's Resource Book page 97)			
2	**Activities** page 15	**Grammar:** Present Simple: *I/you/we* **Vocabulary:** holidays **Can do:** talk about your daily routine **Skills:** **reading:** read about different types of holiday **listening:** listen to an interview with a holiday rep	**Grammar:** Present Simple: *he/she/it* **Vocabulary:** verbs **Can do:** write about a daily routine **Skills:** read about different and unusual jobs **pronunciation:** /s/, /z/, /ɪz/ **listening:** listen to two people talking about Jeanette Ewart's job **speaking:** ask and answer questions about a daily routine	**Grammar:** *this, that, these, those,* noun plurals **Vocabulary:** everyday objects; colours; some adjectives **Can do:** identify everyday objects **Skills:** **pronunciation:** /ɪ/ and /ɪː/ **listening:** listen to dialogues and identify where the people are **Lifelong learning:** finding plurals of words	**Can do:** ask simple questions for information and understand simple answers
		Film bank: Unreal City (page 132) **Photocopiable materials:** Vocabulary, Grammar and Communication (Teacher's Resource Book page 102)			
3	**Free time** page 25	**Grammar:** Present Simple: negative **Vocabulary:** basic leisure activities; days of the week **Can do:** talk about your free time **Skills:** **listening:** listen to people talking about traffic jams **reading:** read about Alistair Standing **speaking:** talk about your daily routine	**Grammar:** *can/can't* **Vocabulary:** sports, games and activities; *play/go/do* + sport **Can do:** talk about what you can and can't do **Skills:** **reading:** read about Tony Hawk **pronunciation:** *can* and *can't* **speaking:** talk about abilities	**Functions:** making suggestions; using the phone **Vocabulary:** large numbers **Can do:** understand and leave a simple phone message **Skills:** **listening:** listen to telephone messages **reading:** read about the Mobile Phone Olympics **pronunciation:** /i/ and /iː/	**Can do:** talk about other people's abilities
		Film bank: Deborah's day (page 133) **Photocopiable materials:** Vocabulary, Grammar, Communication (Teacher's Resource Book page 107)			
4	**Food** page 35	**Grammar:** countable and uncountable nouns; *How much?/How many?* **Vocabulary:** food and drink **Can do:** talk about quantities and numbers **Skills:** **reading:** read about different families	**Grammar:** *a/an, some* and *any* **Vocabulary:** containers; adjectives describing physical and emotional states **Can do:** talk about your diet and lifestyle **Skills:** **listening:** listen to a TV programme about food **pronunciation:** /æ/ and /ʌ/ **reading:** read a problem page **writing:** write an answer to a problem	**Grammar:** object pronouns; *I'd like* **Vocabulary:** menus, prices **Can do:** order food in a fast food restaurant **Skills:** **listening:** listen to a dialogue in a fast food restaurant **speaking:** act out ordering food in a restaurant	**Can do:** shop for food at a market
		Film bank: Two soups (page 134) **Photocopiable materials:** Vocabulary, Grammar and Communication (Teacher's Resource Book page 112)			

Syllabus outline

	UNIT	LESSON 1	LESSON 2	LESSON 3	COMMUNICATION
5	**Home** page 45	**Grammar:** *there is/there are* **Vocabulary:** equipment and furniture **Can do:** talk about your home **Skills:** **reading:** read about ResidenSea **listening:** listen to an interview with Jon Nott **speaking:** act out buying and selling a house **Lifelong learning:** learning new vocabulary	**Grammar:** *have got* **Vocabulary:** possessions; furniture; houses **Can do:** ask and talk about possessions **Skills:** **listening:** listen to descriptions of rooms **pronunciation:** /d/ and /æ/ **speaking:** describe a room in a house **writing:** write about people's homes and possessions	**Grammar:** modifiers (*very, quite, really*) **Vocabulary:** adjectives to describe places **Can do:** write an informal email about your country **Skills:** **listening:** listen to descriptions of different places **pronunciation:** strong and weak syllable stress **Lifelong learning:** identifying word stress	**Can do:** talk about furnishing an apartment
		Film bank: ResidenSea (page 135) **Photocopiable materials:** Vocabulary, Grammar and Communication (Teacher's Resource Book page 117)			
6	**City life** page 55	**Grammar:** past of *to be*: all forms; Past Simple of regular verbs: positive **Vocabulary:** buildings **Can do:** talk about your past **Skills:** **reading:** read about different buildings **listening:** listen to people talking about buildings **pronunciation:** /t/, /d/, /ɪd/ **speaking:** talk about your past	**Grammar:** Past Simple: question forms and short answers **Vocabulary:** prepositions of place **Can do:** understand and give simple directions **Skills:** **reading:** read about Robin Andrews **Lifelong learning:** remembering vocabulary	**Grammar:** Past Simple: negative **Vocabulary:** transport **Can do:** describe your last holiday **Skills:** **reading:** read about navigation **pronunciation:** stress patterns **writing:** write about holidays	**Can do:** understand a store guide and ask for things in shops
		Film bank: Amazing buildings (page 136) **Photocopiable materials:** Vocabulary, Grammar and Communication (Teacher's Resource Book page 124) **Test 2: Units 4–6** (Teacher's Resource Book page 202)			
7	**People** page 65	**Grammar:** pronoun *one/ones* **Vocabulary:** adjectives for describing people **Can do:** write a letter describing family members **Skills:** **reading:** read a letter from a friend **listening:** listen to *The Girl from Ipanema* **Lifelong learning:** opposite adjectives	**Grammar:** possessive pronouns **Vocabulary:** ordinal numbers; months **Can do:** say who objects belong to **Skills:** **listening:** listen to descriptions of different people **pronunciation:** /ð/ /θ/	**Grammar:** Past Simple: irregular vergs **Vocabulary:** phrasal verbs **Can do:** understand an article **Skills:** **reading:** read an article about a jigsaw puzzle **pronunciation:** /w/ and /h/ **speaking:** ask and answer *wh-* questions	**Can do:** identify a person from a simple description
		Film bank: Great Expectations (page 137) **Photocopiable materials:** Vocabulary, Grammar and Communication (Teacher's Resource Book page 129)			
8	**Day to day** page 75	**Grammar:** Present Simple; adverbs of frequency **Vocabulary:** clothes **Can do:** write a request to a colleague **Skills:** **reading:** read about what clothes to wear **writing:** write a letter requesting advice about clothes	**Grammar:** Present Continuous; adverbs of manner **Vocabulary:** activities; rooms; clothes **Can do:** describe what you are doing now **Skills:** **listening:** listen to a description of a reality TV show **pronunciation:** identify strong syllables **speaking:** ask and answer questions about what people are doing	**Grammar:** Present Simple and Present Continuous **Vocabulary:** the weather; health **Can do:** take part in a factual conversation **Skills:** **pronunciation:** /əʊ/ and /ɒ/ **reading:** read an extract from a website **speaking:** talk about the weather **Lifelong learning:** nouns and adjectives	**Can do:** make a complaint in a shop; write a simple letter of complaint
		Film bank: The Notting Hill Carnival (page 138) **Photocopiable materials:** Vocabulary, Grammar and Communication (Teacher's Resource Book page 134)			

	UNIT	LESSON 1	LESSON 2	LESSON 3	COMMUNICATION
9	**Culture** page 85	**Grammar:** comparison of adjectives **Vocabulary:** news media **Can do:** compare people and things **Skills:** **reading:** read about different news sources **pronunciation:** /ə/ **writing and speaking:** write and talk about things you like and don't like	**Grammar:** superlative adjectives **Vocabulary:** films **Can do:** write a short film review **Skills:** **listening:** listen to an interview about films **reading and speaking:** read a movie quiz; talk about the questions **writing:** write a review	**Grammar:** *prefer* + noun/*-ing* forms; *will* for spontaneous decisions and offers **Can do:** talk about personal preferences **Skills:** **reading:** read about different works of art **listening:** listen to a conversation about art **pronunciation:** intonation	**Can do:** discuss and plan activities
		Film bank: Spirit of the city (page 139) **Photocopiable materials:** Vocabulary, Grammar and Communication (Teacher's Resource Book page 139) **Test 3: Units 7–9** (Teacher's Resource Book page 208)			
10	**Journeys** page 95	**Grammar:** Present Perfect (*been* with *ever/never*): *I/you/we/they* **Vocabulary:** travel; holiday activities; sports **Can do:** talk about personal experiences **Skills:** **reading and listening:** read about TV; listen to an extract from a TV programme **pronunciation:** /ɪ/ and /iː/ **speaking:** talk about experiences	**Grammar:** Present Perfect with regular and irregular verbs (*he/she/it*) **Vocabulary:** holidays **Can do:** understand key points in a brochure; write a postcard to a friend **Skills:** **reading:** read about the Seagaia holiday resort **pronunciation:** /iː/ and /ɪ/ **speaking and writing:** to us about a weekend away; write a postcard **Lifelong learning:** irregular past participles	**Grammar:** *-ing* form as a noun (subject only) **Vocabulary:** types of transport **Can do:** book a travel ticket **Skills:** **reading and listening:** read about and listen to two people's journeys to work **listening:** listen to a conversation about booking a holiday	**Can do:** understand basic hotel information; book a hotel room
		Film bank: Commuting (page 140) **Photocopiable materials:** Vocabulary, Grammar and Communication (Teacher's Resource Book page 144)			
11	**Learning** page 105	**Grammar:** *can/can't, have to /don't have to* **Vocabulary:** road rules and signs; traffic offences and penalties **Can do:** understand signs and rules **Skills:** **reading:** read an article about a traffic school **pronunciation:** /f/ and /v/ **speaking:** compare rules in the USA and your country	**Grammar:** *wh-* questions **Vocabulary:** types of school; education **Can do:** understand and produce a simple explanation **Skills:** **reading and vocabulary:** read about different types of education **listening:** listen to an interview **pronunciation:** intonation **speaking:** talk about your education **writing:** write an article	**Grammar:** Present Continuous for future **Vocabulary:** education **Can do:** talk about future arrangements **Skills:** **reading:** read an email describing education plans **listening:** listen to four people talk about adverts for educational courses **speaking:** discuss your opinions about the different types of learning **Lifelong learning:** recognising word groups	**Can do:** make future arrangements and appointments
		Film bank: Rock climbing (page 141) **Photocopiable materials:** Vocabulary, Grammar and Communication (Teacher's Resource Book page 149)			
12	**Ambitions** page 115	**Grammar:** *be going to* for intentions **Vocabulary:** future time expressions **Can do:** talk about intentions **Skills:** **reading and vocabulary:** read an article about travel between continents **pronunciation:** /t/; stress patterns for *going to* **speaking:** talk about future intentions	**Grammar:** infinitive of purpose; revision of *be going to* **Vocabulary:** ambitions **Can do:** write an informal letter **Skills:** **listening:** listen to the song *Fame!* **Reading and writing:** read a letter; write a letter to a relative or close friend	**Grammar:** verbs + infinitive/*-ing* form (*want, would like, like, etc.*) **Vocabulary:** leisure **Can do:** talk about likes, dislikes and ambitions **Skills:** **reading:** read an article **listening:** listen to a telephone enquiry **pronunciation:** /aɪ/ and /eɪ/ **speaking:** talk about your ambitions	**Can do:** plan study objectives
		Film bank: Ten great adventures (page 142) **Photocopiable materials:** Vocabulary, Grammar and Communication (Teacher's Resource Book page 154) **Test 4: Units 10–12** (Teacher's Resource Book page 214)			

Introduction

Teaching and learning are unpredictable experiences. Learners can be dynamic and engaged one lesson and then demotivated, tired or even absent the next. The aim of *Total English* is two-fold: firstly to set new standards in terms of interest level, teachability and range of support materials; and secondly to address the reality of most people's unpredicatable teaching experience as it is, not as we hope it will be.

Research for *Total English* suggested three classroom 'realities' that need to be addressed in a coursebook: 1) learners often lack direction and purpose – they are often not sure about the relevance of what they are learning and where they are going with English; 2) learners need to be genuinely engaged in coursebook content just as they are in the newspapers, TV programmes and films that they see around them; 3) learners often miss lessons and this creates extra work for the teacher to make sure that no-one falls behind.

Finding direction and purpose

Learners need a clear sense of where they are going and how they are going to get there. They need to know what they are learning, why they are learning it and how it can be applied outside the classroom. Clear goals and objectives are crucial. *Total English* contains a clear grammar syllabus and plenty of practice. Each input lesson is organised on a double-page spread and has a grammar and *Can Do* learning objective clearly stated at the start. The *Can Do* objectives give a purpose and reason for learning and mean that students know why they are studying that lesson and how they can use the new language.

The learning objectives in *Total English* are derived from the *Can Do* statements in the Common European Framework which means teachers can feel confident that *Total English* covers the language areas their students need. The levels of *Total English* correlate to the Common European Framework in the following way:

Elementary	Covers A1 and goes towards A2
Pre-intermediate	Covers A2 and goes towards B1
Intermediate	Covers B1 and goes towards B1+
Upper Intermediate	Covers B1+ and B2
Advanced	Covers C1

Engaging learners' interest

Motivation through engagement is equally important for successful language learning. *Total English* lessons give a new twist to familiar topics – topics that reflect learners' needs and interests. This ensures that learners will always have something to say about the content of the lesson. There are frequent opportunities for learners to exchange ideas and opinions and engage with the material on a personal level. Activities have been designed to be as realistic as possible so that learners can see how the language they're learning can be applied outside the classroom.

In addition to the wide range of topics, texts and activities, each level of the *Total English* Students' Books has a DVD, which adds an extra dimension to the course. Containing a range of authentic material from film and TV, the DVDs expose learners to a variety of different English media and give them a feel for how the language is used in real life. Each unit of the Students' Books has a corresponding DVD extract and the Film banks at the back of the Students' Books offer material to use in class or at home while watching the DVD.

Helping learners catch up

One of the most common problems that teachers face is irregular attendance. Learners often have busy lives with work, study or family commitments and attending English classes on a regular basis is not always possible. *Total English* recognises this problem and has been designed to help learners catch up easily if they miss lessons. In addition to the practice exercises in each lesson, there is a Reference page and a Review and practice page at the end of each unit. These provide an accessible summary of the main grammar and vocabulary covered.

The *Total English* Workbooks also have freestanding CD-ROMs that include interactive self-study 'catch-up' material to present and practise language from any lessons learners have missed. With this extensive range of animated presentations, interactive practice exercises and games, *Total English* ensures your students don't get left behind if they miss lessons.

The course package

Total English has five levels and takes learners from Elementary to Advanced. Each level consists of the following:

- **Students' Book**

The *Total English* Students' Books are divided into 10–12 units and contain approximately 80–120 hours of teaching material. Each unit contains a balanced mix of grammar, vocabulary, pronunciation and skills work including writing.

- **DVD**

The 'with DVD' version of the Students' Books has a freestanding DVD which provides additional listening practice linked to the topic areas in the Students' Books.

- **Video**

The DVD material is also available on video (PAL and NTSC).

- **Class Cassettes/CDs**

Total English Class Cassettes/CDs contain all the recorded material from the Students' Books.

- **Workbook**

The *Total English* Workbooks contain further practice of language areas covered in the corresponding units of the Students' Books.

- **Workbook 'Catch-up' CD-ROM**

The *Total English* Workbook CD-ROMs provide extra support for students who miss lessons. In addition to the recorded material from the Workbooks, the Workbook CD-ROMs feature 'catch-up' material related to the key grammar areas covered in the Students' Books.

- **Teacher's Resource Book**

The *Total English* Teacher's Resource Books provide all the support teachers need to get the most out of the course. The Teacher's Resource Books contain teaching notes, photocopiable worksheets, DVD worksheets and tests.

- **Website**

Total English has its own dedicated website. In addition to background information about the course and authors, the website features teaching tips, downloadable worksheets, links to other useful websites as well as special offers and competitions. Join us online at www.longman.com/totalenglish.

The Students' Book

Each unit of the *Total English* Students' Books follows the same structure making the material very easy to use:

- **Lead-in page**
  - acts as a springboard into the topic of the unit and engages students' interest.
  - introduces essential vocabulary related to the topic so that students start with the same basic grounding.

- **Input lessons**
  - three double-page input lessons, thematically linked, offer interesting angles on the unit topic.
  - each input lesson leads towards a *Can Do* learning objective in line with the Council of Europe's *Can Do* statements.
  - each 90-minute lesson focuses on a specific grammar area and includes vocabulary, pronunciation and skills work.
  - each unit contains at least two reading texts and a substantial listening element.
  - How to... boxes develop students' competence in using language, in line with the Common European Framework.
  - Lifelong learning boxes offer tips and strategies for developing students' study skills.

- **Communication page**
  - revises language taught in the previous three lessons in a freer, more communicative context.
  - each communication task practises a range of skills and has a measurable goal or outcome.

- **Reference page**
  - summarises the main grammar points covered in each unit and provides a list of key vocabulary.
  - helps learners to catch up if they miss lessons and is an essential revision tool.

- **Review and practice page**
  - provides a range of exercises to consolidate key grammar and vocabulary covered in the unit.
  - can be used to check progress, enabling teachers to identify areas that need further practice.

- **Film bank pages**
  - support the DVD which is attached to the back of the 'with DVD' version of the Students' Books.
  - feature a range of exercises designed to stimulate interest in each DVD extract and make the authentic material contained on the DVD accessible to students.

The *Total English* Students' Books also feature the following:

- **Do you know?**
  - an optional page to be covered before learners start the course which teaches basic language areas such as the alphabet, numbers and classroom language.

- **Writing bank**
  - provides models and tips on how to write emails, letters and postcards as well as guidance on different writing skills such as punctuation, spelling and paragraph construction.

- **Pronunciation bank**
  - provides a list of English phonemes, guidance on sound-spelling correspondences and weak forms.

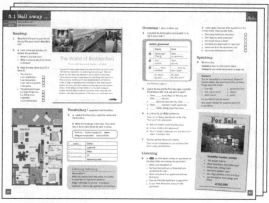

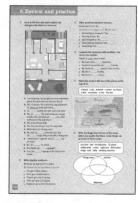

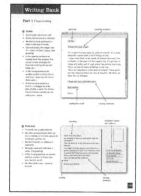
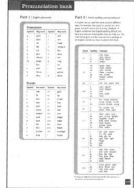

The Workbook

The *Total English* Workbooks contain 10–12 units which correspond to the Students' Book material. Each Workbook contains:

- **Additional practice material**
  Extra grammar, vocabulary, skills and pronunciation exercises practise language covered in the corresponding units of the Students' Books.

- **Review and consolidation sections**
  These occur after units 3, 6, 9 and 12 and contain cumulative practice of the grammar and vocabulary covered in the previous three units.

- **Vocabulary bank**
  This provides further practice in the key vocabulary areas covered in each unit of the Students' Books. Students can refer to this after studying a particular topic and record the new vocabulary they have learned. They can also add new items as they come across them.

The Workbook CD-ROM

In addition to the recorded material from the Workbook, the 'catch-up' section of the CD-Rom contains the following:

- **Grammar presentations**
  Simple, accessible grammar explanations summarise the target language of each unit in a succinct and memorable way.

- **Self-check practice exercises**
  A range of practice exercises (two for each grammar point) enable students to practise the target language.

- **'Can do' game**
  This provides communicative practice of the target language.

The Teacher's Resource Book

The Teacher's Resource Books are divided into the following sections:

- **Introduction**
This explains the aims and rationale of the course and provides a complete description of the course package.

- **Teaching notes**
These provide step by step instructions on how to exploit each unit as well as background notes and suggestions for warm-up, lead-in and extension activities.

- **Photocopiable resource banks**
The photocopiable resource banks contain 60 photocopiable worksheets (5 worksheets for each unit of the Students' Books). The worksheets are designed to practise the grammar and vocabulary covered in the Students' Book units in a freer, less structured and enjoyable context. Detailed instructions on how to use each worksheet are also provided in the Teacher's Resource Book.

- **DVD worksheets**
In addition to the Film bank pages in the Students' Books, the Teacher's Resource Books also have 12 DVD worksheets. Containing Before viewing, While viewing and Post viewing activities, the DVD worksheets provide more detailed exploitation of the DVD material. Instructions on how to use each worksheet including warm-up and extension activities are also provided.

- **Tests**
Four photocopiable progress tests are included in the Teacher's Resource Books. Each test covers grammar, vocabulary, reading, listening and writing skills and is designed to be used after every third unit.

Teaching approaches

Grammar

Total English covers all the main language areas you would expect at each level and gives learners a thorough foundation in grammar based on the following principles:

- **Clear presentation/analysis**
  Each double-page lesson has a clear grammar aim which is stated at the top of the page. New language items are presented in context via reading and/or listening texts and grammar rules are then analysed and explained via the Active grammar boxes which are a key feature of each lesson.

Active grammar

I'm starting the course next month ...
Geoff is working in the US again in March ...

1 Which tense are the sentences?

2 Has Joanna decided to do the course?

3 Has Geoff organised his stay in the States?

4 Are the sentences describing an action in the present or in the future?

Total English takes a 'guided discovery' approach to grammar and learners are actively invited to think about grammar and work out the rules for themselves.

- **Varied, regular practice**
  Once learners have grasped the important rules, all new language is then practised in a variety of different ways so that learners are able to use the grammar with confidence. Practice activities include form-based exercises designed to help learners manipulate the new structures as well as more meaningful, personalised practice. Additional grammar practice exercises can be found in the Review and practice sections at the end of each unit as well as in the Workbooks and on the Workbook CD-ROMs. The Teacher's Resource Books also contain an extensive bank of photocopiable grammar activities which are designed to practise the language in freer, more communicative contexts.

- **Accessible reference material**
  In addition to the explanations contained in the Active Grammar boxes, there is a Reference section at the end of each unit which summarises the rules in greater detail and provides extra information and examples.

Vocabulary

Total English recognises the central role that vocabulary plays in successful communication. The emphasis is on providing learners with high-frequency, useful vocabulary which is regularly practised and revised. New vocabulary is presented and practised in a variety of different ways – via the Lead-in pages which provide a springboard into the topic of each unit enabling teachers to elicit vocabulary that learners already know as well as pre-teach essential vocabulary for the rest of the unit; via the reading and listening texts and related exercises; via special vocabulary sections in the main lessons. Additional vocabulary practice is provided in the Review and practice sections of the Students' Book, in the practice exercises in the Workbook and special vocabulary worksheets in the Teacher's Resource Book.

Speaking

The key aim for most learners is spoken fluency but low level learners cannot express themselves easily without support. *Total English* develops spoken fluency in a number of ways – by giving learners discussion topics they want to talk about; by setting up situations where they are motivated to communicate in order to complete a specific task; by providing clear models and examples of how to structure discourse and by encouraging them, wherever possible, to express their own ideas and opinions. All lessons feature some speaking practice and there are regular How to... boxes throughout the course which focus on the words and expressions learners need to carry out specific functions.

HOW TO...	order in a fast food restaurant	
	Ask questions	_____ you have salads?
	Say what you want	I'd _____ a cheese sandwich, please.
	Ask about prices	How _____ is that?

Communication pages at the end of each unit engage learners in a variety of problem-solving tasks and involve learners in a number of different skills – including speaking. The photocopiable activities in the Teacher's Resource Book are also specifically designed to promote speaking practice.

Listening

Listening is one of the most difficult skills to master and *Total English* pays particular emphasis to developing learners' confidence in this area. Listening texts include short dialogues as well as longer texts (conversations, interviews, stories and songs). There are lots of simple 'Listen and check your answer' exercises as well as more challenging activities where learners have to listen to longer extracts in order to find specific information. The recorded material features a variety of accents including British, American, Australian and some non-native speakers. There is additional listening practice in the Workbooks and the DVDs further enhance learners' confidence in understanding the spoken word.

Pronunciation

Total English pays particular attention to pronunciation which is integrated into all the lessons which present new language. The pronunciation syllabus includes word and sentence stress, weak forms, intonation and difficult sounds. The Pronunciation banks at the back of the Students' Books include a list of English phonemes, guidance on sound-spelling correspondences and weak forms. There is additional pronunciation practice in the Workbooks and on the Workbook CD-ROMs.

Reading

There is a wide variety of reading texts in *Total English* ranging from simple forms and advertisements to short texts from newspapers and magazines. Texts have been chosen for their intrinsic interest as well as for their usefulness in providing a vehicle for the particular grammar and vocabulary points in focus. Many of the texts have been adapted from authentic, real-life sources (magazines, websites etc.) and related tasks have been carefully selected to develop learners' confidence in dealing with written texts. Activities include comprehension and vocabulary work as well as practice in dealing with different reading sub-skills such as reading for gist. There are a number of jigsaw readings where learners work together and share information. The length and complexity of the texts get more challenging as the course progresses.

Writing

With the growth of email, writing is becoming an increasingly important skill. *Total English* acknowledges this by including regular writing tasks in the Students' Books. These are carefully structured with exercises and examples designed to ensure that learners are actually able to carry out the tasks. Models of different types of writing – emails, postcards, formal and informal letters are provided in the Writing Bank at the back of the Students' Books as well as additional advice and guidance on different writing sub-skills such as punctuation, spelling and paragraph construction.

Revision and testing

There are plenty of opportunities for revision in *Total English* and language is constantly recycled throughout the course. At the end of every unit, there are special Review and practice pages which take the form of mini- progress checks enabling learners to identify areas where they might need further practice.

In addition to the Review and practice pages, there are four Review and consolidation sections in the accompanying Workbooks, and a whole range of additional practice material on the 'Catch-up' CD-ROMs. The Teacher's Resource Books include four photocopiable progress tests which are designed to be used after units 3, 6, 9 and 12.

Learner training

Total English places a strong emphasis on learner training and good study habits are encouraged and developed via the Lifelong learning boxes which are a featured in many lessons. The Lifelong learning boxes provide useful tips and suggestions on how to continue learning outside the classroom. In addition, the Vocabulary banks in the Workbooks not only encourage students to record vocabulary from particular lessons, but also to revisit and add further vocabulary items as they arise.

Lifelong learning
Personalise it!
When you want to learn new words, it is useful to write them in a personal sentence.
fridge – *My fridge is very old – it's useless!*
cupboard – *I have a big cupboard in my bedroom.*

Total English and exams

The table below shows how the different levels of *Total English* relate to the Common European Framework levels and the University of Cambridge ESOL main suite examinations in terms of the language taught and the topics covered. While *Total English* is not an examination preparation course, a student who has, for example, completed the Upper Intermediate level would have sufficient language to attempt the Cambridge ESOL FCE (First Certificate in English) examination. Many of the exercises in the *Total English* Students' Books, Workbooks and photocopiable tests are similar in format to those found in the Cambridge ESOL main suite examinations but specific training is required for all EFL examinations and we would strongly recommend this.

For further information on the University of Cambridge ESOL examinations, contact:

Cambridge ESOL
1 Hills Road
Cambridge
CB1 2EU

Tel. +44 (0) 1223 553355
Fax. +44 (0) 1223 460278
Email: ESOL@ucles.org.uk
www.CambridgeESOL.org

	CEF levels	Cambridge ESOL Exams	TOTAL ENGLISH LEVELS					
Proficient user	C2	CPE						
	C1	CAE						■
Independent user	B2	FCE					■	
	B1+						■	
	B1	PET				■		
	A2	KET			■			
Basic user	A1			■				
			STARTER	ELEMENTARY	PRE-INTERMEDIATE	INTERMEDIATE	UPPER INTERMEDIATE	ADVANCED

Total English authors

Total English Elementary

Mark Foley has worked in English language teaching for over 23 years and has extensive experience in teaching (mostly in the UK and Spain), teacher training, examining and materials writing. He is the co-author of a number of publications, including the Longman ELT advanced titles, Distinction and Advanced Learner's Grammar. He is co-author, with Diane Hall, of *Total English* Elementary Students' Book and Workbook.

Diane Hall has worked in English language teaching for over 25 years and has extensive experience in teaching (mostly in the UK and Germany), publishing and materials writing. She is co-author of a number of publications, including the Longman ELT advanced titles, Distinction and Advanced Learners' Grammar. She is co-author, with Mark Foley, of *Total English* Elementary Students' Book and Workbook.

Total English Pre-intermediate and Upper Intermediate

Richard Acklam lives in North London and has been involved in English Language teaching since 1982. He has taught and trained teachers in Egypt, France and the UK and has an M.A. (TEFL) from the University of Reading. His publications include components of the 'Gold' series and he is co-author, with Araminta Crace, of *Total English* Pre-intermediate and Upper Intermediate Students' Books.

Araminta Crace lives in North London with her two young daughters, Petra and Lola. She has been involved in English Language teaching since 1984 and has taught and trained teachers in Brazil, Egypt, Portugal, Spain and the UK. Her ELT publications include Language to Go and Going for Gold. She is co-author, with Richard Acklam, of *Total English* Pre-intermediate and Upper Intermediate Students' Books.

Total English Intermediate and Advanced

Antonia Clare graduated from University College London in Psychology, and has enjoyed teaching (both adults and younger learners), and teacher training in Europe, Asia and South Africa. She is now a full-time writer and freelance teacher trainer based in the UK. Her publications include Language to Go Upper Intermediate and she is co-author, with JJ Wilson, of *Total English* Upper Intermediate and Advanced Students' Books and Workbooks.

JJ Wilson trained at International House London and has taught in Egypt, Lesotho (where he ran a student theatre), Colombia, the UK, Italy and the U.S. His main interests in the field include vocabulary acquisition and the development of innovative methods and materials for the classroom. His short fiction is published by Penguin and Pulp Faction. He is co-author, with Antonia Clare, of *Total English* Upper Intermediate and Advanced Students' Books and Workbooks.

Your life

Overview

Summary

Lesson 1: Ss listen to people describing the countries and nationalities of famous people and ways of asking people where they are from.

Lesson 2: Ss learn about the Bundy family, stars of an American TV programme. They then listen to two people discuss the various people in a photograph.

Lesson 3: Ss read an application form taken from a webpage. They then listen to someone helping a friend fill in the form.

Communicative focus: Ss practise introducing themselves, starting conversations and exchanging personal information with each other.

> **Film bank: Meeting people** (3'48")
> A selection of seven clips from famous British films.
>
> Each clip in *Meeting people* shows people greeting or introducing themselves. The clips are humorous and entertaining and the language is appropriate for early Elementary students.
>
> Possible places to use this short film are:
>
> ▶ after the Unit Opener on page 5 to extend the work on greetings
>
> ▶ before the Communication Focus on page 12 to introduce greetings
>
> ▶ at the end of the unit to round up the topic and language
>
> For ways to use this short film in class, see Students' Book page 131 and Teacher's Book page 189.

Lead-in

> **OPTIONAL WARMER**
> Ss discuss in pairs what type of party they like best: one where there are lots of people they don't know or one where they already know most of the other guests.

1a ▶ Ss look at the dialogues and use the expressions from the box to try to complete the sentences. Ss check answers in pairs and then listen to recording 1.1 to see if they were correct.

> **Answers:** 1 A: Hi, I'm Jana. What's your name? B: Hi Jana. My name's Dominik 2 A: What's your name, please? B: It's Patricia Pérez 3 A: Hello, my name's David Cooper. B: Hi, I'm Lisa Smith. Nice to meet you.

▶ Emphasise to Ss the importance of using the contracted forms (*I'm; My name's; It's*) in order to sound natural and start using English speech patterns and rhythms.

b ▶ Ss match the three dialogues to the photos with a partner.

> **Answers:** 1 B 2 A 3 C

c ▶ Ss practise saying the dialogues to each other.

2a ▶ Ask Ss: *How do you remember phone numbers? Do you write them down? Do you have a different way to remember phone numbers?*

▶ Ss listen to recording 1.2 and repeat the phone number. Draw Ss attention to the long vowel sound in phone /əʊ/.

b ▶ Ss listen to recording 1.3 and write down the phone numbers they hear. They check answers in pairs, then as a whole class.

> **Answers:** 1 02096 659 248 2 951 327 946 3 01542 984 731 4 951 372 964 5 02096 639 247

c ▶ Ss practise saying and identifying the numbers with each other.

> **EXTEND THE LEAD-IN**
> Ss circulate in large groups or as a whole class (depending on the size of the class) and find out the name and phone number of each member of the group. They must also find out how each student got their name (e.g. it was my father's name; my mother loves Greta Garbo, etc.) and how they like to be called in their English class (e.g. shortened versions of their name; nicknames; by their surname, etc.). If Ss already know each other well, have each student think of an English name which they like.

1.1 People and places

In this lesson Ss listen to people describing the countries and nationalities of famous people and ways of asking people where they are from.

OPTIONAL WARMER

Ss look at the map in pairs. If the group is multi-cultural, each student shows their partner where they are from. In monolingual groups, each student can show their partner where they were born, and which countries they have visited.

Vocabulary

1 ▶ Ss look at the map in pairs and find the countries. The first one has been done for them.

> **Answers:** B Brazil C Spain D Britain E France F Germany G Italy H Poland I Finland J Greece K Turkey L Russia M China N Japan O Australia

▶ Help Ss with the pronunciation and stress of the countries. Write each country on the board. Say the name and have Ss identify which syllable is stressed for each one. (E.g. T: Italy Ss: syllable one). Ss say the countries aloud.

OPTIONAL EXTENSION

Game: Ss close their books. For large classes, divide Ss into groups of ten or so. Ss sit in a circle. One student says a country, the next student must say another country which begins with the last letter of the previous country and so on. (E.g. England, Denmark, Kenya, etc.) If any student can't think of a country, he or she drops out and the next student begins a new list of countries. The game continues until only one student is left in each group. As you monitor, help Ss with the names and pronunciation of unfamiliar countries.

2a ▶ Ask Ss if they know the name of anyone famous (not necessarily from modern times) or a famous product from the list of countries in Ex. 1. Elicit a few suggestions. Use this as an opportunity to review the pronouns *he/she/it* (singular) and *they* (plural).

▶ Ask Ss to look at the four questions. Ask: *What is the difference between 'Who' and 'What'?* ('Who' is for people; 'what' is for things).

▶ Help with the *Wh* sound /h/ and /w/ in *Who* and *What*.

▶ Ss then look at the pictures with a partner. In pairs, they identify the people from the names in the box by asking and answering the questions. Ss take it in turns to ask the questions.

> **Answers:** 1 Paulo Coelho; Will Smith; Roman Polanski 2 Penélope Cruz; Gong Li; Nicole Kidman 3 a Nokia phone; a Gucci handbag; a Jaguar car 4 Catherine Deneuve and Gerard Depardieu 5 Ralf and Michael Schumacher

b ▶ Ss match the person to the country in pairs. Do not correct their answers at this stage as Ss will find the correct information on the recording in Ex. 3b.

3a ▶ Model the examples in Ex. 3 to Ss. Ss repeat the examples. Ask Ss to model another example as a whole class. (E.g. Student A: *Where is Nicole Kidman from?* Student B: *She's from Australia*). Ss continue the exercise in pairs. Monitor and correct any pronunciation or grammatical errors you hear. Do not correct the content as Ss will check their answers by listening to the recording.

b ▶ Play recording 1.4 once. Ss listen and check the nationalities.

> **Answers:** Paulo Coelho – Brazilian Will Smith – American Roman Polanski Polish Penélope Cruz – Spanish Gong Li – Chinese Nicole Kidman – Australian Nokia phone – Finnish Jaguar car – British Catherine Deneuve and Gerard Depardieu – both French Ralf and Michael Schumacher – both German

4 ▶ Ss cover their books. Say: *Nicole Kidman is from Australia. She's Australian.* Ask Ss: *Are the words the same or different?* (different). Ss open books and look at the table in Ex. 4. Play the recording a second time. Ss write in the missing words. Ss check answers in pairs, then as a whole class.

> **Answers:** 2 America 3 Brazilian 4 Italian 5 Germany 6 Spain 7 Polish 8 British 9 Finland 10 Chinese 11 France

Pronunciation

5a ▶ Play recording 1.5. Ss listen and repeat the nationality words. Pay particular attention to *Italian* and *Chinese* as the word stress changes in the adjective form for these.

b ▶ Write *Australian* on the board. Say: *Australian*, enunciating each syllable clearly (Aus-tral-ian). Ask: *How many syllables are there?* (three) *Where is the stress?* (tral, syllable two). Underline the stressed syllable on the board.

Play the recording again. Ss listen and write the words, underlining the stressed syllable as they do so.

> **Answers:** Aus<u>tral</u>ian A<u>mer</u>ican Bra<u>zil</u>ian I<u>tal</u>ian <u>Ger</u>man <u>Rus</u>sian <u>Span</u>ish <u>Pol</u>ish <u>Brit</u>ish <u>Finn</u>ish <u>Turk</u>ish Chi<u>nese</u> <u>Japan</u>ese French Greek

c ▶ Ss practise asking and answering about the people in the unit.

6a ▶ Ss complete the exercise by writing in the name of the person. Compare answers in pairs, then as a whole class.

> **Answers:** 1 Will Smith 2 Ralf and Michael Schumacher 3 Penélope Cruz 4 Gong Li 5 Gerard Depardieu and Catherine Deneuve

b ▶ Ss work in pairs and practise asking and answering questions. Model an example with a student in the class first so that everyone is clear they have to imagine they are this person.

Grammar

7a ▶ Ask Ss to look at the statements in Ex. 6a again. Write the first two on the board. *I'm from Philadelphia. We're from Germany*. Underline I'm and We're.

Ask Ss: *Which is singular and which is plural?* (*I'm* is singular and *We're* is plural.)

Focus on the apostrophe. Ask: *What does this mean?* (two words together, the way we say it).

Ss complete the Active grammar box by writing in the second word of the contractions listed (*am/is/are*). Ss check answers in pairs, then as a whole class.

> **Answers:** am is is is are are are

▶ Direct Ss to the reference section on page 13.

b ▶ Ss complete the exercise in pairs.

> **Answers:** 1 is – She 2 re – We 3 are – from – m 4 that/this – s 5 they – re

> **OPTIONAL EXTENSION**
>
> Ss think of a famous person and write that person's name on a piece of paper. If they can't think of anyone, they can use the names of people mentioned in the unit. Emphasise that it must be someone whom all the other Ss would know. Gather up the names and mix them up in a bag. Each student chooses a piece of paper with a name on it and sticks it on the back of another student with sticky tape so that each student has the name of someone famous on their back, but they don't know who it is. Ss work in small groups of four or five. Ss take it in turns to ask one question at a time about 'themselves' (e.g. *Am I American?, Am I a man?, Am I old?*, etc.) and in this way try to guess who they are. Don't worry if Ss have the same names on their back, as this can be amusing for the others in the group who see it.

8 ▶ Ss works in pairs. Each pair says the name of a country to another pair. The pairs then have two minutes to write as many names of famous people and things from the country as they can.

▶ Tell the pairs to swap their lists to check them, and then check the work as a whole class.

1.2 Family ties

In this lesson Ss learn about the Bundy family, stars of a popular American sitcom on TV. They also listen to two people discussing people in a photograph. Through this context, Ss learn the possessive *'s* form, possessive adjectives, *yes/no* questions with *to be* and how to exchange information about their families.

> **OPTIONAL WARMER**
>
> Ask all the Ss to stand up. Label the four corners of the room in the following way: oldest child in the family; youngest child in the family; middle child in the family; only child (explain only child, no brothers or sisters). Ask Ss to go to the corner of the room which corresponds to their position in their own family.
>
> In the four groups, Ss have to think of one good thing and one bad thing about being in that position in the family. (E.g. youngest child; good: having an older brother or sister to help with a problem; bad: old (hand-me-down) clothes from older brother or sister). Don't worry about Ss making mistakes during this activity. Ss will only be able to express their ideas in very basic language.

Vocabulary

1 ▶ Ss look at the pictures. Ask Ss if they recognise anyone in the pictures. Elicit answers. In pairs Ss decide what the relationship between the two people in each photo is.

> **Answers:** 1 D (Spanish singers Julio and Enrique Iglesias) 2 E (American popstar Madonna and her daughter Lourdes) 3 C (British Princes William and Harry) 4 A (American tennis players Venus and Serena Williams) 5 B (former U.S. president Bill Clinton and his wife Senator Hillary Clinton)

> **OPTIONAL EXTENSION**
>
> Review nationalities from lesson 1. Ask Ss where each person is from. (E.g. *Where's Bill Clinton from? He's American* or *He's from America*.)

2 ▶ Ss match the sentence halves. Ss check answers in pairs, then as a whole class.

> **Answers:** 1 c 2 a 3 b 4 e 5 d

▶ Focus on the second column. Ask Ss: *What do you notice about the people's names in each column?* (the apostrophe *'s* at the end of the name).

Grammar

3 ▶ Ss look at the two sentences and choose the correct one. Ss check answers in pairs, then as a whole class.

> **Answer:** Sentence 2

▶ Ask: *What does the 's mean?* It shows possession. Here it is used to indicate the relationship of <u>Bill</u> to Hillary. Hillary is <u>Bill's</u> wife shows the relationship of Hillary to Bill.

With more than two people, the apostrophe *'s* goes after the second name (e.g. Julio Iglesias is Julio José and Enrique's father, not Julio José's and Enrique's father).

4a ▶ *Married with Children* is a popular American TV sitcom about the Bundy family. Ask Ss if they know this programme. If so, personalise it a little. Ask Ss: *Is it good? Do you like it? Who are the main characters? Who are your favourite characters?*, etc.

▶ Ss complete the family tree in pairs.

b ▶ Ss use the *'s* to make sentences about the family.

> **Answers:** Al is Peggy's husband Kelly is Bud's sister Bud is Kelly's brother Peggy is Kelly and Bud's mother Al is Kelly and Bud's father Kelly is Al and Peggy's daughter Bud is Al and Peggy's son

> **OPTIONAL VARIATION**
> If Ss are more familiar with the *Simpsons* than *Married with Children*, the Simpson family could be used instead for Ex. 4a and 4b. Homer and Marge (parents), Bart, Lisa and Maggie (son and two daughters). Personalise in the same way as for Ex. 4a.

5a ▶ Ss match the family words to the meanings. Ss check answers in pairs, then as a whole class.

> **Answers:** 2 g 3 a 4 e 5 b 6 h 7 c 8 f

b ▶ Ss find the meanings of the words in their dictionaries. Ss check answers in pairs, then as a whole class.

Pronunciation

6a ▶ Write /ʌ/ on the board. Explain that this is a sound in English. Write *m<u>o</u>ther* and *br<u>o</u>ther*. Underline the sound. Play recording 1.6. Ss listen to identify the sound.

b ▶ Play recording 1.7. Ss listen and repeat, then underline the five /ʌ/ sounds. Ss check answers in pairs, then as a whole class.

> **Answers:** 1 h<u>u</u>sband 3 grandm<u>o</u>ther 6 c<u>ou</u>sin 7 <u>u</u>ncle 9 grands<u>o</u>n

Grammar

7 ▶ Teach *a crazy family* (not a typical family, a bit wild) and *married to* (husband and wife).

> **OPTIONAL GRAMMAR LEAD-IN**
> Focus on the picture of the Bundy family in Ex. 4a. Establish who everyone is and what their relationship to each other is. Tell Ss to close their books. Dictate the short text in 7. *Meet the Bundy family ... a crazy family!* Ss check their dictation in their books.

▶ Ss read the texts, focusing on the underlined words.

Ask: *Which words are for singular nouns?* (my, his, her). *Which words are for plural nouns?* (our, their).

▶ Ss complete the Active grammar box.

> **Answers:** my his her our their

▶ Write on the board *This is Al. This is <u>Al's</u> wife Peggy. This is Peggy. This is <u>Peggy's</u> daughter.*

Underline the words *Al's* and *Peggy's*. Ask Ss: *Which words could go instead of Al's and Peggy's?* (his and her).

Establish that in English we use *This is his wife. Wife* is a feminine noun but it is still his wife because Al is masculine.

▶ Refer Ss to the reference section on page 13.

8 ▶ Ss complete the gaps by using possessive adjectives. Ss check answers in pairs, then as a whole class.

> **Answers:** 1 My 2 their 3 our 4 your 5 your 6 her 7 your 8 his

Grammar

9 ▶ Ss focus on the completed questions in Ex. 8 and use them to complete the Active grammar box using either *is* or *are* in the spaces provided.

> **Answers:** Is is Are are

▶ Ask: *Is 'are' for plural and 'is' for singular?* (Yes, but remember '*you*' can be both singular and plural).

> **OPTIONAL EXTENSION**
> Ss think of five questions they would like to ask their partner. (E.g. *How old are you? Where is your mother from?* etc.) Ss ask and answer in pairs.

Listening

10a ▶ Ss focus on the dialogue between two people, one asking questions about a photograph and the other answering. Ss complete the dialogue with *she, he, my, your, is* or *are*.

> **Answers:** 1 your 2 is 3 he 4 is 5 your 6 are a my, is b 's c my d she e 's, 's f 's

b ▶ Play recording 1.8. Ss match 1–6 to a–f.

> **Answers:** 1 d 2 b 3 c 4 f 5 a 6 e

Person to person

11 ▶ Ss write down five names of people in their family. In pairs, they ask and answer about who the people are. Don't worry about Ss making mistakes during this activity.

1.3 Work on the web

In this lesson Ss read an application form taken from a webpage. They then listen to someone helping a friend fill in the form.

> **OPTIONAL WARMER**
>
> Elicit all the names of jobs Ss can think of. Put them on the board.
>
> Ss work in pairs. They take it in turns to mime one of the jobs on the board to their partner and the other tries to guess which job it is.

Vocabulary

1a ▶ Ss look at the photos with a partner and match the job to the correct photo. Draw Ss' attention to the language suggested in the coursebook before they start.

> **Answers:** A a journalist   B a police officer
> C a doctor   D a lawyer   E a computer programmer
> F an architect   G a shop assistant   H unemployed
> I an electrician

b ▶ Ss write the correct job beside the photo. Help Ss with the pronunciation of these words. Focus in particular on the initial /dʒ/ sound in *journalist* and *judge* and the /ɔː/ sound in *lawyer* and *warden* as these can cause difficulty for some Ss.

▶ Ask Ss: *Which of the jobs do you like best?* See which is the most popular job in the class.

> **OPTIONAL EXTENSION**
>
> Ss look at the list of jobs and categorise them into jobs where you work in one place (e.g. an office, a school, etc.) and jobs where you work in different places (a police officer; an artist, etc.). There will be some overlap.

Grammar

2 ▶ Direct Ss to the jobs in Ex. 1a again. Ask Ss to focus on the article (the first word). Ask: *Is it always 'a'?* (No, sometimes 'an'.) Ask Ss to decide when it is *a* and when *an* and to complete the Active grammar box.

> **Answers:**   She's an artist. He's a lawyer.

▶ Write *They are _____ artists.* Ask: *What goes in the space?* (nothing, no article.) *Why?* (*A* and *an* are only for singular nouns.) Point out that *unemployed* doesn't have *A* or *an* either – *unemployed* is an adjective.

▶ Refer Ss to reference section on page 13.

3 ▶ Ss write *a* or *an* beside the words. Ss check answers in pairs, then as a whole class.

> **Answers:**   1 an   2 an   3 a   4 a   5 an   6 a
> 7 a   8 a

▶ Draw Ss attention to the initial /h/ sound in hamburger and handbag. Some Ss may be inclined to see it as a silent letter and use *an*.

Demonstrate the elision that occurs with *an*. It sounds like: a nanswer, a nuncle. /nɑːnsə/ /nʌŋkəl/. Ss practise saying an answer, an uncle, a hamburger, etc.

Person to person

4a ▶ Ss work with someone they don't know well in the class. They think of a job, then try to guess each other's jobs. Limit the questions to ten guesses. Ss can give the initial letter of their job if their partner is finding it hard to guess.

b ▶ Extend the activity to ask about the jobs of other members of the family.

> **OPTIONAL WARMER**
>
> Elicit all the names of jobs Ss can think of. Put them on the board.
>
> Ss work in pairs. They take it in turns to mime one of the jobs on the board to their partner and the other tries to guess which job it is.

Grammar

5 ▶ Ss look at the dialogue in Ex. 4a and 4b. Write on the board *Are you a taxi driver? No, I'm not a taxi driver. Is your brother a manager? No, he isn't.* Ask: *Is this positive or negative?* (negative). *What word shows you it's negative?* (not).

▶ Explain to Ss that we use the contracted forms in spoken English and informal writing.

▶ Ask Ss to complete the Active grammar box. Ss check answers in pairs, then as a whole class.

> **Answers:**   'm not   isn't   isn't

Help Ss with the /z/ sound in isn't.

6 ▶ Ss complete the sentences using the correct negative forms. Ss check answers in pairs, then as a whole class.

> **Answers:**   1 isn't   2 'm not   3 aren't   4 isn't
> 5 aren't   6 'm not

▶ Ss practise saying the sentences. Correct any pronunciation errors, especially non-use of the contracted forms.

Reading

▶ Teach *application form* to Ss (showing one is the easiest way). Elicit from Ss some of the reasons we fill out application forms (e.g. applying for a job; joining a club; getting a passport, etc.). Direct Ss to the example in their coursebooks.

▶ Ask: *Where is this form?* (on a website on the Internet). Elicit if Ss use the Internet to fill out forms or if they prefer hard copy (paper) forms. Elicit the types of questions found on forms (name, address, etc.).

7 ▶ Ss look at the questions. In pairs, they match them to the parts of the form. Teach *mobile phone* (show one) and *email address* (write one on the board) first. Teach Ss how to say an email address (. = dot; @ = at) as they will need to know this for the listening exercise in Ex. 8. They should be able to work out 'place of origin' and 'occupation' from the context.

> **Answers:** b 8   c 2   d 7   e 4   f 9   g 1   h 6   i 5

Listening

▶ Ask Ss if they like filling in forms. Do they ask someone to help them or to check their answers?

8a ▶ Play recording 1.9 once. Ss listen to find out who the two people are. Tell them you will play the recording a second time in a minute.

> **Answer:** Marta and Jake attend the same English class in London.

b ▶ Play the recording again. This time Ss listen for the details and fill in the form in Ex. 7.

> **Answers:** 2 Nowak   3 22   4 Lublin, Poland
> 5 Polish   6 36, Mill Lane, London
> 7 marta.nowak@hotserve.com   8 020 87306589
> (home) 03743 5485 132 (mobile)   9 student

c ▶ Ss look at the example dialogue and check their answers by asking their partner similar questions.

Speaking

9 ▶ Ss copy the form in Ex. 7 into their exercise books and fill it out for their partner. They practise using the questions in Ex. 7: *What's your first name? What's your surname?*, etc.

> **OPTIONAL EXTENSION**
>
> Ss imagine their partner wants to sell a TV. They write an email to a friend who is interested in buying a TV, passing on the contact details, (name, address, telephone number(s) and email address.) Begin the email 'Hi ____. A friend from my English class has a TV for sale ...' and end it 'Best wishes ____'.

▶ See Writing bank on page 143 for an example of an email layout.

10 ▶ Ss work in pairs. Each pair looks at a different page. Student A looks at page 11 and student B looks at page 125. Each student has part of the completed form for Anne and David. They must ask and answer questions, in turns, to find out the missing information. E.g. What is Anne's surname?

Communication: Making conversation

> **OPTIONAL WARMER**
>
> With multi-cultural classes, Ss can tell others the typical way of greeting and saying goodbye to others in their cultures. Is it different for formal and informal situations?
>
> With monolingual groups, Ss can tell others how they greet family members, friends, colleagues, a stranger, etc. (kiss on cheek, hug, nothing, etc.).

▶ Elicit from Ss all the ways they know of saying *hello* and *goodbye* in English.

1a ▶ Ss quickly read through the expressions and then listen to recording 1.10. They tick the expressions which they hear. Ss check answers in pairs. Do not give feedback yet until Ss have completed the How To box.

> **Answers:** Excuse me   See you later   Bye   Hi
> Good morning   Goodbye

b ▶ Ss listen again and complete the How To box.

> **Answers:** Start: Hello   Excuse me   Hi   Good morning.   Finish: See you tomorrow   See you later
> Bye   Goodbye

▶ Ask Ss to categorise the words into three groups: informal, formal and both. Discuss the different categories with the students. You may need to draw their attention to the /h/ sound in *hello* and *hi*.

2a ▶ Ss complete the dialogues. Explain *single* (not married). Ss check answers with a partner.

b ▶ Ss listen to recording 1.11 to see if they were correct.

> **Answers:** 1 B: Hello, Maria, I'm Clara.   2 A: Excuse me. Are you Silvio?   3 B: I'm from Barcelona.
> 4 A: What's your email address?   5 A: What's your job?   6 B: No, I'm not. I'm single.

3 ▶ Ss practise asking and answering the questions in Ex. 2a with their partner, using real information about themselves.

4a ▶ Review *form* from Lesson 3. Ss check the meaning of the headings in the application form by matching the words in a–d to the correct heading on the form.

> **Answers:** a 3   b 5   c 13   d 15

b ▶ Ss complete the forms using information about themselves.

5a ▶ Ss each speak to five other Ss in the class. They exchange their forms and try to find Ss who correspond to the headings in Ex. 5a.

b ▶ Try to keep the feedback short. Ask: *Who is married?* Have Ss shout out the answers about the others they have spoken to. They cannot answer about themselves.

Review and practice

Do you know?

1b ▶

Answers: /eɪ/ j k /iː/ e g p t v /e/ n s x z /aɪ/ y /uː/ u w

2a ▶

Answers: 1 one 2 two 3 three 4 four 5 five
6 six 7 seven 8 eight 9 nine 10 ten

b ▶

Answers: 14 fourteen 16 sixteen 17 seventeen
19 nineteen 22 twenty-two 30 thirty 50 fifty
70 seventy 80 eighty 90 ninety

3a ▶

Answers: 1 Look at page... 2 Listen 3 Ask and
answer 4 Read E Write 5 Complete 6 Match
7 Repeat 8 Correct 9 Check your answers

4a ▶

Answers: Food/drink: cola Family: father, daughter
Equipment: Tv Sport: football Transport: car
Colours: blue

Unit 1

1 ▶

Answers: 1 his 2 my 3 their 4 Our 5 her
6 Her 7 my 8 Tessa's 9 his

2 ▶

Answers: 1 Elizabeth is from the United States. She
is American. 2 Ivan and Katia are from Russia. They
are Russian. 3 I am from France. I am French.
4 You are from Britain. You are British. 5 Pavlos is
from Greece. He is Greek. 6 His camera is from Japan.
It is Japanese. 7 I am from Poland. I am Polish.

3 ▶

Answers: 4 Are 5 aren't 6 are 7 Russia
8 Is 9 from 10 is 11 Is 12 No 13 isn't

5 ▶

Answers: 1 Is Andreas your first name? 2 Where are
you from? 3 How old are you? 4 What do you do?
5 Who are they? 6 Are they German?

6 ▶

Answers: 1 an 2 an 3 a 4 a 5 a 6 a 7 an

7 ▶

Answers: Jobs: teacher, retired, dentist, taxi driver,
student, traffic warden, nurse, engineer, electrician;
Family: son, niece, nephew

Notes for using the Common European Framework (CEF)

CEF References

1.1 Can do: talk about where you are from

CEF A1 descriptor: can describe him/herself, what he/she does and where he/she lives (CEF page 59)

1.2 Can do: exchange information about your family

CEF A1 descriptor: can ask and answer questions about themselves and other people, where they live, people they know, things they have (CEF page 81)

1.3 Can do: understand and complete a simple form

CEF A1 descriptor: can write numbers and dates, own name, nationality, address, age, date of birth or arrival in the country, etc. such as on a hotel registration form (CEF page 84)

CEF quick brief

The Common European Framework is a reference document for teachers. It is about 260 pages long. You can download it for free from www.coe.int. The CEF recommends that Ss use a *Portfolio*. This is a document that aims to help Ss reflect on, record and demonstrate their language learning. There is a free downloadable *Total English* Portfolio.

Portfolio task

Download the Total English Portfolio free from www.longman.com/totalenglish.

Objective: help Ss to understand the purpose and value of the Portfolio.

This task can be done in Ss' own language.

▶ Make sure that each student in your class has a copy of the Total English Portfolio.

1 ▶ Ask Ss to complete their personal details on the Portfolio and explain its purpose: to help Ss learn more effectively and demonstrate their language abilities and experiences to others.

2 ▶ Explain that you will ask them to update their Portfolio at regular intervals but you will not 'mark' their Portfolio – it is an aid to learning, not a focus for learning itself.

2 Activities

Overview

Lead-in	**Vocabulary:** activities; the time
2.1	**Grammar:** present simple: *I/you/we*
	Vocabulary: holidays
	Can do: talk about your daily routine
2.2	**Grammar:** Present Simple: *he/she/it*
	Vocabulary: verbs
	Can do: write about a daily routine
2.3	**Grammar:** *this*, *that*, *these*, *those*, noun plurals
	Vocabulary: everyday objects; colours; some adjectives
	Can do: identify everyday objects
Com. Focus Reference Practice	Holiday routines

Summary

Lesson 1: Ss read an advertisement for Fun Club package holidays and an advertisement for a job as a holiday rep. They then listen to Jenny describing her typical routine as a holiday rep and the various activities she organises and participates in.

Lesson 2: Ss read descriptions of the daily routines involved in the jobs of three people: a hairdresser at a wax museum, an inventor of new rides at a theme park and a tank cleaner at the zoo.

Lesson 3: Ss listen to a description of a car boot sale, where people can buy and sell second-hand goods. They also listen to a dialogue between an airport official and a passenger at the security bag check at an airport.

Communicative focus: Ss discuss and write about each other's holiday routines.

Film bank: Unreal City (5'14")
An animation set in London (no dialogue).

Unreal City is a short animation about a man bored with his life. He escapes through his imagination and at the end of the film his dreams come true. Though *Unreal City* has no dialogue, it offers plenty of opportunity to practice the language of Unit 2.

Possible places to use this short film are:

▶ after the Unit Opener on page 15 to review the vocabulary

▶ after lesson 2 to extend work on the Present Simple

▶ at the end of the unit to round up the topic and language

For ways to use this short film in class, see Students' Book page 132 and Teacher's Book page 189.

Lead-in

OPTIONAL WARMER

Ask Ss: *What time of day do you prefer to do these things? : Study, read the paper, go to a film, phone friends, go to the gym...*, etc.

In feedback, establish whether most of the class are morning, afternoon, evening or night people.

1a ▶ Ask Ss to cover the names of the activities. Ask them to look at the pictures and discuss with a partner what the people are doing. Don't worry if they don't know the exact words/phrases for the activities at this point.

2a ▶ Ss look at the headings and match them to the pictures. Check answers as a whole class.

Answers: A leave work B get up C have dinner D get home

---

b ▶ Ss match the activities to the time of day.

Answers: in the morning: have breakfast, go to work, leave home in the afternoon: have lunch in the evening: leave work, get home, have dinner at night: go to bed

---

2a ▶ Ss listen to recording 2.1 and write in the correct times. Ss check answers with a partner and then as a whole class.

Answers: 1 half past 2 quarter to 3 o'clock 4 quarter past

---

b ▶ Ss write in the times and ask and answer with a partner to find out what times each has written down.

Answers: 1 two 2 ten 3 twelve 4 one

OPTIONAL VARIATION

In pairs. Ss think of their favourite period of day and write down the time this period usually starts and when it usually ends, e.g. The morning when I get up and before I leave the house for work. Quarter past seven till eight o'clock. The other student asks when their favourite time of day is and why (I have the house to myself; I listen to the news on the radio; I feel great after a shower, etc.).

EXTEND THE LEAD-IN

Ss make two columns (1) my working day and (2) my day off, and write in the various activities and times they do things, noting in particular any differences. They write up a piece comparing the two.

E.g. *On work days I get up at quarter past seven but on my day off I get up at around ten*, etc.

2.1 Fun Club

In this lesson Ss read two advertisements, one for a package holiday tour operator called Fun Club and one for a job as a holiday rep. They then listen to Jenny, a holiday rep working for Fun Club, describing her typical daily routine and the various activities she does as part of her job. Through this context, Ss learn the Present Simple (*I/we/you*) to describe daily routines and use it to talk about their own daily routines.

Reading

> **OPTIONAL WARMER**
>
> Give Ss two minutes to make a list in pairs of all the different types of holidays they can think of. Find out which pair had the most ideas. E.g. *skiing*, *camping*, *beach*, *bus tour*, etc.
>
> Elicit their suggestions and put them on the board. Ask which type of holiday they like best.

▶ Teach *package holiday* (a holiday company where everything is arranged for you. Club Med is fairly well known internationally.).

1 ▶ Ss look at the two texts and decide which is an advertisement for a package holiday and which for a job. Ss check answers in pairs and then as a whole class.

> **Answers:** advertisement for a package holiday = 2
> advertisement for a job = 1

▶ Ask Ss if they would like this type of holiday. Explain this job is called 'a holiday rep'.

> **OPTIONAL EXTENSION**
>
> Ask Ss to work with a partner. They list two things they would like about this job (holiday rep) and two things they would not like.

Vocabulary

2a ▶ Ss look at the pictures A–F and match them to the words. Ss compare answers in pairs and then as a whole class.

> **Answers:** 1 E 2 F 3 D 4 B 5 A 6 C

b ▶ Ss work in pairs and match the verbs in the left column with the nouns in the right column. The first one is done for them.

> **Answers:** 2 e 3 f 4 b 5 a 6 d

c ▶ Finally, Ss match each pair to advertisement 1 or 2.

> **Answers:** Advertisement 1: 2 e 3 f 6 d.
> 2: 1 c 4 b 5 a

Listening

3a ▶ Explain to Ss that only eight activities are mentioned, two are not. Play recording 2.2. Ss tick the activities mentioned as they listen. Ss check answers in pairs and then as a whole class.

> **Answers:** Have breakfast and Go to the office are not mentioned.

b ▶ Ss look at Jenny's diary. Play the recording again. Ss listen and complete the blanks in the diary by filling in the times and activities mentioned.

> **Answers:** 2 about eleven 3 quarter past eleven
> 4 2 o'clock 5 half past three 6 quarter to eight
> 7 half past ten 8 half past one

Grammar

> **OPTIONAL GRAMMAR LEAD-IN**
>
> Write out a selection of questions and answers from the tapescript on strips of paper, one question or answer for every student. Include varied questions (*Yes/No* questions and *Wh-* questions). Ss mingle, those with question cards ask the question and try to find the student with the matching answer. With small classes, this can be done with the whole class. With larger classes, divide them into groups.

4 ▶ Ss look at the tapescript and complete the Active grammar box.

> **Answers:** have Do you play do; don't do you go

Sometimes we <u>have</u> special parties; <u>Do you play</u> the games?; Yes, I <u>do</u>; No, I <u>don't</u>.; Where <u>do you go</u> for dinner?

▶ Make sure Ss are clear about the two types of questions. Put up some questions and answers on the board. Ask Ss: *What do you notice about the different answers to the questions?* (Some *Yes/No* and some more information answers.) *Which questions go with which type of answer?* ('Do you' questions and question word questions.)

5 ▶ Ss match the questions to the answers. Do the first one as a whole class. Ss work alone, then check answers with a partner before checking answers as a whole class. Draw Ss' attention to *What do you do?* as a way of finding out about a person's job rather than *What is your job?*

> **Answers:** 1 c 2 e 3 d 4 b 5 a

▶ Help Ss with the pronunciation of the questions, especially the weak /ə/ sound of the auxiliary verb *do*. Ss practise asking and answering these questions in pairs. Monitor closely and correct mistakes.

6a ▶ Ss work in pairs and complete the dialogue.

Answers: 1 do 2 Do 3 do 4 do 5 When
6 have 7 you 8 don't 9 do 10 work 11 nurse

b ▶ Ss listen to recording 2.3 to check if their answers were correct. Ask two Ss to say the dialogue for whole class feedback. Correct as necessary. Then Ss practise saying the dialogue in pairs.

> **OPTIONAL EXTENSION**
>
> Ss play a 'What's my Job?' game. Before Ss start the game, elicit as many different types of jobs as they know. Refer Ss to Ex. 1 in lesson 1.3 for a list of jobs. Put the suggestions on the board. Ss work in small groups of four or so. One student thinks of a job. The other Ss take turns to ask ten *Yes/No* questions to try to guess what the job is. (Some examples of questions are contained in 6a but you may want to elicit other types of questions they might ask first. E.g. *Do you work alone?*, *Do you wear special clothes?*, etc.)

7 ▶ Ss look at the diary in Ex. 3b. They create their own diary entries, focusing on their daily routines. Don't conduct feedback yet, as Ss will use their diaries for Ex. 8.

8 ▶ Ss complete the How to box, using the language and information they completed in Ex. 6.

Answers: do/do do At do work

Person to person

9 ▶ Ss show their diary entries to a partner. Encourage Ss to ask lots of questions about their partner's diary, focusing particularly on routines, times and places as in the How to box. Don't worry about Ss making mistakes during this activity. Encourage them to use all the language they have. Make a note of obvious errors to deal with later.

> ▷ **TIP** It is a good idea to vary the student pairings regularly to add variety to exercises. Ss have already discussed aspects of their routines with other Ss in the class, so make sure they are working with someone new. If it is difficult to move around in the classroom, this can be achieved by moving one student from the end of each row to the other end.

2.2 A very special job

In this lesson Ss read about what is involved in the jobs of three people: a wax model hairdresser at Mme Tussaud's, a theme park ride inventor and a shark tank cleaner in a zoo. Through this context, they learn the *he/she/it* forms of the Present Simple to talk and ask questions about habits and activities we do regularly. They also learn how to write about someone's daily routine.

> **OPTIONAL WARMER**
>
> Ss work in small groups of three or four. They describe to the others in the group (1) an activity they enjoy doing in their job and (2) an activity they don't enjoy doing in their job.

Reading

1a ▶ Ss look at the photos and discuss what the jobs are with a partner. Do not give the names of the jobs yet as Ss will find out in the reading.

b ▶ Scanning. Explain to Ss that they will read the three texts twice, the first time very quickly and the second time much more slowly. Explain that they do not need to understand the text fully at this point. Stop the activity after a minute. Ss compare answers in pairs and then as a whole class.

Answers: top photo: wax model hairdresser
middle photo: shark tank cleaner
bottom photo: theme park ride inventor

c ▶ Ss read the texts more slowly, this time focusing on the words in italics. First teach *theme park* (e.g. Disneyworld, in Florida) and *zoo* (a place where exotic animals are kept, not a farm). Ask Ss to try to guess the meanings of the words in italics from the surrounding words and to match the words to the labels in the pictures. Ss check answers in pairs and then as a whole class.

Answers: A the wax model B the hairdresser
C the shark D the shark tank E the theme park ride

2 ▶ Ss read the text again to find out which of the three people does the five activities.

Answers: 1 Jo 2 John 3 Jo 4 John 5 Jeanette

> **OPTIONAL EXTENSION**
>
> Ss discuss with a partner which of the three jobs they would like most and which least. They must explain why. E.g. *I like Jeanette's job best. I love animals and I think sharks are very interesting.* or *I don't like Jeanette's job. I think sharks are very scary. I hate their big teeth*, etc.

Vocabulary

3 ▶ Ss work in pairs. They match verbs from the texts to the pictures. Check answers as a whole class.

> **Answers:** a walk b swim c watch d wash
> e listen f feed g invent.

Grammar

4a ▶ Direct Ss to the texts in Ex. 1. Ask them to find the sentences in the texts and fill in the blanks in the sentences in Ex. 4. Ss check answers in pairs.

> **Answers:** 1 washes dries. 2 cleans 3 has

b ▶ Ss complete the Active grammar box with their partner.

> **Answers:** s 1 es. 2 ies 3 has.

▶ Refer Ss to the reference section on page 13.

c ▶ Ss look at text 2 and find the sentence.

> **Answer:** *Engineers* is plural and is the same as *I/you/ we*. It does not take *s* after the verb.

▶ Write *John invents new rides* and *The engineers make the rides*. Draw Ss' attention to the *s* in the first sentence but not in the second.

5 ▶ Ss complete the sentences using the verbs in the box. They check answers in pairs, and then as a whole class.

> **Answers:** 1 cleans 2 talks 3 washes 4 plays/ watches 5 helps 6 watch/play 7 have

Pronunciation

It is important for Ss to listen to the different word endings without repeating the sounds first. Complete Ex. 6a and 6b before moving on to repeating the verb endings.

6a ▶ Ss close books and listen to the three verbs in recording 2.4. Tell them to focus on the endings of the words. They should be able to hear the different endings. Ss check the sounds in their books.

b ▶ Direct Ss to the completed sentences in Ex. 5. Play recording 2.5. Ss complete the table according to the verb ending they hear.

> **Answers:** /s/ talks helps /z/ cleans plays
> /ɪz/ washes watches

▶ Ss repeat the sentences, paying particular attention to the verb endings. Ss should be able to see which verbs take the /ɪz/ sound fairly easily as it corresponds to the spelling. It is more difficult for them to pick up on the voiced and unvoiced sounds. It is enough to recognise the different sounds at this point.

OPTIONAL EXTENSION

Put all the verbs from this unit on the board. Add a few more e.g. *listen*, *play*, *work*, *clean*, *talk*, *go*, *watch*, etc. Ss work in pairs. Call out the names of jobs.

Ss have two minutes to think of sentences about the daily routine of a person with that job, using the verbs on the board. E.g. *A teacher: She/He listens to students*; *She/He works in a school*. The pair with the most sentences gets a point – but only if they get the grammar and pronunciation of the verbs right. Ss who use a verb no one else thought of also get a point. The pair with the most points wins.

Listening

7a ▶ In pairs, Ss look at the dialogue and guess what the missing words might be. Do not give feedback yet as they will get the information from the recording.

b ▶ Ss listen to recording 2.6 to see if they were right.

> **Answers:** Does does Does feeds Does works

8 ▶ Tell Ss to use the completed dialogue from Ex. 7b to choose the correct form. They cross out the incorrect words in the questions. Draw Ss' attention to the differences between *they/the sharks* and *she/Jeanette* in this tense when asking questions.

▶ Focus on the use of the auxiliary verb *do/does* and point out that you drop the *-s* after the verb (not *Does she feeds the sharks?*) Direct Ss to the reference section on page 23.

> **Answers:** 2 Do/cleans 3 Do/likes

9 ▶ Ss complete the questions using the correct form of the verbs. The first one is done for them.

> **Answers:** 1 Does/like 2 Do/watch 3 Does/invent
> 4 Do/talk 5 Does/have

Speaking

10 ▶ Ss work in pairs. Student A's card is on page 125 and Student B's card is on page 129. Give Ss a minute or two to read their cards. Ss can use their dictionaries. They should not look at their partner's card.

Ss follow the instructions on the card and ask and answer questions about Rob's routine. Don't worry if Ss make mistakes during this activity.

Writing

11 ▶ Ss choose one part of Rob's day and write sentences using the verbs they have underlined.

OPTIONAL VARIATION

Ss interview each other about their jobs and daily routine and write up a 'A Day in the Life' type article about their partner.

2.3 The car boot sale

Car boot sales are becoming increasingly popular. People fill their cars with all kinds of objects they no longer want and drive to a designated field or car park where they try to sell the objects. A similar phenomenon in the U.S. and Australia is a yard sale where people sell objects from their gardens or garages.

Teach *second-hand* (not brand new). Elicit the kind of things and places where you can buy things second-hand (eBay on the Internet; second-hand book store or clothing shops; jumble sales in schools; special magazines, etc.).

Vocabulary

1a ▶ Ss look at the photo and answer the questions in pairs.

b ▶ Play recording 2.7. Ss check their answers.

> **Answers:** They are at a car boot sale. some people sell things and other people buy.

Make sure Ss understand the difference between a car boot sale and a market.

> **OPTIONAL EXTENSION**
>
> Ss work in small groups. They discuss whether or not they would buy something at a car boot sale or on eBay (over the Internet) and explain their reasons.

2a ▶ Ss look at the picture and see if they know the names for any of the items. They then label the objects in pairs. Check answers.

> **Answers:** 1 books 2 watches 3 lamps 4 suitcase 5 DVD player 6 video camera 7 laptop computer 8 bags 9 pictures 10 shoes

b ▶ Ss listen to recording 2.8 and tick the items they hear. Check answers in pairs, then as a whole class.

> **Answers:** laptop computer watches shoes lamps suitcase

▶ Help Ss with the pronunciation of these words. 'Suitcase', in particular, can be difficult for Ss to pronounce.

> **OPTIONAL EXTENSION**
>
> Ss categorise the objects into things they would be happy to buy second-hand and things they would not. Ss compare categories with a partner.

3 ▶ Ss find examples of the different colours in the pictures with a partner. The first one is done for them.

> **Answers:** the lamps are yellow the printer is grey the chair is brown the dishes are white the watch is pink the suitcase is red the watch is orange the picture is blue the books are purple the bag is green the DVD player is silver the shoes are gold.

> **OPTIONAL EXTENSION**
>
> Ss discuss in pairs what their favourite colour is for (1) a car, (2) a phone and (3) a winter coat.

Grammar

4a ▶ Ask Ss: *What are the things in the pictures?* Ss listen to recording 2.9 and fill in the missing words.

> **Answers:** 1 this, a DVD player 2 that, a picture 3 these, mobile phones 4 those, dishes.

This (singular) and *these* (plural) are for things near to us; *that* (singular) and *those* (plural) are for things farther away. Use gestures to demonstrate the point to Ss.

▶ Help Ss with the pronunciation of the contracted form and the /ð/ sound in the four words. Direct Ss to the reference section on page 23.

b ▶ Ss correct the underlined words. Check answers in pairs, then as a whole class.

> **Answers:** 1 that/this 2 are 3 Is 4 This

▶ Emphasise to Ss that *those/these* are plural and take 'are', e.g. *Those/these* are cars. *This/that* are singular and take 'is' e.g. *That/this* is a car.

Pronunciation

5a ▶ Put the /ɪ/ and /iː/ vowel sounds on the board. Play recording 2.10 and write *this* and *these* under the correct sound.

b ▶ Play recording 2.11. Ss put the words in the correct side of the table.

> **Answers:** /ɪ/ listen, pink, sister, think
> /iː/ green niece read teacher

▶ Ss repeat the sounds. Dictate further words to Ss. Ss add them to the table. (E.g. *sheep, bit, sleep, keep, lip, sit.*)

Vocabulary

▶ Show Ss two things which are the complete opposite of each other (e.g. two money notes – one brand new and the other old and worn; or two books – one very large and the other very small). Ask Ss: *What is the difference between these two books/notes?* The difference should be immediately obvious to them.

6a ▶ Ss look at the words in the box, using a dictionary for the words they don't know and match the opposites. Ss check answers in pairs, then as a whole class.

> **Answers:** big – small horrible – nice modern – old-fashioned old – young useful – useless

b ▶ Ss choose six of the adjectives and write sentences about themselves using the adjectives.

Listening

7a ▶ Ss close their books. Teach *Madam* and *Sir* as a way of addressing people in a formal or official situation. Ask them to listen to the three dialogues and find out where the people are. Play recording 2.12. Ss check answers in pairs, then as a whole class.

> **Answer:**   At the security bag check at an airport.

b ▶ Ss look at the pictures. They identify the objects in the bags with a partner. Play the recording again. Ss listen and match each dialogue to the correct picture. Check answers in pairs, then as a whole class.

> **Answers:**   1 B   2 A   3 C

c ▶ Ss look at the tapescript on page 151. In pairs, they find six more words for everyday objects.

Grammar

8a ▶ Ss complete the Active grammar box in pairs.

> **Answers:**   books   lamps   phones   s

b ▶ Ss complete the table. Check answers in pairs, then as a whole class. Direct Ss to reference section on page 23.

> **Answers:**   bags   cameras   shoes   watches   dishes   scarves

Lifelong learning

c ▶ Ask Ss if they know any other irregular nouns like person – people. They probably know a few already, e.g. foot – feet. Explain they are going to learn how to use the dictionary to find the plurals of words. Teach the abreviation 'pl.' which is sometimes found in dictionaries.

▶ Ss look at the dictionary entry for *diary*. In pairs, they find the plurals of the other words.

> **Answers:**   men   women   children   wives   dictionaries   addresses   families   nieces   classes   buses

Speaking

9 ▶ Ss play the game. Elicit some examples of possible questions before they start. Don't worry if Ss make mistakes during this activity. Note down any obvious errors to deal with later.

> **OPTIONAL VARIATION**
>
> Ask Ss to imagine they are going to go to a monastery or temple for a month of solitude and meditation. In pairs, Ss discuss what three personal items they would bring from home.

Communication: Holiday routines

> **OPTIONAL WARMER**
>
> Put the three headings on the board: *in the city*; *in the mountain*; *at the beach*. In pairs, Ss discuss which location is the best for a city holiday, a holiday in the mountains and a beach holiday. They must give reasons for their choices. (E.g. *I think Bondi beach in Australia is the best beach holiday. It's good for scuba diving and I love kangaroos*). Elicit suggestions from the class in feedback. Find out which is the most popular destination for each type of holiday.

1 ▶ Ss look at the photos that show different holiday destinations. In pairs, they match the captions to the photos in pairs.

> **Answers:**   1 B   2 C   3 A

2a ▶ Ss look at the words in the box. In pairs, they complete the questions using one of the words for each gap. In feedback, help Ss with the *Wh* sounds in the questions.

> **Answers:**   2 get   3 Who   4 do   5 When   6 do   7 What   8 time/go

b ▶ Ss match the answers to the questions. Check answers in pairs, then as a whole class.

> **Answers:**   1 b   2 h   3 g   5 c   6 d   7 f   8 e

c ▶ Ss think about their own answers to these questions and write them in note form in the 'you' section of the questionnaire. Encourage them not to write full sentences at this point.

3a ▶ Ss work in pairs and ask each other about their holiday routines using the questions from Ex. 2a. Encourage Ss to answer at length, without worrying about making mistakes. As you monitor, note down any obvious errors, which you can deal with later.

b ▶ Based on the information gathered during Ex. 3a, Ss decide which type of holiday would suit their partner best.

4a ▶ Have a number of Ss describe their partner's holiday routines to others in the class. With large classes, Ss can work in groups.

b ▶ Ss write about their partner's holiday routines.

> **OPTIONAL VARIATION**
>
> Ss work in small groups. Together they must decide on a group holiday which will please all the members of the group. They must choose
>
> (1) a destination, (2) a type of accommodation and (3)a time of year for their holiday.

Review and practice

1 ▶

> Answers: B He reads his emails at half past nine.
> C He eats a sandwich at a quarter to one.   D He
> finishes work at half past six.   E He watches the news
> at ten o'clock.   F He goes to bed at half past eleven.

2 ▶

> Answers: 1 get up   2 Does/have   3 go   4 cleans
> 5 do/do

3 ▶

> Answers: 1 What does she do in the afternoon?
> 2 Where does he have lunch?   3 Do you take the train
> to work?   4 When does he finish work?   5 What do
> you do in the evening?

4 ▶

> Answers: 1 holidays   3 parties   4 pizzas
> 5 sandwiches   8 knives

5 ▶

> Answers: 1 these/sandwiches   2 that/shark
> 3 What's that? It's a nightclub   4 What are those?
> They're dictionaries

6a ▶

> Possible answers: Personal: book, scarf, handbag,
> shoes, magazine, wallet, mobile phone, watch;
> House/home: dish, lamp, desk, picture; Travel:
> suitcase; Equipment: printer, camera, fax machine,
> scissors, computer

b ▶

> Answers: Ss' own answers.

c ▶

> Answers: 1 hairdresser   2 mechanic   3 shop
> assistant   4 inventor   5 teacher   6 cleaner
> 7 bank clerk

Notes for using the Common European Framework (CEF)

CEF References

2.1 Can do: talk about your daily routine

CEF A1 descriptor: can ask and answer simple questions, initiate and respond to simple, statements in areas of immediate need or on very familiar topics (CEF page74)

2.2 Can do: write about a daily routine

CEF A1 descriptor: can write simple phrases and sentences about themselves and imaginary people, where they live and what they do (CEF page 62)

2.3 Can do: identify everyday objects

CEF A1 descriptor: has a basic vocabulary repertoire of isolated words and phrases related to particular concrete situations (CEF page 112)

CEF quick brief

The Common European Framework is produced by the Council of Europe. The Council of Europe is concerned with issues like human rights, European identity, education and more. This identity is based on diversity and the Common European Framework gives equal importance to all languages of Council of Europe member nations.

Portfolio task

Download the Total English Portfolio free from www.longman.com/totalenglish.

Objective: help Ss to use the Portfolio to assess their skills.

This task can be done in Ss' own language.

▶ Portfolios are divided into three main sections. The first section is called the 'Passport'. The Passport is designed to summarise relevant language learning experiences and qualifications. This can be shown to others, for example new teachers, employers, etc. Firstly, however, it is helpful for learners to give their own assessment of their abilities in the different skills areas.

1 ▶ Help Ss to understand the self-assessment grids (there are many translations available as this is a standard document) for levels A1 to B1.

2 ▶ Ask Ss to assess their own abilities in the different skills areas (listening, reading, spoken interaction, spoken production, and writing). Ss complete the language skills profile by shading in the relevant boxes.

3 ▶ Explain that Ss can update this profile as they progress and they can fill in profiles for other languages.

3 Free time

Overview

Lead-in	**Vocabulary:** free time activities
3.1	**Grammar:** Present Simple: negative
	Vocabulary: basic leisure activities; days of the week
	Can do: talk about your free time
3.2	**Grammar:** *can/can't*
	Vocabulary: sports, games and activities; *play/go/do,* + sport
	Can do: talk about what you can and can't do
3.3	**Functions:** making suggestions; using the phone
Vocabulary:	large numbers
Can do:	understand and leave a simple phone message
Com. Focus:	The perfect job
Reference	
Practice	

Summary

Lesson 1: Ss listen to people describing what they do to pass the time in traffic jams and read about what Alistair does during his lunch break.

Lesson 2: Ss read about Tony Hawk, who counts being world skateboard champion among his many abilities and achievements.

Lesson 3: Ss listen to phone messages and read about texting and phone throwing events at the Mobile Phone Olympics.

Communication focus: Ss discuss four people's abilities and hobbies in order to suggest suitable jobs for them.

Film bank: Deborah's day (4'46")
A short film about an actor and her free time.

Deborah's day is about an actor and what she does in her free time. We see Deborah's house and the places she goes to exercise, shop and relax. Deborah talks to the camera throughout.

Possible places to use this short film are:

▶ before the Unit Opener on page 25 to introduce the topic of free time

▶ after lesson 1 to review the Present Simple with *he/she/it*

▶ at the end of the unit to round up the topic and language

For ways to use this short film in class, see Students' Book page 133 and Teacher's Book page 190.

Lead-in

OPTIONAL WARMER

Ask Ss to imagine it is Sunday morning and they have no work or anything they have to do. Tell their partner what they would do with their time. E.g. Read the paper, listen to music, go for a walk with the dog, stay in bed, etc. Don't worry about Ss making mistakes. Write their suggestions on the board.

1a ▶ Ss look at the photos and choose verbs and verb phrases in the box that describe them.

Answers: A go to the gym   B cook   C go shopping   D go to a concert

---

b ▶ Direct Ss to the box and ask them to check the words they don't know with a partner. Draw their attention to the use of the definite and indefinite article: go to a concert/ go to the gym; play football/play the guitar; watch TV/ watch a video; listen to music/listen to the radio. Ask Ss which of the activities they enjoy doing?

c ▶ Ss organise the words according to the table in pairs. There will be some overlap between the categories. Encourage Ss to discuss these.

Possible Answers: At home: cook, listen to music, play the guitar, read a book or magazine, sunbathe, watch TV or a video; In the park: listen to music, go for a walk, meet friends, go to a concert, play the guitar, read a book or magazine, sunbathe, play football; At the shops: go shopping, meet friends; At a nightclub: dance, meet friends, listen to music; At a concert hall: dance, go to a concert, listen to music, meet friends; At a sports centre/swimming pool: go to the gym, listen to music, meet friends, play football, sunbathe, read a book or magazine, swim

---

▶ Encourage Ss to add as many activities as they can to the list.

2a ▶ Ss write the activities. Draw Ss' attention to the language *in the morning/evening; at the weekend; on Mondays.*

b ▶ In pairs, Ss ask and answer questions about their free time.

c ▶ Ss tell the class about their partner. With larger groups ask: *Who else plays the guitar? Who else likes reading?* to speed up the feedback.

EXTEND THE LEAD-IN

Game. Ss work in small groups. Each student thinks of an activity and the others ask up to five questions to guess what it is. E.g. *Do you do it alone? Do you do it in a special place? Do you need special clothes?*, etc.

3.1 Drive time

In this lesson Ss focus on what people do in their free time. They listen to people describing what they do to pass the time in traffic jams and read about what Alistair does during his lunch break. Through this context they learn the Present Simple negative and how to talk and write about their own free time activities.

Listening

1 ▶ Ask Ss to focus on the picture. Teach *traffic jam*. Ask students how people feel when they are stuck in traffic (angry/bored/worried they will be late, etc.). Elicit ideas about the kind of things people do in traffic jams (listen to music/the radio; put on make-up, etc.). Put suggestions on the board. Try to elicit some of the key vocabulary from the text during feedback (e.g. mobile phone, CD player, diary, computer games, shave).

2a ▶ Tell Ss they are going to listen to five people talking about what they do in traffic jams. Ss read through the texts first and try to guess what the missing words/ phrases might be. They check answers with a partner. Play recording 3.1 once and Ss listen to see if they were right.

> **Answers:** 1 write 2 listen to 3 hate 4 watch
> 5 play 6 call

b ▶ Ss cover the reading text and then read the five sentences. Play the recording again. Ss listen to see if the statements are true or false. After listening, Ss check answers with a partner and then as a whole class.

> **Answers:** 1 F 2 F 3 T 4 F 5 F

Grammar

> **OPTIONAL GRAMMAR LEAD-IN**
>
> Focus on the false statements from Ex. 2b. E.g. *Her daughter likes traffic jams.* Ask: *Why is this false? What is the right answer?* Her daughter doesn't like traffic jams.
>
> Nathan listens to CDs. *Why is this false? What is the right answer?* Nathan doesn't listen to CDs.
>
> Put the new sentences on the board and ask Ss what they notice about them.

3a ▶ Ss find the negatives in the text and underline them. Write the sentences on the board. Underline the negative verb in each sentence.

> **Answers:** doesn't like don't make doesn't have
> don't like

▶ Ask: *Do you notice anything different about the four sentences?* (My daughter *doesn't* like traffic jams. I *don't* make phone calls.) Third person singular changes from <u>do</u> to <u>does</u> + <u>n't</u>. *What happens to the verb after 'doesn't' and 'don't'?* (Infinitive without <u>to</u>).

b ▶ Ss complete the Active grammar box. Write the grammar box on the board and elicit the correct answers for the gaps in feedback.

> **Answers:** don't doesn't don't

▶ Direct Ss to the reference section on page 23.

4a ▶ Direct Ss to Ex. 2b. Ss make the negative sentences in pairs. Elicit answers from the whole class.

> **Answers:** 1 Melanie's daughter doesn't like traffic jams. 2 Nathan doesn't listen to CDs. 4 Lauren and Emily don't work on their computers. 5 Lauren and Emily don't think mobile phones in cars are dangerous

b ▶ Ss tick correct answers about themselves and rewrite the false answers to make them correct.

> **OPTIONAL EXTENSION**
>
> In pairs Ss make sentences about themselves or other students in the class. Give a few minutes to prepare their sentences. Each pair reads out their sentences and the others have to guess whether the sentences are true or false.
>
> E.g. *I don't like chocolate. X gets up early on Saturday. X doesn't have a pet. X sings in the shower.* etc.

Vocabulary

5a ▶ Ss order the days of the week, then listen to recording 3.2 to check their answers.

> **Answers:** 6 Friday 2 Monday 7 Saturday
> 1 Sunday 5 Thursday 3 Tuesday 4 Wednesday

▶ Focus on the pronunciation of the words, especially *Tuesday, Wednesday* and *Thursday*. Ask: *What day is today? What day is tomorrow?* Teach the expressions *the day after tomorrow* and *the day before yesterday*.

> **OPTIONAL LEAD-IN**
>
> Ss discuss their own lunch break in pairs. Put the following headings on the board to guide their conversation. *how long?/food?/who with?/activities during lunch break?*

b ▶ Ss look at the pictures and decide what the various activities are. Play recording 3.3. Ss listen and mark which day for each activity. Ss check answers in pairs. If Ss are having difficulty, play the recording a second time before checking answers as a whole class.

> **Answers:** A Monday B Wednesday C Saturday
> D Sunday E Thursday F Friday

Reading

6a ▶ Ss read silently. They find and correct the three mistakes and check answers with a partner.

> **Answers:** On Tuesdays he goes to the gym. On Wednesdays he sometimes meets friends in a restaurant. On Fridays he works.

b ▶ Ss write the correct sentences. Elicit answers from the whole class.

> **Answers:** 1 He doesn't watch a film on Thursdays. 2 On Fridays he works. 3 He doesn't play football on Saturdays. 4 On Sundays he sleeps.

Speaking

7a ▶ Direct Ss to the chart. Ask them to read through the activities and tick the ones that apply to them, then write in when they do this activity, e.g. *on Sunday mornings/on Saturday evenings/at night/in the morning/ at the weekend*.

b ▶ Ss interview each other about what they do in their free time and complete the chart for their partner.

> **OPTIONAL VARIATION**
>
> Class survey. Put the following headings on the board. *Every day/Once a week/Sometimes/Never* (If Ss are confident, you can increase the number of headings: e.g. *rarely*, *often*). Elicit *How many of us watch TV every day?*, *How many never go to the gym?*, etc. Collate the information under the different headings. Find out the most popular activities in the class. With larger classes, Ss can work in groups for this.
>
> Ss write the results of the survey, e.g. *70% of us go for walks once a week*, etc.

Writing

8a ▶ Ss work alone and brainstorm ideas about their free time.

b ▶ Prepare a short model article in advance to show Ss (handout, overhead or on the board). Ss write their articles based on their notes for Ex. 8a. With smaller groups, help with errors as they write. Otherwise take notes and mark errors later.

> ▷ **TIP** Use a marking code, rather than correcting the errors yourself. There is no need to correct every error, just the important ones for this stage of the course. Ss can then correct their own errors.

3.2 Skateboard style

In this lesson Ss read about Tony Hawk, who counts being world skateboard champion among his many abilities and achievements. They learn *can/can't* to describe ability and how to speak about what they can and can't do themselves.

Vocabulary

1a ▶ Ss focus on the pictures and match them to an activity in the box.

> **Answers:** A football B yoga C sailing D aerobics E running F computer games G judo H skiing I swimming J tennis

▶ Ask Ss to categorise the words into (1) indoor/outdoor activities and (2) activities which we do alone/in teams.

b ▶ Ss complete the table and check answers with a partner, and then as a whole class.

> **Answers:** DO: yoga, judo GO: sailing, swimming, skiing PLAY: computer games, tennis

▶ Draw Ss' attention to the fact that *play* is usually used with activities done in teams or games. *Do* is usually used with non-game activities which we do alone. Ask Ss what they notice about what is usually used with *go* (the *-ing* form of the verb).

c ▶ Ss ask and answer questions about the activities in pairs. Review the phrases *on Mondays*; *at the weekend*; *in the morning* to help them.

> **OPTIONAL EXTENSION**
>
> Ss cover books. They take it in turns to mime one of the activities to another student, who must guess what it is and give the whole expression: *go swimming*, *play football*, *do yoga*, etc.

See www.tonyhawk.com for further information on Tony Hawk, successful skateboarder, businessman and writer.

Reading

2a ▶ Direct Ss to the photos of Tony Hawk and discuss the questions as a whole class.

b ▶ Tell Ss they are going to read the first part of a newspaper article about Tony Hawk. Pre-teach *champion* (the best at something, e.g. gold medal at the Olympic Games (not the silver).

Ss look at the questions first and then read the short text. Elicit answers as a whole class.

> **Answers:** 1 He's from America. 2 He's a businessman. 3 He's 34 years old and a skateboarder.

3a ▶ Scanning. Direct Ss to the longer text about Tony Hawk. Explain that they will read the text twice, the first time very quickly and the second time much more slowly. Direct them to the questions in Ex. 3a and tell them they have one minute to find this information in the text as quickly as possible. Explain that they do not need to understand the text at this point. Stop the activity after a minute and have Ss call out the answers.

> **Answers:** 1 34 2 Spencer, 4 3 Hawk – Occupation: skateboarder

b ▶ Ss look at the questions for Ex. 3b. Explain *prize* (what you get when you come first, e.g. money) and *show* (entertainment like a circus or musical). Put the words *tricks*, *competitions* and *perform* on the board and encourage Ss to guess the meaning of these words. Ss read the text again, at their own pace. Explain they do not need to understand every word in the text.

▶ Ss compare answers in pairs before whole-class feedback.

> **Answers:** 1 73 2 tricks 3 a skateboard 4 all around the U.S. and Canada 5 skateboarding tricks and music

Grammar

4a ▶ Say: *Tony can ride a skateboard* and then write it on the board. Ask: *Is he good at skateboarding?* Elicit if anyone else likes skateboarding. Find a student (or yourself) who doesn't skateboard. Write X (name of person) can't skateboard on the board. Establish that X is not good at it.

▶ Ss cover the text and with a partner try to remember what Tony can and can't do. They look at the list of activities in Ex. 4a and in pairs mark a ✓ at what he can do and an X at what he can't do. Ss check their answers in the text.

> **Answers:** play the guitar X ride a skateboard ✓ use a computer ✓ sing X play rock music X perform tricks ✓

b ▶ Ss complete the sentences using *can* and *can't* and the question form. Put *can* and *can't* on the board and point to the correct answer during feedback. Ss complete the Active grammar box.

> **Answers:** 1 can 2 can 3 can't 4 Can 5 can't, can

▶ Ask Ss if they notice anything different about the verb *can*: It never changes, (no *s* after He/She can); It doesn't need another verb to make it negative or to ask a question (*I don't can swim. Do you can swim?*); It almost always has another verb with it (*I can swim*).

▶ Direct Ss to the reference section on page 33.

> **OPTIONAL EXTENSION**
>
> Ss work in pairs to make sentences and the other Ss guess who or what they are describing. E.g. *It can fly. It can talk. It can't sing.* (a parrot). He can fly. He can lift heavy objects. He can't do magic. (Superman).

Pronunciation

5 ▶ Tell Ss they are going to listen to two mothers describing what their children can and can't do. Ss look at the list of activities. Play recording 3.4 once. Ss check answers with a partner, then check with the whole class.

> **Answers:** play the piano – S sing – J, S dance – S play football – J play tennis – J, S ski – S speak French – J, S speak Spanish – S ride a bike – J drive a car – S

6a ▶ Play recording 3.5. Ss note how *can* and *can't* are pronounced. Put the phonetic sounds on the board and say the sentences for the Ss, emphasising the different vowel sounds. Ss repeat the sentences after the recording. Draw Ss' attention to the final /t/ ending in can't.

b ▶ Direct Ss to Ex. 5 again. Model a few questions about what Jonny and Susie can do with the whole class. Ask: *Can Susie speak Spanish?* Ss Answer *Yes, she can*, or *No, she can't*. Ss continue the exercise in pairs.

c ▶ Ss work in pairs and ask and answer questions about themselves based on the activities listed in Ex. 5. Monitor and correct any errors you hear.

Speaking

7a ▶ Ss work in small groups. They look through the various activities and discuss their own abilities in relation to them. Encourage Ss to respond to what others can and can't do. E.g. St1: *I can play the saxophone.* St2: *Oh, when did you learn? Is it difficult?* etc. It is not important if they make mistakes during this activity.

b ▶ One student from each group describes their overall findings to the rest of the class.

> **OPTIONAL VARIATION**
>
> Give each student one of the abilities from Ex. 7a. They circulate and ask other Ss if they can do that activity. If the answer is 'No', they move on, but if the answer is 'Yes', they have to find out two more things about that activity and that person.
>
> E.g. *Can you speak three languages? Yes. Which languages? Where did you learn French?*, etc.

3.3 Phone fun

In this lesson Ss listen to phone messages and read about the Mobile Phone Olympics. They learn how to make suggestions and requests and how to leave a simple phone message.

Listening

▶ Ask Ss: *What are the good things about having a mobile phone?* (can always be reached; texting, etc.). Ask: *Are there any bad things about them?* (can extend the working day; interruptions, etc.).

1 ▶ Ss answer the questions in Ex. 1 in pairs. Establish whether Ss make more 'social calls' or 'work calls' on their mobiles during class feedback.

> **OPTIONAL WARMER**
>
> Have Ss work in small groups to discuss the following questions. *How many phones do you have in your house?; Which rooms are they in?; Are there times when you don't answer the phone (e.g. during dinner, etc.)?*
>
> In whole-class feedback, establish who uses the phone the most in each group.

2a ▶ Tell Ss they are going to listen to five different phone messages. Ss read the five names first. Play recording 3.6 once and Ss listen to find out which name relates to which message. The first one is done for them.

> **Answers:** Damian 4   Mary Wilde 5
> Benson Cameras 3   Steve Henshaw 2

b ▶ Ss read through the written messages in their books. Play the recording again. Ss complete the texts with the missing words. Check answers in pairs and then as a whole class.

> **Answers:** 1 Jane, cinema   2 call, -0752   3 Brown, camera, week, 6.30   4 dinner, Italian, office
> 5 391, call

c ▶ Play message 5 again. Ss listen to how we say *88*.

> **Answer:** double eight

3a ▶ Ss work in pairs to put the sentences into the correct order. The first one is done for them.

> **Answers:**   2 Hello, can I speak to Laura, please?
> 3 She isn't here right now. Can I take a message?
> 4 Yes, please ask her to phone Jeffrey.   5 OK. What's your number?   6 It's 011 908 5561.   7 OK. Bye.

b ▶ Ss practise saying the dialogue in pairs. Monitor Ss correcting any obvious mis-pronunciation you hear.

4 ▶ Ss practise making phone calls in pairs. Give Ss time to read their individual cards. Student A's card is on page 125. When Ss have finished, ask one pair to model the phone call to the others.

Reading

▶ Write the following text messages on the board *C u l8r* and *R u coming 2nite*? Ask Ss if they know what they are and where they might see them. (*See you later* and *Are you coming tonight?* are informal text messages.) Establish that we would not use this type of language in a formal situation.

> **OPTIONAL ACTIVITY**
>
> Ss discuss in pairs when they would text rather than phone someone. Put these headings on the board to guide the discussion. *Who?/Why?* (reason for the call)/*When?* (time of day), etc.

5a ▶ Tell Ss they are going to read about the Mobile Phone Olympics. Elicit suggestions as to the kind of activities which might happen at this event.

▶ Scanning. Explain to Ss that they will read the text twice, the first time very quickly and the second time much more slowly. Direct them to the questions and tell them they have one minute to find this information in the text as quickly as possible. Teach *throw* (mime throwing a ball). Explain that they do not need to understand the text fully at this point. Stop the activity after a minute and have Ss call out the answers.

> **Answers:**   a 2   b 3   c 1

b ▶ Ss look at the columns. Explain *user* (someone who uses a service). Ss predict what the answers will be with a partner. Do not give feedback as they will find the answers in the text.

▶ Pre-teach *fan* and *the average phone user* (football fan and the typical phone users). Check they remember *champion* from Lesson 3.2. Ss read the text again silently and complete the matching exercise as they read. The first one is done for them. Ss check answers in pairs, then as a whole class.

> **Answers:**   1 d   3 e   4 f   5 c   6 b   7 a

6 ▶ In pairs, Ss match the figures to the written number in the box. Then they listen to recording 3.8 to see if they were right.

> **Answers:**   16 sixteen   60 sixty   600 six hundred
> 6,000 six thousand   60,000 sixty thousand
> 600,000 six hundred thousand   6,000,000 six million
> 6,000,000,000 six billion

Pronunciation

7a ▶ Play recording 3.9. Ss listen and underline the strong sounds.

> **Answers:**   six<u>teen</u>   <u>six</u>ty   four<u>teen</u>   <u>for</u>ty

▶ Teach the phonetic symbols /i/ and /iː/ to help emphasise the point. Ss repeat the words after you.

b ▶ Ss listen to recording 3.10 and tick the number they hear. Check answers with a partner, then as a whole class.

Answers: 1 forty 2 eighty 3 seventeen
4 thirteen 5 ninety 6 sixteen

c ▶ Ss practise saying the weak and strong forms to each other.

OPTIONAL EXTENSION

Ask Ss if these numbers have any significance as ages in their country (e.g. driver's licence at 16; voting at 18; women retiring at 60, etc.).

---

8 ▶ Direct Ss to the phone messages they listened to in Ex. 2a. Put *suggestion* and *request* on the board. Establish the purpose of each of the calls: making suggestions (we want to do something with another person) in call 1 and 3; making requests (we want someone else to do something) in calls 2, 4 and 5. Call 3 also includes a request. In pairs, Ss read the messages and complete the How to box.

> Answers: meet for dinner the Italian restaurant
> ask him to call

▶ Explain to Ss that *Why don't we ...?* and *How about ...?* both take question marks when we write them but are not real questions. The appropriate response to *Why don't we meet at five?* is not *Because ...* but something like *Ok* or *No/Sorry, I can't/don't like it*.

9a ▶ Ss write the times in full.

> Answers: 1 twenty past three 2 five to nine
> 3 half past six 4 twenty five past eight

▶ Ss practise saying the times. Draw their attention to the weak sound /ə/ in five <u>to</u> nine and ten <u>to</u> eight.

OPTIONAL EXTENSION

Time Bingo. Ss write down six numbers in pairs using the 24-hour clock (e.g. 17.20). Call out times at random (e.g. twenty past five). Ss tick their times if you call it. Continue until one pair has ticked all six times and calls Bingo.

---

b ▶ Ss write the suggestions and requests. Check answers in pairs and then as whole class.

> Answers: 1 Let's have dinner at the Chinese restaurant at twenty to nine. 2 Can you come to the office tomorrow at five to ten? 3 How about lunch in the Greek café in Belmont St at ten past three? 4 Why don't we go to the bar at a quarter to eleven?

10a ▶ Ss look at the list of activities. In pairs, tick the activities that people do in their area and note down where and when they can do them.

b ▶ Ss practise making and responding to suggestions in pairs. Ss order the activities according to which they would like to do best.

Communication:
The perfect job

1a ▶ Ss work in pairs to match the abilities to the jobs. Encourage Ss to use dictionaries.

> Answers: 2 i 3 a 4 b 5 j 6 h 7 c 8 e 9 f
> 10 d

OPTIONAL EXTENSION

Ss work in small groups and decide which of the jobs they consider (1) most interesting, (2) most difficult, (3) most boring, (4) most stressful.

---

b ▶ Ss extend the list of jobs and abilities. Give them a few prompts to get started (e.g. doctor, Prime Minister).

2a ▶ Elicit ways of looking for a job (ads in the paper, sending letters to companies, etc.) Explain what an *employment agency* is. Direct Ss to the Perfect Employment Agency notes for four people. Make sure Ss understand *qualifications* (diploma; exams). Teach *a degree* and *notes* (pieces of important information, not full sentences).

▶ Ss read about Jane Danuby and Brian Winter and complete the employment agency notes for them. Check answers in pairs and then as whole class.

> Answers:
> Jane: 32; a degree in Art; can speak Spanish and German, can paint and draw, can take digital photos and change them on her computer; likes the Internet
> Brian: 25; none; can repair cars and engines, can repair houses, can make furniture in wood and metal, can drive; doesn't like cold weather

b ▶ Ss listen to recording 3.11 and complete the information for the other two people in the notes. Ss check answers with a partner after the first listening. Play the recording a second time then check answers.

> Answers:
> David: 22; certificate in computer programming; can play the piano and guitar, can drive; dislikes computer programming
> Lizzie: 26, a college diploma in sports medicine; football, basketball, tennis, aerobics, dancing, can speak Portuguese; likes dancing

3a ▶ Ss work in groups of three or four and decide on the best job from the list in Ex. 1 a for each of the four people. Remind Ss of *can* and *can't*, the Present Simple and the language of suggestions, which have been covered earlier in the units, before they start.

b ▶ Encourage Ss to explain and justify their views. It is not important if Ss make mistakes during this activity. During monitoring, note down any obvious errors and deal with them in a general way when the activity has finished.

Review and practice

1 ▶

> **Answers:** 1 Malcolm doesn't have a job. 2 Malcolm doesn't have an address. 3 Malcolm doesn't go to work every morning. 4 Malcolm carries his things in a bag. 5 Malcolm doesn't eat in restaurants.
> 6 Ss own answers.

2 ▶

> **Answers:** Ss' own answers.

3 ▶

> **Possible answers:** 1 Computers can check spellings/can't play football. 2 Sharks can swim/can't understand Russian. 3 Mobile phones can send photos/can't clean a shark tank. 4 Cats can run/can't invent text messages.

4 ▶

> **Answers:** Andrea can do a lot of things he can play basketball he can't play tennis he doesn't like tennis he plays the guitar he sings too he doesn't dance he can't play the piano.

5 ▶

> **Answers:** 1 Let's meet at six o'clock. 2 How about lunch at the Italian restaurant? 3 Can you take a message? 4 Let's get a takeaway from MacDonald's. 5 Can you give me your phone number? 6 Why don't we watch a video this evening? 7 How about dinner on Saturday?

6 ▶

> **Answers:** 1 go 2 invite 3 take 4 go 5 cook
> 6 go 7 play 8 do 9 go 10 go 11 watch

Notes for using the Common European Framework (CEF)

CEF References

3.1 Can do: talk about your free time

CEF A1 descriptor: can interact in a simple way but communication is totally dependent on repetition at a slower rate of speech, rephrasing and repair (CEF page 74)

3.2 Can do: talk about what you can and can't do

CEF A1 descriptor: can reply in an interview to simple direct questions spoken very slowly and clearly in direct non-idiomatic speech about personal details (CEF page 82)

3.3 Can do: understand and leave a simple phone message

CEF A1 descriptor: can manage very short, isolated, mainly pre-packaged utterances, with much pausing to search for expressions, to articulate less familiar words, and to repair communication (CEF page 129)

CEF quick brief

The Common European Framework describes itself as 'a common basis for the elaboration of language syllabuses, curriculum guidelines, examinations, textbooks, etc'. It is not intended to be a definitive description of what to teach but it is designed to offer a 'framework' which the user can build on.

Portfolio task

Download the Total English Portfolio free from www.longman.com/totalenglish.

Objective: help Ss to complete the 'language learning and intercultural experiences' section of their Passport.

This task can be done in Ss' own language.

1 ▶ Remind Ss that their Passport enables them to demonstrate their relevant experiences and qualifications.

2 ▶ Explain that language learning and intercultural experiences are important in this. The Total English Portfolio has a section for Ss to give information about these.

3 ▶ Give some examples of your own relevant experiences (exchange trips, holidays, courses, friends with that first language, etc).

4 ▶ Ask Ss to write a list of their own relevant experiences and show a partner.

5 ▶ Ask Ss to complete this section of their Passport.

6 ▶ Remind Ss that they can update this at any time.

4 Food

Overview

Lead-in	**Vocabulary:** food and drink
4.1	**Grammar:** countable and uncountable nouns; *How much?/How many?*
	Vocabulary: food and drink
	Can do: talk about quantities and numbers
4.2	**Grammar:** *a/an*, *some* and *any*
	Vocabulary: containers; adjectives describing physical and emotional states
	Can do: talk about your diet and lifestyle
4.3	**Grammar:** object pronouns; *I'd like*
	Vocabulary: menus, prices
	Can do: order food in a fast food restaurant
Com. Focus	Shopping at a market
Reference	
Practice	

Summary

Lesson 1: Ss read about the shopping and eating habits of 3 different families, the Ronayne family from the United States, the Ukita family from Japan and the Costa family from Cuba.

Lesson 2: Ss listen to part of a TV programme looking at people's diet. They then read several letters to a problem page in a magazine describing problems with diet and a reply to one of those letters.

Lesson 3: Ss listen to two people ordering food in a fast food restaurant. They then read the menu for the restaurant.

Communicative focus: Ss buy and sell food at a market.

Film bank: Two soups (3'22")
An extract from a British TV comedy programme.

Two soups is a classic sketch from a comedy series called As seen on TV. The show starred Victoria Wood (who also wrote the show) and Julie Walters (who appears here). In this sketch, two customers have to cope with a waitress who has a poor memory and unsteady hands.

Possible places to use this short film are:

▶ after lesson 3 to extend the work on restaurants and ordering

▶ at the end of the unit as an entertaining end to the topic of food

For ways to use this short film in class, see Students' Book page 134 and Teacher's Book page 190.

Lead-in

OPTIONAL WARMER

Ss work in small groups of three or four. They tell each other what their favourite food is in the following situations (1) in bed when you're not feeling well, (2) at the beach on a hot day, (3) at the cinema, (4) served with a drink in a bar.

---

1 ▶ Ss look at the painting and the photos. They match eight of the words in the box to the food in the pictures. Check answers in pairs, then as a whole class.

Answers: A cheese   B bread   C butter
D cherries   E rice   F apples   G eggs   H milk

2a ▶ Ss ask a partner or use dictionaries to find the meanings of the other words. They put the words under the correct column in the table. Give them a time limit of three minutes for this to add an element of fun to the list making. See which pair has the longest list.

▶ In groups Ss talk about the different places they buy their food (supermarket, market, local shop, etc). Then they discuss how they pay (cash, cheque, credit card).

3 ▶ Ss match the words in the box to the pictures. Ss work in pairs to ask and answer questions 1 and 2. Elicit answers as a whole class.

Answers: A credit card   B coin   C note   D cheque
E receipt   Pictures B and C show cash.

EXTEND THE LEAD-IN

Ss imagine they have been asked to do the cooking in the restaurant of a friend who is ill and needs their help. Based on their own cooking skills, they must decide what to include on the menu. They must have a choice of two starters, two main courses and two desserts for the menu.

Ss then compare menus with another pair, who must say what they would choose to eat from the menu.

4.1 Shopping lists

Big supermarkets and giant out-of-town shopping malls have become more and more popular and these shops are often open until very late, or even 24 hours a day in some cases. People are leading increasingly busy lives, leading to the rising popularity of fast food restaurants and convenience foods like frozen and ready-made dinners.

OPTIONAL WARMER

Put the questions from Ex. 2b on the board (except for *has a ration book?*). In pairs, Ss discuss the questions in relation to their own families' eating habits.

Vocabulary

1 ▶ Ss look at the family in the picture. Ask: *Where do you think this family is from?* Tell Ss they will read about this family in a minute. First they look at the labelled pictures and match them to the words in Ex. 1. The first one has been done for them.

Answers: orange juice B   cereal E   bananas F
carrots G   cola C   water D

▶ Teach *a packet of* (cereal), *a carton of* (orange juice), *a bottle of* (water).

Reading

2a ▶ Scanning. Explain to Ss that they will read the text twice, the first time very quickly and the second time much more slowly. Direct them to the list of countries in Ex. 2a and tell them they have one minute to find this information in the text as quickly as possible. Explain that they do not need to understand the text fully at this point. Stop the activity after a minute and have Ss call out the answers.

Answers: United States   Japan   Cuba

b ▶ Ss look at the questions. Explain *ration book* (the government decides how much of a particular item you can buy, not the shopper, due to shortages, e.g. during a war) and *fast food restaurants* (McDonald's or Burger King). Ss read the text again, this time at their own pace. Explain that they do not need to understand every word in the text. Explain *hot dog* (a sausage in a roll) and *cereal* (e.g. Corn Flakes).

▶ Put the word *convenience food* and *tropical* on the board before they read, and encourage Ss to guess the meaning of these words if they don't know them rather than look them up in the dictionary. Ss compare answers in pairs before whole-class feedback.

Answers: 1 Ukita   2 Costa   3 Costa   4 Ronayne
5 Ronayne   6 Ukita and Ronayne (only once a week)

▶ Ss decide in pairs which family is most like their own.

Grammar

3a ▶ Direct ss to the picture. Ss decide which of the items they can count (the eggs) and which they cannot (the cereal). Count the eggs for the Ss (1, 2, 3, 4 eggs). Put the words *countable* and *uncountable* on the board.

OPTIONAL GRAMMAR LEAD-IN

Ss focus on the picture again. Ask: *What time of day is this?* (breakfast). Ask: *How do you know?* (eggs and Corn Flakes are typical breakfast food in English speaking countries). Ask: *What do you usually have for breakfast?* Elicit various suggestions and put them on the board. Put two headings on the board, *countable* and *uncountable*. Ask Ss which column the suggestions should go under, e.g. coffee, bread, tea, orange juice, etc., for uncountable; biscuits, apples, etc., for countable. Try to elicit details *how many cups of coffee*, *how many pieces of toast*, etc. Put x cups of coffee, 2 pieces of toast, etc., in the countable column.

b ▶ Direct Ss to the shopping list. Ss decide whether the red and blue words are countable or uncountable and how each are measured. Check answers in pairs.

Answers: 1 a countable   b uncountable   c plural
2 use quantity words like litres or kilos in front of them.

c ▶ Ss complete the Active grammar box.

Answers: 1 Countable nouns   2 Uncountable nouns

Uncountable nouns have no plural forms but we can say two cups of coffee or two litres of milk. We rarely say <u>one</u> banana or <u>one</u> apple when speaking of a singular noun. We usually say <u>a</u> banana or <u>an</u> apple instead.

4a ▶ Ss look at the two shopping lists and decide whether the food words are countable or uncountable.

Answers: Countable: watermelons, papayas, bananas, pizzas, eggs, tomatoes   Uncountable: pasta, coffee, cereal, rice, milk, tuna, beef, cola.

OPTIONAL VARIATION

Ss close their books. Dictate the food words from the shopping lists while Ss write the words in the correct column in their exercise books. To make it a little more challenging, dictate the countable words in the singular (e.g. *banana* rather than *bananas*).

b ▶ Ss read the two questions and complete the Active grammar box. Check answers in pairs, then as a whole class.

Answers: 1 500g of coffee   2 one pineapple
many   much

▶ Direct Ss to the reference section on page 43.

5a ▶ Ss complete the dialogues in pairs using the words and phrases from the box.

> **Answers:** 1 much   2 2 kg   3 tomatoes   4 six
> 5 coffee   6 many

b ▶ Play recording 4.1. Ss listen to check their answers.

6 ▶ Play recording 4.2. Ss listen and complete the quantities. Ss check answers in pairs.

> **Answers:**   1 seven litres   2 one and a half kilos
> 3 twelve   4 two hundred and fifty grammes
> 5 four hundred and seventy-five grammes

▶ Play the recording again. Ss focus on the quantities stated. Write the quantities on the board and say them for Ss. Ss repeat the expressions. Highlight the use of <u>and</u> in high numbers: one hundred <u>and</u> fifty, four hundred <u>and</u> seventy-five.

7 ▶ Ask Ss about (1) where and (2) when they usually do their weekly shopping, (e.g. supermarket, street market, small shops; Thursday nights, Saturday mornings, etc.). For multi-cultural groups ask about typical opening and closing times in their countries (Lunch hour breaks? Late opening nights? 24 hour shops? Open on Sundays? etc.).

▶ Tell Ss about typical shopping routines in English speaking countries. 24 hour shopping is common; shops don't close during lunchtimes; late opening varies but is typically Thursday or Friday nights. Ss work in pairs and find out about each other's weekly shopping. They ask each other questions similar to those in Ex. 5a.

> **OPTIONAL EXTENSION**
>
> Ss write up a shopping list for their partner for the following week, based on the results of the questions in Ex. 7.

4.2 Trash tales

People are becoming more and more interested in eating a healthy, balanced diet and leading healthy lifestyles. Problem pages in magazines specifically devoted to health and diet are common.

> **OPTIONAL WARMER**
>
> Ss work in small groups of three or four. They decide on what they consider to be the 'Five Main Rules' for healthy living. (E.g. Drink lots of water. Eat lots of fruit and vegetables. Drink green tea. Get exercise, etc.) In feedback, elicit suggestions and put them on the board.

Vocabulary

1a ▶ Ss look at the advert. Explain *rubbish* (what people throw away) and *bin* (show them in the picture). Ss discuss the three questions in pairs.

> **Answers:**   1 what people have in their rubbish bins and what it tells us about their diet.   2 Laurence Redburn. 3 Ss' own opinions.

▶ Use this opportunity to teach *a healthy diet*, *an unhealthy diet*, and *to be on a diet*. They need to know this for the listening text.

b ▶ Ss use their dictionaries to find the meanings of the words they don't know. Ss check answers in pairs, then as a whole class.

Listening

2a ▶ Play recording 4.3 once. Ss listen to decide which of the bins are being described. Ss check answers in pairs.

> **Answers:**   Bin 1 = B   Bin 2 = A

b ▶ Play the recording a second time. Ss listen and write the names of the foods in the correct column. Check answers in pairs, then as a whole class.

> **Answers:**   Healthy food: potatoes, carrots, fruit, bananas, apples, juice, milk, water, fish.
> Unhealthy foods: cola, instant coffee, pizza, biscuits.
> Tea bags are mentioned but it is not clear whether Laurence considers them to be healthy or not.

Person to person

3 ▶ Ss discuss the three questions in pairs.

> **OPTIONAL VARIATION**
>
> Refer Ss back to the list of food categories which they met in Lesson 4.1 (Meat/Fish/Dairy/Fruit/Vegetables/Other/Cold drinks/Hot drinks). Ss interview their partner about everything their partner ate yesterday. (E.g. *For breakfast? For dinner? Anything else?*). When both Ss have finished, they look at the two lists to see if they each have a balanced diet.

Grammar

4 ▶ Ss focus on the examples taken from the recording and complete the Active grammar box.

> Answers: a/an   some   some   any

▶ Refer Ss to the reference section on page 43.

5a ▶ Ss complete the exercise in pairs. Check answers as a whole class.

> Answers: 1 some / some   2 an   3 a   4 some / a
> 5 any

b ▶ Ss read the paragraph and correct the underlined mistakes. Check answers in pairs, then as a whole class.

> Answers: some pasta   some minced beef   some
> tomatoes   a bottle   any chicken   some vegetables.

Pronunciation

6a ▶ Write the two words, *pasta* and *some* on the board. Play recording 4.4. Ss listen to identify the two vowel sounds. Show the phonetic symbols for two sounds.

b ▶ Ss read the sentences. Play recording 4.5. Ss listen and underline the /æ/ and /ʌ/ sounds.

> Answers: 1 He has lunch on Sundays in his club.
> 2 My family travels by taxi, but my young cousin takes
> the bus.   3 Anne and Sally have butter on their pasta.

▶ Draw Ss' attention to the weak stress on <u>on</u> in connected speech. Refer Ss to the Pronunciation bank on page 148.

> **OPTIONAL EXTENSION**
>
> Say one of the three sentences several times at increasing speed, like a tongue twister. Ss repeat after you. Ss say the other sentences to each other at increasing speed.

Vocabulary

7a ▶ Ss look at the pictures and match the pictures to the adjectives. Check answers in pairs.

> Answers: A healthy   B unhealthy   C fit   D tired
> E happy   F unhappy   G hungry   H thirsty

b ▶ Ss categorise the adjectives in pairs. Check answers as a whole class.

> Answers: Positive: healthy, fit, happy
> Negative: unhealthy, tired, unhappy, hungry, thirsty

Reading

8a ▶ Explain *problem page* to Ss (people write in to magazines about their problems). Tell Ss they are going to read three problems written to Laurence in a magazine. Review *convenience food* from the previous lesson.

▶ Ss look at the three summaries first. Then they read the three letters to decide which summary matches each letter. Ss check answers in pairs, then as a whole class.

> Answers: 1 B   2 A   3 C

b ▶ Focus on question 1 first. Ask Ss to read and match Laurence's answer to the correct letter. Write *energy* on the board and ask Ss to guess what this word means as they read. Focus on questions 2 and 3. Ss look at the lesson again to see how Laurence starts the letter and the language he uses to make the two suggestions. Ss check answers in pairs, then as a whole class.

> Answers: 1 It matches letter C.   2 Dear Karin
> 3 Why don't you take some exercise? and How about
> a walk every evening after work?

▶ Write the two suggestions on the board. Underline the language of suggestion. <u>*Why don' t you*</u> *take some exercise?* and <u>*How about*</u> *a walk after work?*

Writing

9a ▶ Ss look at Laurence's notes for the other two letters. They match each suggestion to the appropriate letter. The first one is done for them. Check answers in pairs, then as a whole class.

> Answers: 2 A   3 A   4 B   5 B   6 A

b ▶ Ss make further suggestions for the two writers in pairs. (E.g. *join a gym*; *go on a diet*; *get a different job*; *get a chef to cook your meals*.) In feedback, put all the suggestions on the board so Ss have lots of ideas for the writing activity in 9c.

c ▶ In pairs, Ss write a letter in response to one of the writers. They decide which letter they will respond to and choose which suggestions they like best. Ss swap letters with another pair who make corrections and improvements. Draw Ss attention to the Writing bank at on page 144 for help with punctuation.

> **OPTIONAL EXTENSION**
>
> Ss roleplay a conversation in pairs between Laurence and one of the letter writers from Ex. 8a. Student A explains his/her problem and Student B is Laurence and gives some suggestions to the other student. In feedback, ask Ss which was the best suggestion they got from Laurence.

4.3 Ready to order?

Fast food restaurants are very common in English-speaking countries. There are fast-food chains like McDonald's, Burger King and Kentucky Fried Chicken. In Britian and Ireland there are chip shops (or chippies) selling fish and chips. Indian and Chinese Takeaway restaurants are also very popular where people order meals over the phone which are then delivered to their homes. Take away pizza delivery is also very common.

> **OPTIONAL WARMER**
>
> Elicit the types of fast food restaurants available. (E.g. McDonald's type restaurant; sandwich bar, take away restaurant, etc.). In pairs, Ss list the occasions when they go to a fast food restaurant or use a take away restaurant, e.g. late night shopping after work; taking children out for an outing; take away on Friday night, etc.

Listening

1 ▶ Ss look at the photo of a food court. They decide where the place in the photo is and discuss in pairs whether this is somewhere they like eating.

2a ▶ Ss listen to recording 4.6 twice, the first time to get a general understanding of the conversation and the second time to listen for more detailed information. Ensure Ss understand *fries* (potato chips).

▶ Play the recording once. Ss listen and mark which items are ordered by Jenny and which by Sam. Check answers in pairs.

> **Answers:** cheese sandwich S   fries S   salad J   coffee S   water J

b ▶ Play the recording a second time. Ss listen and fill in the missing words in the bill. Explain they will not find out the bill total yet. Check answers in pairs, then as a whole class.

> **Answers:** 1 fries   2 medium   3 large   4 water

▶ Ask Ss what they think *mineral water* is (water bought in a bottle) and the terms *small, medium* and *large* (fries).

3a ▶ Play the second part of recording 4.7. Ss listen and fill in the total on the bill. Check answers in pairs, then as a whole class.

> **Answer:** $16.70 (sixteen dollars and seventy cents).

b ▶ Play recording 4.7 a second time. Pre-teach *vegetarian* (no meat). Ss listen and answer the questions. Check answers in pairs, then as a whole class.

> **Answers:** 1 vegetarian pizza   2 How much is that?
> 3 by credit card

> **OPTIONAL EXTENSION**
>
> Explain what *service and tax included* means on a bill. There is an example on the bill in Ex. 2b. Teach *to leave a tip* (extra money you leave for the waiter). In pairs, Ss discuss (1) when they tip in a restaurant (always; if the service is very good; in expensive restaurants, etc.), (2) how much they usually tip (10%, 15%, etc) and (3) how they usually tip (leave it on the table, include it on the credit card bill, etc). Tell Ss about the typical conventions in English-speaking countries in relation to tipping – most people tip in restaurants (other than fast food restaurants). They usually leave between 10 and 20%.

4a ▶ Ss look at the menu. Ask: *Is this an expensive restaurant?* (No, a fast food one). Ss look at the headings. Do not explain *side orders* to Ss yet. Ask them to work it out for themselves as they read. Ss read the menu and match the headings to A–C. Check answers in pairs, then as a whole class.

> **Answers:**   A Main dishes   B Side orders
> C Drinks

> **OPTIONAL EXTENSION**
>
> Ss discuss what they might choose from this menu in pairs.

b ▶ Teach *How much is a burger? How much are fries?* Direct Ss to the bill in Ex. 2b again. Demonstrate to Ss how to say the prices in the bill. E.g. A coffee is $2.95 (two dollars ninety five). A mineral water is $2.25 (two dollars twenty five), etc.

▶ Ss work in pairs. Student A looks at the prices on page 125. Student A asks about the prices in the menu and fills in the gaps.

Grammar

5a ▶ Play recording 4.8 once. Ss listen to the extracts from the conversation in Ex. 3a and fill in the missing words. Check answers in pairs. Do not give feedback yet as Ss will see the correct answers in the tapescript.

> **Answers:**   1 him/me   2 us   3 them   4 you   5 her

b ▶ Ss turn to the tapescript on page 153 and complete the Active grammar box.

> **Answers:**   him   her   us   you   them

6 ▶ Ss look at the cartoon. Ask: *Why is she holding the meal?* (it is for someone). *What is the problem?* (she can't find who the meal is for). Ss imagine they are speaking to the waitress and make sentences with their partner about the meal using the object pronouns. Check answers as a whole class.

> **Answers:**   1 him   2 her   3 us   4 them

▶ Refer Ss to the reference section on page 43.

7a▶ Elicit ways of ordering food in a restaurant. Ask Ss how they would get a waiter's attention in a restaurant. Establish how to do it in an English-speaking country (arm raised or a nod, not clicking fingers or calling 'Waiter').

▶ Ss look at the beginnings and endings of sentences from the recording. Elicit the answer to the first one as a whole class, then Ss work in pairs to match the sentence halves.

> Answers: 1 c   2 d   3 f   4 e   5 g   6 a   7 b

b▶ Ss check their answers by reading the tapescript on page 153. They complete the How to box.

> Answers: Do   like   much

▶ Say the expressions for the Ss and ask them to repeat them. Help with the pronunciation and intonation patterns. Draw Ss' attention to the /d/ sound in *I'd like* (not *I like*).

c▶ Ss complete the dialogue with words from Ex. 7a.

> Answers: can   I'd   Do   want   like   much   can

When checking Ss' answers, draw their attention to the use of *would* for asking questions in this context. (*Do you like fries?* and *I like a vegetarian burger* are both incorrect for this conversation. The correct answer is *Would you like fries?* and *I'd like a vegetarian burger*).

Speaking

8▶ Ss work in groups. Try to ensure Ss are working with new people for this activity. One student is the waiter/ waitress taking orders and the others are customers placing orders from the menu in Ex. 4a. They use the language learned in Ex. 7.

> **OPTIONAL ACTIVITY**
> Ss imagine they have been on a desert island for the last two years and have just returned to their country again. In pairs, Ss tell each other what meal they would choose the first evening back home.

Communication: Shopping at a market

▶ Ss focus on the photo of the market. Teach *stall* (a shop at a market).

> **OPTIONAL WARMER**
> Ss talk about markets in pairs. Put the following headings on the board: *Do you like markets? Why/ Why not? What do you buy/not buy? Prices*

1a▶ Tell Ss they are going to hear a woman shopping at a market. Ss look at the food words and the three exercises. Play recording 4.9 once. Ss listen and tick the correct blue boxes. Ss check answers in pairs.

> Answers: apples, bananas, melon from stall one
> beef, tuna, chicken from stall two

b▶ Play the recording a second time. Ss listen and check the red boxes. Check answers in pairs.

> Answers: bananas and apples from stall one
> beef and chicken from stall two

c▶ If necessary, play the recording a third time. Ss check answers in pairs, then as a whole class.

> Answer: 18.50 euros

2a▶ Write *How much are apples?* on the board and demonstrate the rise and fall of the intonation pattern. Draw arrows up and down to show Ss how to mark intonation. Play recording 4.10. Ss listen and mark the intonation. Check answers in pairs, then as a whole class.

> Answers: apples (up) melon (down)
> beef (up), tuna (up), chicken (down)

▶ Ask: *Why does the voice go down at the end of the list?* (to show it is the last thing on the list).

b▶ Play the recording again. Ss listen and repeat.

c▶ Ss work in groups of ten or so. With small classes play the game as a whole class. One student starts the list, choosing a food item from the box. Each student continues the list, using the correct intonation to mark the end of the list. Correct errors in intonation during the game.

3a▶ Divide Ss into shoppers and shop assistants. Shoppers decide on their shopping lists and shop assistants decide which food they sell (based on the letter A, B, C, D given to them) and the prices. Give Ss about five minutes to prepare. When Ss are ready, they start buying and selling the groceries. Shoppers cannot go over their budget of 25 euros.

b▶ Ss tell the class about what they have bought/ sold. Compare prices and find out which pair was most successful. E.g. *Who bought the cheapest bananas?*, etc.

Review and practice

1 ▶

> Answers: 2 e 3 f 4 c 5 a 6 b

2 ▶

> Answers: 1 many 2 water 3 2 4 much 5 much

3 ▶

> Answers: 1 some 2 a 3 some 4 any 5 any
> 6 some 7 a 8 any

4 ▶

> Answers: 1 We/them 2 She/us 3 They/them
> 4 He/it 5 We/her

5 ▶

> Answers: 1 I 2 He 3 him 4 they 5 them
> 6 me 7 her 8 She 9 me

6a ▶

> Answers: 1 tuna 2 burger 3 bread
> 4 watermelon 5 tomatoes 6 chicken
> 7 milk 8 pizza 9 rice

b ▶

> Answers: 1 trout (fish) 2 fries (cooked)
> 3 sugar (non-dairy) 4 sandwich (not a drink)

Notes for using the Common European Framework (CEF)

CEF References

4.1 Can do: talk about quantities and numbers

CEF A1 descriptor: can handle numbers, quantities, cost and time (CEF page 80)

4.2 Can do: talk about your diet and lifestyle

CEF A1 descriptor: can ask and answer simple questions, initiate and respond to simple statements in areas of immediate need or on very familiar topics (CEF page 81)

4.3 Can do: order food in a fast food restaurant

CEF A1 descriptor: can ask people for things and give people things (CEF page 80)

CEF quick brief

The Common European Framework believes that language learning can be measured not by how much grammar or vocabulary a learner knows, but by what a learner can achieve with the language that they know. Grammar and vocabulary are only important in terms of what they empower a learner to do. This is an 'action-oriented' approach to language.

Portfolio task

Download the Total English Portfolio free from www.longman.com/totalenglish.

Objective: help Ss to complete the qualifications section of their Passport. This task can be done in Ss' own language.

1 ▶ Remind Ss of the purpose of the Portfolio and the Passport.

2 ▶ Explain that their formal qualifications are also important and that this is the other section of the Passport to complete.

3 ▶ Ask Ss to list their formal qualifications and compare with a partner.

4 ▶ Ask Ss to complete this section of their Passport.

5 Home

Overview

Summary

Lesson 1: Ss read a brochure for World of ResidenSea, a complex of luxury apartments aboard a ship. They then listen to a conversation between an estate agent and potential buyer for one of the apartments.

Lesson 2: Ss listen to Pete Morgan describe his studio apartment to Amanda.

Lesson 3: Ss listen to five people talking about where they are from and describing the landscape there. They also read an email in which Monica describes Australia to a friend and asks her to visit.

Communicative focus: Ss decide together how to furnish a new apartment and how much to pay for each item of furniture.

Film bank: ResidenSea (2'44")
A short documentary showing life on the ship *The World of ResidenSea.*

ResidenSea continues the topic of lesson 1. The film shows *The World of ResidenSea* inside and outside and the narrator gives us interesting facts about the ship.

Possible places to use this short film are:

▶ before lesson 1 to introduce the topic and language

▶ after lesson 1 to review and extend the topic and language

▶ at the end of the unit to round up the topic and language

For ways to use this short film in class, see Students' Book page 135 and Teacher's Book page 191.

Lead-in

1a ▶ Ss look at the photos to identify the different rooms.

> **Answers:** A bedroom B bathroom C living room D kitchen

OPTIONAL WARMER

Ss discuss the following in pairs. Ask: *Which room do you usually spend the most/the least time in? What do you do in that room?*

(E.g. *I spend most time in my kitchen. There is a big table and I study there too. When friends come, we have dinner in the kitchen.*)

b ▶ Ss look at the words in the box and match them to the activities. The first is done for them. Ss check answers in pairs, then listen to recording 5.1.

> **Answers:** 1 You can cook in the kitchen. 2 You can sleep in the bedroom. 3 You can have a shower in the bathroom. 4 You can put your car in the garage. 5 You can eat in the dining room/kitchen. 6 You can watch TV in the living room.

2a ▶ Direct Ss to the photos again. Ask: *Do you think all the rooms are in the same house?* Teach *the same* (the opposite of different). *Why/Why not?* (different views out of the windows). Teach *landscape* (what you can see when you look out of a window). Ss look at the list of landscapes, then tick which ones they can see in the photos. They can use their dictionaries for this exercise. Ss check answers in pairs, then listen to recording 5.2.

> **Answers:** a mountain a forest

▶ Help Ss with the pronunciation of these words, especially desert.

b ▶ Ss extend the list of different kinds of landscapes in pairs. E.g. fields; a castle; a park, etc. In feedback, elicit all the suggestions and put them on the board. Ask Ss: *Which landscape do you like most?*

c ▶ Ss look at the diagram. Teach *in the north/south/ east/west/centre of the country.* Ss ask and answer the two questions with a partner.

3 ▶ Ss work in groups. Each student thinks of a country and describes its landscape to the others, who try to guess the country. An example is given in their book.

EXTEND THE LEAD-IN

Ss look at the photos and decide which rooms they like best/don't like etc. In pairs, Ss discuss what they think are the best/worst colours for different rooms. (E.g. *I don't like bright orange or red in a bedroom because it keeps me awake.*) Teach *bright*, *pale*, and *dark* before Ss start.

5.1 Sail away...

In this lesson Ss read about the World of ResidenSea, a luxury apartment complex aboard a ship. They then listen to a conversation between an estate agent and potential buyer for one of the apartments. Through this context, Ss learn *there is/there are*, vocabulary associated with rooms, and how to talk about their homes.

Reading

1▶ Ss close their books. Elicit the different kinds of houses/homes people live in (apartment, semi-detached house, cottage, castle, etc.).

> **OPTIONAL WARMER**
>
> Ss tell partner about the location of their 'dream' house – the house they would buy if they were very rich (in the country/city centre/ by the sea/in the mountains, etc.) and why.

2a▶ Ss look at the photos. Ask: *What kind of house is this?*

▶ Scanning. Direct Ss to the text in their books. Explain that they will read the text twice, the first time very quickly and the second time much more slowly. Direct them to the questions and tell them they have one minute to find this information in the text as quickly as possible. Explain that they do not need to understand the text fully at this point. Stop the activity after a minute and have Ss call out the answers.

> **Answers:**   1 a brochure for ResidenSea apartments   2 they're luxury apartments on a boat

b▶ Ss look at the questions. Explain *terrace* (show in the picture), *private* (not shared, not public) and *well-equipped kitchen* (elicit the types of machines people have in a kitchen). Ss read the text again. Explain that they do not need to understand every word in the text. They mark the statements true or false, check answers in pairs, then as a whole class.

> **Answers:**   1 a (T)   b (F)   c (T)   d (F)   2 (T)   b (F)   c (F)   d (T)

▶ Ask Ss: *Would you like to live in one of these apartments? Why/Why not?* Elicit the reasons why they would like/not like to live in a ResidenSea apartment.

Vocabulary

3a▶ Ss look at the floor plan for one of the ResidenSea apartments. They label the rooms and furniture.

> **Answers:**   terrace, bedroom 1, bed, sofas, chairs, bathroom, kitchen, bedroom 2

b▶ Ss work in pairs. They put the headings in the correct place in the table and add two or three items to each heading. Teach *facilities* (buildings and services near

where you live – e.g. supermarket, library, playgrounds, etc.). Explain the difference between *furniture* and *equipment*.

> **Answers:**   1 rooms (also living room, bathroom, etc.)   2 furniture (also bed, table, etc.)   3 kitchen equipment (also cooker, dishwasher, etc.).
> Note: People in Britain often have their washing machines in the kitchen.   4 living room equipment (also DVD, CD player, etc.)   5 ship's facilities (also gym, restaurants, etc.).

> **OPTIONAL VARIATION**
>
> Ss close their books and write the headings in their books. Call out the words to go under the various headings at random. Ss write each word into the correct category (e.g. bedroom, microwave, CD player, etc.)

Lifelong learning

▶ Talk to Ss about writing new words and expressions in a vocabulary journal as a useful way of remembering them. Discuss the various ways to categorise the new words (alphabetically, thematically, etc.). Direct Ss to the note on personalising new vocabulary as a useful way to learn and remember new vocabulary.

Grammar

4▶ Ss use the text on The World of ResidenSea to complete the Active grammar box.

> **Answers:**   are   isn't   aren't   Is   Are   isn't   are

▶ Explain that we use *there is* and *there are* to talk about what is in particular places. Help Ss with the pronunciation of the contracted forms: *there's, there isn't,* (singular) *there aren't* (plural). No contraction for *there are.*

> **Short Answers:**   no contraction for Yes, there is. Not Yes, there's.

▶ Review *some* and *any* from the previous unit: *There are some chairs/There aren't any tables.* Refer Ss to the reference section on page 53.

5▶ Ss look at the text and floor plan of the ResidenSea apartments again and complete the sentences. Check answers in pairs.

> **Answers:**   1 are/aren't   2 Are/aren't   3 's   4 Is/isn't

6a▶ Ss return to Ex. 2b and make sentences using *There is/isn't; There are/aren't.* An example is given.

b▶ Ss ask and answer questions about the floor plan in Ex. 3a using *there is/there are.*

7▶ Ss work with a new partner. They describe their home to their partner.

> **OPTIONAL VARIATION**
>
> Ss draw a floor plan of their own house and show it to their partner, describing where each room is, who sleeps where, etc.

Listening

▶ Tell Ss they are going to listen to a conversation between Jon and an estate agent for ResidenSea apartments. Elicit some examples of the kind of questions Jon might ask (*How much is it? How big is it? How many bedrooms are there?* etc.).

8a ▶ Ss look at the questions. Play recording 5.3 once. Ss listen and answer the questions. Check answers in pairs.

> **Answers:** 1 an apartment on The World of ResidenSea
> 2 two bedroom apartments only 3 two million dollars 4 Yes 5 Possibly, he says he will think about it. But maybe he doesn't want to say it is too expensive for him.

b ▶ Play the recording again. Ss number Jon's questions in the correct order and then answer them. Check answers in pairs, then as a whole class.

> **Answers:** 1 4 (2 bathrooms) 2 1 (Yes, of course)
> 3 5 (100 sq metres and 120 sq metres) 4 2 (There are three two-bedroom apartments for sale)
> 5 6 (2 million dollars) 6 3 (two and three bedrooms)

Speaking

> **OPTIONAL LEAD-IN TO ROLEPLAY**
>
> Write the following on the board: *garden/how many bedrooms/how many bathrooms/facilities nearby/ price/landscape from windows*. Ss work in small groups of three or four and discuss together which of the headings are important/not important to them when choosing where to live. (E.g. *What do you think is important? The landscape is important for me. I like to look out of the window in the evening. A garden is important for me. I enjoy gardening at weekends*.)
> Don't worry if Ss make mistakes during this activity.
>
> In feedback, establish what is important to most Ss when choosing where to live.

9 ▶ Ss conduct an estate agent and buyer roleplay in pairs. Student A looks at the information he/she needs to find out. Student B looks at the information about the house for sale on page 126. Give Ss a minute or two to prepare. Ss conduct the roleplay in pairs. Don't worry about Ss making mistakes during this activity.

▶ When Ss have finished they swap roles and read the new information. Student A is now the estate agent and Student B is interested in buying. In feedback ask: *How many bought the country cottage? How many bought the town house?*

5.2 To have and have not

In this lesson Ss listen to Pete Morgan describing his studio apartment and what is in it to Amanda Myers. Through this context they learn *have/has got* and how to ask and talk about important possessions.

> **OPTIONAL WARMER**
>
> Ss look at the four different rooms. In pairs they decide who they think might live there: a single woman, a single man, two friends, a married couple – no children, a family with young children, a family with teenage children, an old couple. They must give reasons for their opinions. (E.g. *I don't think a family with young children live in C. It is too small. I think a family lives in B but I think there are teenage children because there are no toys*, etc.)

Vocabulary

1a ▶ Ss look at the four rooms and tell their partner which room they prefer and why. (E.g. *I like A because you can see the mountains from the window*.)

b ▶ Ss have three minutes to list all the things they can see in the pictures. Have Ss call out the things and write them on the board.

c ▶ Ss close their books. They tell their partner everything they remember from the pictures. Ss check answers by looking again in their books. Review furniture vocabulary from the previous unit, especially *terrace, laptop computer, mobile phone, microwave, sofa* which come up in the listening.

Listening

2a ▶ Play recording 5.4 once. Ss listen and decide which of the four photos is being described. Check answers in pairs.

> **Answer:** C

b ▶ Play the recording again. Ss listen and tick the items which Pete has got in his flat and cross the things he hasn't got. Check answers in pairs, then as a whole class.

> **Answers:** studio apartment (✓) house (✗)
> garden (✗) terrace (✓) fridge (✓) cooker (✓)
> sink (✓) chairs (✓) microwave (✗) coffee
> table (✓) sofa (✓) dining table (✗) TV (✓) music
> system (✓) laptop computer (✓) mobile phone (✓)

Grammar

3a ▶ Ss listen to the first part of recording 5.5 again. They can read the tapescript on page 153 at the same time. They use the tapescript to complete the gaps in the dialogue in their books.

> **Answers:** got haven't 've Has hasn't 's

b ▶ Ss use the dialogue to complete the Active grammar box. Check answers in pairs, then as a whole class.

> **Answers:** 've I/We/You/They hasn't Have Has haven't

▶ Draw a simple version of a room with a table and chairs in it. Ask: *What room is this?* (a kitchen) *What is this?* (pointing at the table) A table. Write *It's got a table* and *It's a table* on the board. For each one ask: *Am I talking about the table or the kitchen?*

▶ Underline the *'s* in each sentence. Establish that *'s* is a contraction of *is* in *It's* a table and a contraction of *has* in *It's* got a table. Help Ss with the pronunciation of the contracted forms.

▶ Draw Ss's attention to the short answers. We don't use *got* in the short answer. *Yes, I have* is correct, not *Yes, I've got*. Direct Ss to the reference section on page 53.

4a ▶ Ss tick the true sentences and correct the false ones. An example is given. They practise saying the correct sentences in pairs, then as a whole class.

> **Answers:** 1, 2, 3, and 4 are true. 5 He's got two chairs. 6 He hasn't got a garden.

b ▶ Ss use the prompts to write sentences using *has/have* got and write true short answers. The first one is done for them.

> **Answers:** 1 Has your town got a theatre? 2 Have your parents got a car? 3 Have you got a computer? 4 Has your teacher got any pens?

Pronunciation

▶ Ss focus on the two sounds, /ɒ/ and /æ/.

5a ▶ Play recording 5.6. Ss listen and identify the different sounds.

> **Answers:** cat is different /ɒ/ got, laptop and watch are /æ/.

b ▶ Ss listen to recording 5.7 and tick the word they hear. Check answers in pairs, then as a whole class.

> **Answers:** 1 hot 2 an 3 top 4 pocket

> **OPTIONAL EXTENSION**
>
> Ss say one of the words to their partner, who must identify which sound it is.
>
> Ss identify the difference in the sounds and practise saying them. Ss practise saying sentences which contain both sounds, e.g. *He's got a packet of coffee in his bag. He's got a laptop in the bottom of the sack.*

▶ Direct Ss to the Pronunciation bank on page 147 for further examples of the sounds.

Speaking

6 ▶ Ss take it in turns to describe one of the rooms in Ex. 1. The second student decides which room is being described. Demonstrate by describing one of the rooms yourself first as a whole class.

> **OPTIONAL VARIATION**
>
> Imagine or look at a picture of a room in a magazine. Ss draw a large rectangle in their exercise books. Describe the furniture in the room to the Ss. (*There's a large sofa in the middle of the room. There's an armchair on the left of the sofa and a coffee table on the right.*) Ss listen to your description and draw the furniture in the correct position in the room. Teach *in the middle, on the left, on the right* before you start.

7a ▶ Ss make a list of family members and important possessions similar to the one in their coursebook.

b ▶ Ss ask each other about their lists and possessions in pairs, noting which items each has that the other hasn't got, and vice versa. Don't worry about Ss making mistakes during this activity.

Writing

8 ▶ Ss look at the sample paragraph in their books and write a similar paragraph about their partner, based on the information gained in Ex. 7b.

▶ Ss look at the sentences in the How to box. They focus on the use of *and* (to add something in a sentence or list) and *but* (to contrast something in a sentence, to show something is different).

> **OPTIONAL EXTENSION**
>
> Gather up the different paragraphs. Read out a selection of the paragraphs to the Ss, but without using the name of the person being written about. The other Ss must try to guess which student it is.

5.3 World class

In this lesson Ss listen to five people talking about where they are from and describing the landscape there. They also read an email in which Monica describes Australia to a friend and asks her to visit. Through this context Ss learn modifiers and how to write an informal email about their country.

OPTIONAL WARMER

Ss work in pairs. They look at the photos and discuss which type of landscape they would like best and which they would like least (1) to live in and (2) for a holiday. They must give reasons for their choice.

Listening

1a ▶ Ss read the list of places and match them to the photos. There is one extra word. Check answers in pairs, then as a whole class.

Answers: Mountain 2   desert 1   forest 4   city 5   lake 3. There is no river in the photos.

b ▶ In pairs Ss try to guess which countries the pictures are from. Do not give the answers yet as the information is on the recording.

2 ▶ Play recording 5.8 once. Ss listen to check which countries are being described.

Answers: 1 Spain   2 Argentina   3 Poland   4 Greece   5 Japan

3a ▶ Review *in the north/south/east/west of the country* before playing the recording again. Ss listen and complete the table. Tell Ss to listen for the adjective as well. Check answers in pairs, then as a whole class.

Answers: 1 famous desert, south   2 Argentina, high mountains   3 Poland, east   4 lovely forest, north   5 Japan, huge city

b ▶ Help Ss with the pronunciation of the adjectives. Ss make sentences about the places they've heard about, using *There is/there are*.

Grammar

4a ▶ Ask Ss to look at the four sentences. See if they remember which place they refer to. (1 = the desert; 2 = Argentina; 3 = Poland; 4 = Osaka).

▶ Play recording 5.9. Ss listen and complete the sentences with the correct word.

Answers: 1 really   2 very   3 quite   4 very/not very

▶ Ask: *Which is the strongest?* (really and very); *Which is the weakest?* (not very). Explain that the modifiers go before the adjective.

b ▶ Ss look at the different thermometer readings and complete the scale. Check answers in pairs, then as a whole class.

Answers: 40° = really hot, very hot   30° = hot   25° = quite hot   15° = not very hot

5 ▶ Ss make sentences in pairs using the prompts given. Ss call out answers in whole-class feedback.

Possible Answers: 1 New Zealand is quite big.   2 Mount Everest is very high.   3 The Pyrenees are high.   4 Mexico City is really busy.   5 Canada is very cold.   6 The United Kingdom is quite cold.

Vocabulary

6a ▶ Ss add two further adjectives from the box to describe a desert in pairs.

b ▶ Ss make word maps for the other nouns using adjectives from the box. There will be some overlap.

Possible Answers: mountain – beautiful, famous, high   Island – beautiful, famous, noisy, huge, green, popular   forest – beautiful, green, huge, famous   beach – beautiful, busy, famous, noisy, popular   city – beautiful, busy, famous, huge, noisy

Pronunciation

OPTIONAL PRONUNCIATION LEAD-IN

Write out the adjectives from Ex. 6a on individual strips of paper, one word per strip. Ss work in groups of ten or so. Give each student a strip of paper. Try to have at least two words of one, two and three syllables for each group. Ss circulate and say the adjective to each other. They group themselves according to the sound of the words. (The connection is the number of syllables in the word.)

7a ▶ Play recording 5.10. Ss listen and answer the questions.

Answers: 1 two syllables   2 weak

▶ The stress is usually on the first syllable in words of two syllables in English.

Lifelong learning

▶ Ask Ss to look up the words in their dictionaries and to see how the syllables are marked (dots) and how the word stress is marked.

b ▶ Ss look at the words. They use their dictionaries to find out which is the strong syllable.

Answers: cen•tre   is•land   Ja•pan   Po•land   Chi•na

c ▶ Play recording 5.11. Ss listen and check their answers.

Speaking

8a ▶ Ss focus on the How to box and review how to (1) say where they live, (2) describe the landscape where they live and (3) give their opinion about whether they like where they live or not.

b ▶ Ss work in pairs. They describe where they live and their country to a partner and speak about which parts of their country they like/don't like.

Writing

> **OPTIONAL EMAIL LEAD-IN**
>
> Ss close their books. Write *cities* and *landscapes* on the board. Elicit all the cities and famous landscapes which the Ss know in Australia and write them on the board under the two headings. (Sydney, Great Barrier Reef, etc.)

▶ Ss work in pairs and draw a rough map of Australia in their exercise books. Student A describes the location of the various cities and places to their partner who marks them on their map. (E.g. *Perth is in the south west of Australia. The Great Barrier Reef is in the north east of Australia*, etc.)

9a ▶ Ask: *Which part of Australia would you visit? Why?* Ss look at the four questions about Australia, then read the email to find the answers. Check answers in pairs, then as a whole class.

> **Answers:** 1 The Great Barrier Reef and some very nice beaches. 2 in the centre 3 Yes, Perth. 4 in the East

b ▶ Ss look at the email again. They scan the text to find the four expressions, then match them to the purpose a–d. Check answers in pairs, then as a whole class.

> **Answers:** 1 c 2 a 3 b 4 d

> **OPTIONAL EXTENSION**
>
> Ss read the email on page 143. They find out who is writing the email (Sylvia); what country is being described (Ireland) and what there is in the South (Cork), East (Dublin), West (mountains, beaches, no big cities) and North (the email doesn't say) of the country.

10 ▶ Ss write a similar email about their country and read them to each other in groups. Review how to use *and* and *but* which Ss met in the previous lesson.

Communication: Furnishing an apartment

1 ▶ Ss look at the photo of the apartment. Ask: *Do you like this apartment? Why/Why not?* Ss discuss with a partner what the apartment has got/not got. Establish that there is a cooker and fridge but nothing else. There are no light fittings either.

2a ▶ Ss look at the list of items and choose ten things that they need to furnish the apartment. Ss should use their dictionaries to look up words they don't know.

b ▶ Ss work in pairs and compare their lists. Together they agree on ten items and rank them in order of importance. (E.g. *I think a bed is very important. You have to sleep at night. You can sit on a bed but you can't sleep in a chair*, etc.) Don't worry about Ss making mistakes during this activity. Encourage Ss to express their opinions as best they can.

▶ Ss compare lists with a different pair.

3a ▶ Ss work in groups of three. Try to ensure that Ss are working with different Ss than they worked with for Ex. 2b in order to generate plenty of discussion.

▶ Each student has different information about home furniture and prices. Student A's information is on page 126, Student B's information is on page 129 and Student C's information is on page 52. Give Ss several minutes to read about the activity and look at their individual information.

▶ Ss then discuss what they will buy and how much to spend on each item. They have a maximum of 1,000 euros to spend.

b ▶ Ss compare their lists with other groups.

> **OPTIONAL VARIATION**
>
> Cut pictures with prices shown out of a home shopping catalogue for Ss to use for this activity.

> **OPTIONAL EXTENSION**
>
> Ss work in pairs. They choose two things they could change or buy for the classroom to make it a nicer room (e.g. *paint the walls yellow, buy a big plant for the window*, etc.).

Review and practice

1 ▶

> **Answers:** 2 Is there 3 there isn't 4 there's
> 5 there isn't 6 there's 7 are there 8 there aren't
> 9 is there 10 there's

2 ▶

> **Answers:** 1 I haven't got a video camera. 2 She
> hasn't got a mobile phone. 3 They haven't got
> a lot of money. 4 Their car hasn't got a CD player.
> 5 England hasn't got a lot of mountains.

3 ▶

> **Answers:** 1 Has Rachel got a laptop computer? Yes,
> she has. 2 Have they got a big house? No, they
> haven't. 3 Has your flat got a garden? No, it hasn't.
> 4 Has Kelly got a washing machine? Yes, she has.
> 5 Has Spain got a King? Yes, it has.

4 ▶

> **Possible answers:** 1 very 2 really 3 not very
> 4 quite 5 really

5 ▶

> **Answers:** A the sea B an island C mountains
> D a city E a forest F a river G a lake H a beach

6 ▶

> **Possible answers:** Living room: coffee table,
> sofa; Overlapping living room /kitchen/bedroom:
> bookshelves, CD player, table; Overlapping living room/
> bedroom: armchair; Kitchen: cupboard, dishwasher,
> fridge, washing machine, cooker; Bedroom: bed

Notes for using the Common European Framework (CEF)

CEF References

5.1 Can do: talk about your home

CEF A1 descriptor: can describe him/herself, what he/she does and where he/she lives (CEF page 59)

5.2 Can do: ask and talk about important possessions

CEF A2 descriptor: can use simple descriptive language to make brief statements about and compare objects and possessions (CEF page 59)

5.3 Can do: write an informal email about your country

CEF A2 descriptor: can write about everyday aspects of his/her environment, e.g. people, places, a job or study experience in linked sentences (CEF page 62)

CEF quick brief

Chapters four and five of The Common European Framework set out 'reference levels' as a way to describe someone's ability in language. There are six basic reference levels: A1, A2, B1, B2, C1, C2 (though these can be subdivided if required). These reference levels are designed to describe ability in any language, not just English.

Portfolio task

Download the Total English Portfolio free from www.longman.com/totalenglish.

Objective: to introduce Ss to the Biography section of the Portfolio.

This task can be done in Ss' own language.

The second section of the Portfolio is the Biography. The Biography is for Ss to keep a more detailed and personal record of their language learning history, objectives and progress.

1 ▶ Explain the purpose of the Biography section of the Portfolio.

2 ▶ Ask Ss to think about their language learning objectives. Give some examples of your own objectives in a different language.

3 ▶ Ask Ss to think about their own language learning objectives and makes a list. Ss compare objectives with their partner.

4 ▶ Ask Ss to complete this section of their Biography.

Overview

Lead-in	**Vocabulary:** places in the city
6.1	**Grammar:** past of *to be*: all forms; Past Simple of regular verbs: positive
	Vocabulary: buildings
	Can do: talk about your past
6.2	**Grammar:** Past Simple: question forms and short answers
	Vocabulary: prepositions of place
	Can do: understand and give simple directions
6.3	**Grammar:** Past Simple: negative
	Vocabulary: transport
	Can do: describe your last holiday
Com. Focus	In shops
Reference	
Practice	

Summary

Lesson 1: Ss read about the changing function of four well-known buildings in various parts of the world. They then listen to four people talking about the four buildings.

Lesson 2: Ss read about Robin Andrews, who went missing for 16 hours. They then listen to an interview with Robin about his experiences. They also listen to Robin asking for directions after he wakes up in a strange town.

Lesson 3: Ss read about the changes in navigation over the centuries and learn about different modes of transport in different cities.

Communicative focus: Ss buy and sell goods in a gift shop.

Film bank: Amazing buildings (3'05")
Five people talk about their favourite building.

This film shows dramatic footage of five buildings in different cities. A different person talks about their unique relationship to each building. The buildings are The Flatiron building in New York, The Guggenhiem Museum in Bilbao, The Eiffel Tower in Paris, The 'Gherkin' in London and The Sydney Opera House in Sydney.

Possible places to use this short film are:

▶ before lesson 1 to introduce the topic of buildings

▶ before lesson 2 to introduce the Past Simple tense in an interesting and different way

▶ at the end of the unit to round up the topic and language

For ways to use this short film in class, see Students' Book page 136 and Teacher's Book page 191.

Lead-in

OPTIONAL WARMER
Ss think of their local town or city. In pairs, they list five reasons why their city is better/worse than the next big city in the area. If you are working with a multi-cultural group, Ss list five reasons why their own city is better/worse than the city/town they are in now. (E.g. *The food in x restaurant is fantastic. The mountains outside the city are really beautiful*, etc.)

1a ▶ Ss look at the photos. They see if they recognise different places in the pictures and match them to the words in the box. Ss can use dictionaries for words they don't know. Check answers in pairs, then as a whole class. Ss may confuse the words *library* and *bookshop*.

> Answers: A café, square, bank B train station
> C art gallery D library

b ▶ Play recording 6.1. Ss listen to the words and count how many syllables each word or phrase has. Play the recording a second time. Ss mark the stressed syllable. Ss check answers in pairs, then as a whole class.

▶ Ss practise saying the words. The first syllable is stressed in all except for museum and police station, where the second syllable is stressed.

> Answers: bar 1 bookshop 2 café 2 church 1
> cinema 3 factory 3 hospital 3 library 3
> museum 3 newsagent's 3 phone shop 2
> police station 4 post office 3 restaurant 3
> school 1 square 1 supermarket 4 train station 3

c ▶ In pairs, Ss ask and answer about what people can do in the various places. An example is given.

2a ▶ Play recording 6.2. Ss listen and complete the sentences with the missing word.

> Answers: 1 Go 2 on 3 Turn 4 Go 5 left

b ▶ Ss match the directions to the diagrams. Check answers in pairs, then as a whole class. There is one extra diagram.

> Answers: 1 F 2 C 3 A 4 E 5 D

▶ Ask Ss to look at picture B again. Ask: *What do you say for this one?* (Turn left at the bookshop).

EXTEND THE LEAD-IN
Ss discuss city life. They list three advantages and three disadvantages of living in a city. (E.g. *lots to do, big shops, noise, expensive houses*, etc.)

6.1 Changes

In this lesson Ss read about the changing function of four well-known buildings in various parts of the world. They then listen to four people talking about the four buildings. Through this context, Ss learn the Past Simple of *to be*, regular verbs and how to talk about their past.

> **OPTIONAL WARMER**
>
> Ss decide in pairs which is (1) their favourite old building and (2) their favourite modern building in the local city/town. Ss compare answers.

Reading

1a ▶ Ss look at the photos. Ask them if they recognise any of the buildings they see. Ss scan the text quickly to find out the names of the buildings.

> **Answers:** 1 the Hoover Building in London 2 the Musée d'Orsay in Paris 3 the Reina Sofía building in Madrid 4 the Smolny Institute in St Petersburg

b ▶ Ss look at the table. Make sure Ss understand the two headings, *now* and *in the past*. Ss read the text again, to find out what each building is now and what it was before. Explain *century* (100 years) and *1930s/40s* (1930–1939/1940–1949) before they read. Check answers in pairs, then as a whole class.

> **Answers:** 2 an art gallery – a train station 3 a museum and art gallery – a hospital 4 an office – a school

> **OPTIONAL EXTENSION**
>
> Think of several buildings in the local city/town which were built for a different purpose to what they function as now (often banks, town halls, offices were originally used for completely different purposes). Write the current names of the buildings on the board. Ss decide what the original function of each building was.

Grammar

2 ▶ Ss look at the four texts again. Ask Ss to underline all the verbs in the sentences. (All the verbs are *is/are* and *was/were*.)

▶ Ss complete the Active grammar box. Check answers in pairs, then as a whole class.

> **Answers:** were wasn't Was wasn't were

▶ Help Ss with the initial /w/ sound in *was* and *were* and the weak vowel sound /ə/ in *was* in affirmative and negative sentences. Show Ss the contracted negative form on the board.

3 ▶ Ss make two true sentences about each of the buildings following the example given.

Person to person

4 ▶ Ss work in pairs. They find out details of where their partner was at the times in the box.

Listening

> **OPTIONAL LISTENING LEAD-IN**
>
> Ss focus on the four buildings again. Explain to Ss that they will hear four people talking about the four buildings and they have to identify which building is being referred to. Write the name of each building, what it is used for now and what it was used for in the past, on the board. Elicit some suggestions of words they might hear for each building. Accept all suggestions, whether they occur in the recording or not. E.g. The Hoover Building – a supermarket now – a factory in the past (Suggestions: shopping; shopping bags; workers, etc.).

5a ▶ Write the dates *1917, 1900, 1937, 1986* on the board. Say them for Ss so they recognise them when they hear them during the recording. Tell Ss they don't need to understand every word but to listen for words which will tell them which building is being described. Play recording 6.3. Check answers in pairs. Play the recording again. Ss note down words that help them decide which building is being described. Check answers as a whole class.

> **Answers:** 1 the Hoover Building (worked there, do my shopping) 2 Reina Sofía building (doctors and nurses, sick people, pictures, works of art, Picasso, painting) 3 Smolny Institute (school, studied there, Russian, Moscow, St Petersburg) 4 Musée d'Orsay (station, trains, journeys, France, museum, painter, tourists)

b ▶ Ss read the summary and find a new piece of information about each building. Ss check answers in pairs, then as a whole class.

> **Answers:** Hoover Building – produced electrical equipment The Reina Sofía – once called the San Carlos Hospital The Smolny Institute – Lenin worked there Musée d'Orsay – France's impressionist collection is there

Grammar

6a ▶ Ss read the summary again. They find the five verbs and note the ending for each. Check answers in pairs, then as a whole class.

> **Answers:** lived worked studied planned opened

b ▶ Ss match the verb endings to the verbs. Ss check answers in pairs, then as a whole class. Direct Ss to the reference section on page 63.

> **Answers:** live – 4 (+ -d) work – 1 (+ -ed) study – 2 (-y + -ied) plan – 3 (+ -n + -ed) open – 1(+ -ed)

c ▶ Ss complete the gaps in the summary with a suitable verb. Ss check answers in pairs, then listen to see if they were correct.

> **Answers:** 1 worked   2 looked   3 turned
> 4 decided   5 opened   6 closed   7 moved

7 ▶ Ss use the prompts to write sentences using the Past Simple. The first one is done for them.

> **Answers:**   1 The Hoover Factory produced vacuum cleaners.   2 Alicia studied at the Sorbonne.   3 My brother started a new job yesterday.   4 My mother married my father in 1977.   5 That church changed to apartments in 2002.

Pronunciation

8a ▶ Ss close their books. Write the three verbs on the board *worked, opened, decided*. Play recording 6.4. Ss listen and note the different endings used for each verb. Ss look at their books to see the correct phonetic sound and repeat the verbs.

b ▶ Ss listen to recording 6.5 and write the verbs in the correct column.

> **Answers:**   /t/: finished, looked, produced   /d/: lived, changed, planned   studied /ɪd/: visited, started

▶ Say: *finished*. Ask: *How many syllables do you hear?* (two, not three syllables). Say: *looked, changed*. Ask: *How many syllables do you hear?* (one, not two) Ask: *When does the past tense ending sound like a new syllable /d/?* (After verbs ending in /t/ and /d/.)

c ▶ Ss practise reading sentences from Ex. 7 in pairs. Ss correct each other. Monitor closely and correct any mis-pronunciation of past tense endings.

Speaking

9 ▶ Ss make notes about their past. Put *lived, moved, studied, worked* on the board as prompts but encourage Ss to use lots of different verbs if they can. Review how to say dates, *1990, 1985*, etc.

▶ Ss work in pairs. They tell each other about their past. Encourage Ss to ask questions and get further details from their partner during the conversation. Don't worry about Ss making mistakes during this activity. Note down any obvious errors to correct later.

> **OPTIONAL EXTENSION**
>
> Ss write a short biography (one paragraph) about their partner.

6.2 Missing!

In this lesson Ss read about Robin Andrews, who went missing for 16 hours. They listen to an interview with Robin about his experiences and to Robin asking for directions after he wakes up in a strange town. Through this context, Ss learn the Past Simple question forms and short answers and how to understand and give simple directions.

> **OPTIONAL READING LEAD-IN**
>
> Teach *disappeared* (no one knows where you are). In pairs, Ss make a list of the reasons why someone disappears (e.g. *kidnap; get lost; lose memory; want to be alone*, etc.). Put all the reasons on the board. Ss will only be able to explain their ideas in very simple English. Tell Ss they are going to read about what happened to Robin.

Reading

1 ▶ Teach *disappeared* and *something strange happened*. Ss look at the three questions and read the text to find the answers. Ss check answers in pairs, then as a whole class.

> **Answers:**   1 16 hours   2 lost, disappeared   3 because he doesn't remember what happened

> **OPTIONAL EXTENSION**
>
> Ss re-read the text and underline all the verbs. All but two are regular verbs in the Past Simple. Review past tense endings and pronunciation of regular verbs which were introduced in the previous lesson.

2a ▶ Tell Ss they will hear an interview between Robin and a reporter. Play recording 6.6. Ss listen and answer the questions. Ss check answers in pairs, then as a whole class.

> **Answers:**   1 in Marbury, lying in front of a library   2 an old man   3 his father

b ▶ Explain to Ss that the interviewer got several details wrong when writing down notes for the newspaper report. Play the recording again. Ss listen and correct the underlined details. Check answers in pairs, then as a whole class.

> **Answers:**   1 3.30   2 two   3 at the phone shop   4 to an Internet café   5 an old man   6 his father

Vocabulary

> **OPTIONAL VARIATION**
>
> Ss close their books. In pairs, they try to remember all the places mentioned in the dialogue in the correct order. Compare with another pair.

3a ▶ Ss look at the list of places. Play the recording again. Ss listen and tick the places mentioned.

Answers: in the bank   at the phone shop   to the Internet café   in front of a library   on the ground under the bridge

b ▶ Play recording 6.7. Ss repeat the phrases.

Lifelong learning

▶ Ss read the vocabulary journal tip. Some Ss remember words best when they have a visual or picture image of the word. Encourage Ss to try to do this with new words to decide if it helps them remember the vocabulary.

4 ▶ Ss look at the diagrams and write the correct preposition in the space provided. Ss check answers in pairs, then as a whole class.

Answers: 1 in   2 next to   3 in front of   4 behind
5 under   6 on   7 between

Grammar

5 ▶ Ss look at the questions which the interviewer asked Robin. Write them on the board. *Did you get lost? Where did you go then? Did you go to sleep?* Ss choose the correct word to complete the rule.

Answers: did   infinitive

▶ Write *Did you walked there?* on the board and then cross out the past tense form in walked and write walk to show Ss that we use the bare infinitive form of the verb to make questions. Direct Ss to the reference section on page 63.

6a ▶ Ss complete the questions, then match the questions to the answers a–d. Ss check answers in the tapescript on page 154.

Answers: 1 Did b   2 Where c   3 Did a   4 what d

b ▶ Ss write questions for the sentences in Ex. 2b using the question words. The first one is done for them.

Answers: 2 How many kilometres did he walk?/How far did he go?   3 Where did he stop?   4 Where did he want to go?   5 Who helped him?   6 Who collected him?

▶ Explain the difference between *Who helped him?* and *Who did he help?*; *Who collected him* and *Who did he collect?*

7a ▶ Elicit some suggestions about what might have happened to Robin. Ask: *What do you think happened to Robin?* (E.g. *aliens stole him; a car bumped into him*, etc.) Accept all suggestions, but do not comment on whether any are right or not.

▶ Divide the class into two groups, As and Bs. Group A work together in pairs, Group B work together in pairs. Group A looks at page 126, Group B looks at page 129. Ss construct a story ending about what happened to Robin based on the pictures and expressions given. Give Ss about five minutes to do this.

▶ When Ss are ready, ask them to form new pairs. Each new pair should have a Student A and a Student B. Ss describe their story to their partner and decide which is the best ending for the story.

b ▶ Ask: *Which story do you like best?* Play recording 6.8. Ss listen and find out which is the correct ending to the story.

Answer: Story A

Person to person

8 ▶ Ss work in pairs. They take turns to ask ten *yes/no* questions in order to find out what their partner did at the time periods mentioned. Ss can only answer *yes* or *no*.

9a ▶ Ask Ss to look at the places on the map. Ask: *Where is the art gallery?* (on Church Rd); *Where is the computer shop?* (On Mill St, between the phone shop and the bar). Establish where the library is on the map as this is the starting point for the directions in recording 6.9.

▶ Tell Ss they are going to hear the conversation between Robin and the old man after he woke up in Marbury. Ask: *Does Robin know Marbury?* (No.) *Do you remember what Robin asked the old man?* (Directions to the police station.)

▶ Play recording 6.9. Ss listen and follow the directions on the map. They find the three places mentioned on the map.

Answers: post office D   bookshop B   police station A

b ▶ Play the recording again. Ss listen and complete the How to box. Ss check answers in pairs, then as a whole class.

Answers: the police station?   at the next road   right into   200 metres   the road   the street

▶ Ss practise saying the directions. Help with the pronunciation of *straight* and *right*. Direct Ss to the Pronunciation bank on page 147 for the sound-spelling correlation of *-igh*.

10 ▶ Ss work in pairs. Using the map, they ask and give directions from and to the places listed. Monitor carefully, correcting any errors you hear.

OPTIONAL EXTENSION

Ss think of two places they often go to near the school. (E.g. *somewhere for lunch; a train station*, etc.) Ss work in small groups of three or four. Each student gives directions to the places they have thought of. The other Ss try to work out where the place is.

11 ▶ Ss write a reply to the email, giving directions from the station to their house.

6.3 Getting around

In this lesson Ss read about the changes in navigation over the centuries and learn about different modes of transport in different cities. Through this context, they learn the Past Simple (negative) and how to describe their last holiday.

Reading

1 ▶ Review *map* (show the picture of a map in their books) Ss discuss the three questions in pairs.

2a ▶ Scanning. Direct Ss to the text. Explain that they will read the text twice, the first time very quickly and the second time much more slowly. Direct them to the question and tell them they have one minute to get a quick idea of what the text is about. Explain that they do not need to understand the text fully at this point. Stop the activity after a minute and ask Ss to decide on a title for the text. Check answers.

> Answer: c

b ▶ Ss read the text again, at their own pace. Explain they do not need to understand every word in the text. Ask Ss not to use their dictionary while they read. Explain that there is a vocabulary exercise on the text to follow. Ss use the words in italics to label the pictures with the italicised words in the text.

▶ Ss check answers in pairs, then as a whole class.

> Answers: A stars   B compass   C satellite
> D sextant   E map

3a ▶ Ss look at the text again. They find the words 1–6 in the text and try to guess what these words mean before matching them to the six meanings given. The first one is done for them. Ss check answers in pairs, then as a whole class.

> Answers: 2 d   3 a   4 b   5 c   6 e

b ▶ Ss complete the sentences with verbs from the text. Ss check answers in pairs, then as a whole class.

> Answers: 1 didn't work   2 were   3 didn't give
> 4 changed

Grammar

4 ▶ Ss choose the correct word to complete the rule based on the negative sentences they read.

> Answers: didn't   infinitive

▶ The verb *to be* does not need the auxiliary *didn't* to form the negative: *he wasn't there*; *they weren't there*. Help Ss with the pronunciation of *didn't*. Direct Ss to the reference section on page 63.

5 ▶ Ss correct the false statements following the example given. Check answers in pairs, then as a whole class.

> Answers: 1 The sextant didn't show the exact location.
> 2 People didn't use cars in the sixteenth century.
> 3 Leonardo da Vinci didn't invent the compass.
> 4 Ancient people didn't play computer games.
> 5 Beethoven didn't paint the Mona Lisa.
> 6 Marco Polo didn't own a mobile phone.

OPTIONAL EXTENSION

Elicit a list of famous explorers and travellers and put their names on the board. (E.g. *Christopher Columbus, Marco Polo, the Vikings*, etc.) Ss work in pairs and make a list of five differences between exploration then and now. (E.g. *There was no contact with people at home. There were more places to explore*, etc.)

Vocabulary

6a ▶ Ask Ss: *How do people get to work every day today?* (car, bus, walk, etc.) and *How did people get to work 100 years ago?* (walk, bicycle, etc.) Elicit the other ways of getting around. Teach *by car, by bicycle/train/taxi/tram/boat/plane* but *on foot*.

▶ Ss look at the photo and discuss the answers to the 2 questions.

b ▶ Ss match the forms of transport to the places.

> Answers: 1 b   2 f   3 e   4 a   5 c   6 d

▶ Find out if Ss have visited any of these cities and elicit if they used any of the forms of transport mentioned.

OPTIONAL EXTENSION

Ss work in small groups of three or four. Ss decide on one advantage and one disadvantage for the different modes of transport mentioned. (Buses are cheap but they are slow, etc.)

7 ▶ Ss discuss the two questions about modes of transport in pairs. Ask them to speak about their preferences for long journeys, short journeys (e.g. to buy the paper), going to work/school, travelling on holiday, etc.

OPTIONAL EXTENSION

Ss have thought about transport systems in the present and the past. Ask them to design a type of transport of the future in small groups of three or four. Don't worry about Ss making mistakes during this activity. Ss will not be able to use future forms of verbs but should still be able to draw and speak about what their vehicle might look like (e.g. video maps on the steering wheel, massage chairs for traffic jams, etc.). This need not be a serious exercise. In feedback, Ss put their designs on a notice board or around the walls.

Pronunciation

8a ▶ Ss close their books. Write *I like trains* on the board. Say it for Ss, using normal stress patterns. Write *Do you like buses?* above the first sentence. Explain that now *I like trains* is an answer to that question. Insert *No,* at the front, e.g. *No, I like trains*. Play recording 6.10. Ss listen and underline the stressed word (trains). Ask: *Why is 'trains' stressed?* (to give emphasis).

▶ Ss open books. They look at the other two examples. Play the recording again, Ss listen and mark the stressed word for each (Rome, horrible). Ss practise saying the sentences.

b ▶ Direct Ss to the prompts in the table. In pairs, Ss practise the dialogues using secondary stress patterns. The first one is done for them.

Writing

9a ▶ Elicit from Ss anything they know about Bangkok. Ask about the weather, the population, attractions, etc. Accept all suggestions and put them on the board. Ask Ss to scan read the paragraph to see if they were right.

▶ Ss read about a visit to Bangkok. They underline all the verbs in the Past Simple in the paragraph. Check answers in pairs, then as a whole class.

> **Answers:** visited   liked   didn't like   was   stayed   were   talked   didn't walk   travelled   was   looked   watched   wanted   visited

b ▶ Ask Ss to make notes about their last holiday using the verbs from Ex. 9a as headings, especially *liked, didn't like, stayed, visited, travelled*. Ss write a paragraph about their own last holiday.

> **OPTIONAL EXTENSION**
>
> Ss interview each other about their last holiday, using the verbs and headings from the previous exercise.

Communication: In shops

> **OPTIONAL WARMER**
>
> Elicit a list of special events when people buy presents for several different people at the same time. (E.g. for religious festivals such as Christmas or for national celebrations such as Chinese New Year). Ss work in pairs. They discuss (1) who they buy for, (2) who is the hardest to buy for and (3) how far in advance they shop for presents.

1 ▶ Teach *department store* (a shop where you can buy clothes, household goods, beauty products, etc., give examples). Discuss the four questions as a whole class. Teach *escalator* (moving stairs), as they need this for the listening exercise.

2a ▶ Teach *on the ground*, *first, second floor* and *in the basement* (draw a map of a building). Play recording 6.11. Ss listen and complete the gaps in the store guide. Check answers in pairs, then as a whole class.

> **Answers:** Fourth floor: furniture   Third floor: music   First floor: men's shoes   Basement: computers

b ▶ Ss listen to the recording again and complete the How to box in their books. Check answers in pairs, then as a whole class.

> **Answers:** can I find   Have you got   I have   much

c ▶ Ss work in pairs. They ask and answer about where to find the items listed in the box. An example is done for them.

> **Answers:** football – sports hall, first floor   CD player – electronic goods, basement   aspirin – pharmacy, fourth floor   printer – computers, basement   women's jeans – women's clothes, second floor   pencil – stationery, ground floor   dictionary – bookshop, basement

3 ▶ Ss work in pairs. A pairs work in a gift shop and B pairs are potential customers. A pairs read the information on page 126, B pairs on page 62. Give Ss time to decide what they sell and what they want to buy. They also decide on the price of the goods for sale and on how much they want to spend.

▶ A pairs set up shops around the room. B pairs circulate, asking about the goods and prices and decide where they will buy the presents. An example dialogue is provided for them.

▶ Do not worry about mistakes during this activity. Monitor and note down any obvious errors to deal with later. In feedback, compare presents and prices.

> **OPTIONAL EXTENSION**
>
> Ss imagine they are the recipient of the gift. They write a 'Thank you' note to their friend. Direct Ss to the writing bank on page 144 for an example of an informal letter to a close friend.

Review and practice

1 ▶

> Answers: + -ed: looked, owned, started, wanted;
> + -d: closed, decided, lived, moved; + -ied: married,
> worried; +consonant + -ed: planned, stopped

2 ▶

> Answers: They were lovely people worked
> in a car factory he owned a car she was a girl
> She married she stayed at home My great-
> grandfather stopped work always carried a
> little bag died too.

3 ▶

> Answers: 1 Was Pablo Picasso Spanish? Yes, he was.
> 2 Did Mozart play the guitar? No, he played the piano.
> 3 Was President Kennedy Russian? No, he was
> American. 4 Did the USA launch GPS satellites in
> 1983? No, they launched them in 1973. 5 Was the
> Hoover Building a factory 70 years ago? Yes, it was.
> 6 Did Alexander Graham Bell invent the computer? No,
> he invented the telephone. 7 Did the ancient Romans
> speak Latin? Yes, they did. 8 Did Neil Armstrong walk
> on a star? No, he walked on the moon.

4 ▶

> Answers: 1 in front 2 on 3 under 4 next to
> 5 in 6 between 7 behind

5 ▶

> Possible answers: 1 café, internet café, bar,
> restaurant 2 supermarket, bookshop, newsagent's,
> pharmacy, department store 3 art gallery, museum,
> church 4 bus station, train station, tram station,
> 5 library, park, church 6 pharmacy, police station,
> post office, bank, bus station, train station, church

Notes for using the Common European Framework (CEF)

CEF References

6.1 Can do: talk about your past

CEF A2 descriptor: can describe plans and arrangements, habits and routines, past activities and personal experiences (CEF page 59)

6.2 Can do: understand and give simple directions

CEF A1 descriptor: can understand questions and instructions addressed carefully and slowly to him/her and follow short, simple directions (CEF page 75)

6.3 Can do: describe your last holiday

CEF A2 descriptor: can tell a story or describe something in a simple list of points, can describe everyday aspects of his/her environment e.g. people, places, a job or study experience (CEF page 59)

CEF quick brief

The reference levels in the Common European Framework (A1–C2) are mostly written in the form of 'Can do' statements. These statements give examples of what a learner Can do at the different reference levels. Teachers, syllabus designers, writers, etc. can write and add their own statements according to the needs of their users.

Portfolio task

Download the Total English Portfolio free from www.longman.com/totalenglish.

Objective: to help learners complete the 'language learning history' section of their Portfolio Biography.

This task can be done in Ss' own language.

▶ By completing details of their language learning history, Ss are encouraged to reflect on successful and unsuccessful language learning experiences and hence to further develop their language learning skills.

1 ▶ Explain the benefits for any language learner of thinking about their history and what has been successful for them.

2 ▶ Ask Ss to write details of their English language learning history (12 years at school, etc.) and compare with a partner.

3 ▶ Encourage Ss to reflect critically on what has been successful and what hasn't been successful for them.

4 ▶ Ask Ss to transfer this information to the language learning history section of their Biography.

7 People

Overview

Lead-in	**Vocabulary:** adjectives to describe people; *belongs to*
7.1	**Grammar:** pronoun *one/ones* **Vocabulary:** adjectives for describing people **Can do:** write an informal letter describing family members
7.2	**Grammar:** possessive pronouns **Vocabulary:** ordinary numbers; months **Can do:** say who objects belong to
7.3	**Grammar:** Past Simple: irregular verbs **Vocabulary:** phrasal verbs **Can do:** understand an article
Com. Focus Reference Practice	Identifying people

Summary

Lesson 1: Ss read a letter from Marianne who is staying with a host family while studying near Ipanema Beach in Brazil. They listen to the song *The girl from Ipanema*.

Lesson 2: Ss find out about Jane and her friends and then listen to a conversation between Jane and her husband about presents for their friends.

Lesson 3: Ss read about how two schoolgirls found thousands of pieces of banknotes on their way to school and what they did with the money.

Communication: Ss identify people based on oral descriptions and complete a police report form for missing persons.

Film bank: Great Expectations (3'24")
An extract from a classic British film.

This film version of *Great Expectations* by Charles Dickens was made in 1945. It is still considered one of the best Dickens adaptations. In this extract Pip, a young boy, goes to see Miss Haversham, an old lady who lives in a big house nearby. The extract offers a nice opportunity to practise the language for describing people from Unit 7.

Possible places to use this short film are:

▶ after the Unit Opener to practise the language of descriptions

▶ before lesson 2 to introduce the Past Simple tense in an interesting and different way

▶ at the end of the unit to round up the topic and language

For ways to use this short film in class, see Students' Book page 137 and Teacher's Book page 192.

Lead-in

OPTIONAL WARMER

Ss work in pairs. They tell each other about their impressions when they meet people for the first time. Ask: *What do you notice first about (1) men and (2) women: face, eyes, body, clothes, etc?*

1a ▶ Ss focus on the pictures. Ask: *Where do you think these people are?* (Coming out of a train station; in the street, etc.)

▶ Ss match the people in the photos to the descriptions 1–10. The first one is done for them. There are several possible answers for some of the adjectives/expressions.

Answers: 2 G 3 A 4 E 5 D 6 G 7 B 8 H 9 F 10 A, B

---

b ▶ Play recording 7.1. Ss listen to check their answers. Discuss variations with Ss during feedback.

▶ Focus on the contracted form of *has got* in spoken English, e.g. *G's got* blue eyes; *A's got* fair hair. Note: Hair is singular in English. Explain to Ss *She's got* a pretty face but *She's* pretty. *She wears* glasses.

2 ▶ In pairs, Ss describe and identify one of the people from the photos. Monitor closely, helping with vocabulary and correcting any obvious errors.

EXTEND THE LEAD-IN

Ss work in small groups. They describe what their ideal partner would look like. (E.g. My ideal partner has blue eyes and dark hair. I don't like beards but I like moustaches.) Don't worry about Ss making mistakes during this activity. In feedback focus on any differences of opinion.

▶ As a follow-on have a whole-class discussion on important possessions in an ideal partner. Ask: *Is money important? Is a car/your own house important? What about his/her books? CDs collection?* Etc. This links in with the next exercise which focuses on what belongs to whom.

3a ▶ Ss look at the four items and the list of who they belong to. They match the items to the people and place. The first one is done for them.

Answers: 2 d 3 a 4 b

---

b ▶ Direct Ss to the dialogue. Write on the board *Who does X belong to?* (X is usually a thing) *It belongs to Y.* (Y is usually a person)

▶ Ss take turns to ask and answer about the things in Ex 3a.

7.1 The girl from …

It is common to stay with host families during short-term study periods overseas. Ss of all ages stay with a local family and live as one of the family. This can be a very effective way of getting to know the culture and practising the language of the host country.

> **OPTIONAL WARMER**
>
> Ss imagine they are going to an English-speaking country to do a course in English. Elicit the types of accommodation available. (E.g. host family, youth hostel, etc.) In pairs, Ss think of two advantages and two disadvantages for the different types of accommodation. (A host family is good because you can practise English with the family. But it is bad because I like to cook for myself, etc.)

Reading and vocabulary

1 ▶ Ss look at the photos. Explain who Marianne is and why she is in Brazil. Ss discuss the two questions.

> **Answers:** 1 It is Ipanema Beach in Rio de Janeiro. 2 Ss' own answers

2a ▶ Teach *host family* (a local family who you stay with if you are visiting a different city or country). Ss look at the three questions and read the text to find the answers. Explain that they do not need to understand the text fully at this point. Write *my age* and *tiring* on the board and ask Ss to try to guess what these words mean as they read. (The same age as me; it makes me feel tired.) Check answers in pairs, then as a whole class.

> **Answers:** 1 She arrived in Rio de Janeiro to do a course. 2 She lives with the Silva family. 3 She usually goes to the beach.

b ▶ Ss read the letter again and match the people to the adjectives. Ss check answers in pairs, then as a whole class.

> **Answers:** 1 c 2 d 3 a 4 f 5 b 6 e

Lifelong learning

▶ Direct Ss to the Lifelong learning box. Point out that it is useful to write the noun too when noting down opposites. For example, *old* can be the opposite of *new* or *young* (depending on who/what we are describing).

3a ▶ Ss look at the adjectives in Ex 2b again and match them to their opposites. Ss check answers in pairs, then as a whole class. The first one has been done for them.

> **Answers:** 1 dark 2 fat 3 nice 4 handsome, pretty 5 young 6 short

▶ We usually use *pretty* to talk about a woman and *handsome* to talk about a man. We use *short* and *tall*

(not long) for people. We use *young* (not new) to talk about people, except for a new baby.

b ▶ In pairs, Ss put the adjectives into the different columns.

> **Answers:** Body: slim, fat Face: pretty, handsome, ugly Skin: tanned, pale, fair, dark Hair: fair, dark Height: tall, short Age: old, middle-aged, young Personality: shy, nice. Fair and dark can be used to describe both hair and skin colour.

> **OPTIONAL EXTENSION**
>
> Ss work in teams of two. Each pair must try to extend the list in each category without using a dictionary. Give Ss two minutes per category. Each team gets one point for each new vocabulary item. The team with the most points at the end wins.

4 ▶ Review modifiers (*really, quite, very, not very*). Ask Ss to look at the letter again and to underline the modifiers. (Very friendly, quite short, very tanned, really handsome, quite shy. Note: He's <u>a bit</u> fat is introduced here.) Ss work in pairs. One student describes someone to their partner, who tries to guess who it is. Ensure Ss describe someone known to their partner, either a famous person or someone in the class.

Grammar

5a ▶ Ss focus on the excerpts from the letter in Ex. 2a. Ask Ss to find the sentences in the letter. Ss match the underlined words to the correct meaning. Check answers in pairs, then as a whole class.

> **Answers:** 1 d 2 a

▶ *One* replaces singular nouns, *ones* replaces plural nouns. We often use *one* and *ones* to replace the noun after an adjective or after *this/these* and *that/those*. We also use *one* after *each* (Ss will hear this in the song in Ex. 6a) and in expressions like *the one/ones on left/right*, etc. Direct Ss to the reference section on page 73.

b ▶ Ss read the paragraph and find four words which could be replaced by *one* or *ones*. Ss check answers in pairs, then as a whole class.

> **Answers:** The second one The third one the one on the second floor The other ones

Listening

> **OPTIONAL VARIATION**
>
> Focus on the *ooh* and *ah* exclamations which come up in the song. Demonstrate saying *ooh*. Ask: *Is this reaction to something nice or something unpleasant?* (nice). Give examples. (When you see something lovely, e.g. opening a present; a dress in a shop.) Ss practise saying *ooh* and *ah* using appropriate intonation and stress patterns.

6a ▶ Ss look at the two questions, then close their books. Play recording 7.2. Ss listen to the song and answer the questions.

> **Answers:** 1 sad because the girl does not notice him. 2 Ss' own answers

b ▶ Ss look at the words of the song. Teach *samba* (a type of dance) and *pause* (stop for a moment). Review *straight ahead* from the previous unit. Ss read through the song and try to guess what the missing words might be. Ss compare answers in pairs.

▶ Play the song a second time. Ss listen and fill in the missing words. Ss check answers in pairs, then as a whole class.

> **Answers:** 1 tanned 2 young 3 goes 4 one 5 walks 6 and 7 one 8 watch 9 her 10 give 11 sea 12 not 13 tanned 14 young 15 Ipanema 16 doesn't

> **OPTIONAL EXTENSION**
>
> Ask: *Marianne and the man in the song have the same problem. What is their problem?* (Both are interested in people they see on the beach in Brazil. Both are too shy to speak to the person.) In pairs, Ss think of advice to give to Marianne and the man. (E.g. Say hello to him/her; Bump into him/her 'accidentally', etc.) Elicit all the suggestions in feedback and decide as a class on the best piece of advice.

Writing

7a ▶ Ss look at the format and structure of Marianne's letter from Ex. 2a. Ss read the letter again and match the statements to the paragraphs. Ss check answers in pairs, then as a whole class.

> **Answers:** She asks Carol to do something – E. She thanks Carol – A. What she does – D. Where she lives – B

b ▶ Ss focus on the beginning and end of the letter and complete the How to box.

> **Answers:** Dear Love

▶ Direct Ss to the writing bank on page 144 for an example of an informal letter.

8 ▶ Write a framework for the letter on the board to guide Ss. E.g.

Dear _____
Paragraph 1 – where you live
Paragraph 2 – describe your family
Best wishes

_____

▶ Ss write the letter.

7.2 Birthday puzzle

In this lesson Ss find out about Jane and her friends and listen to a conversation between Jane and her husband about presents for their friends. Through this context, Ss learn possessive pronouns (mine, etc.) and how to say who objects belong to.

> **OPTIONAL WARMER**
>
> Ss work in pairs. They describe their best friend as a child and their best friend now to each other. They tell their partner the kind of presents they bought/buy for and received/receive from their friends.

Listening

1a ▶ Ss look at the photos of Jane's friends. In pairs, they describe each person in the photos without looking at the sentences (e.g. hair colour, height, etc.). Ss match the descriptions to the photos. Check answers in pairs, then as a whole class.

> **Answers:** Mrs Clark – 3 Davy – 1 Tara – 5 Mr Clark – 2 Gordon – 4

b ▶ Elicit other descriptions about the five people. Ss make guesses about what their jobs might be. An example is given.

2a ▶ Ss look at the presents Jane has bought for her friends. They match the words to the presents. The first one is done for them.

> **Answers:** clock – B electric drill – E wrapping paper – G diary – F handbag – D umbrella – C

b ▶ Ss discuss who the presents might be for following the example given.

c ▶ Play recording 7.3. Ss listen and match the items to the people. Ss check answers in pairs, then as a whole class.

> **Answers:** electric drill – Gordon; trainers – Davy clock – Mr and Mrs Clark handbag – Jane diary – Tara umbrella – Jane and Mike

> **OPTIONAL EXTENSION**
>
> Ss work in pairs. They discuss present giving in their families. *Who usually buys the presents in your family? Do you usually buy individual or shared presents?* (E.g. My mother and I buy a present together for my father.)

Grammar

3a ▶ Ss look at the excerpts from the recording in Ex 2a. They match the underlined words to the correct meaning. Ss check answers in pairs.

> **Answers:** 1 c The trainers are <u>his</u> – Davy's trainers. 2 d It's ours – belongs to us

b ▶ Ss look at the tapescript on page 155 and complete the Active grammar box.

> Answers: mine   his   hers   ours   yours   theirs

▶ Write *It is mine* and *It belongs to me* on the board. Underline the verbs to emphasise the different structures.

It is mine can mean both *It belongs to me* and *It is for me*. Direct Ss to the reference section on page 73.

4 ▶ Ss rewrite the sentences using possessive pronouns. Ss check answers in pairs, then as a whole class. The first one is done for them.

> Answers: 1 yours   2 is mine   3 hers   4 was theirs
> 5 ours   6 his   7 theirs   8 Is this his?

> **OPTIONAL EXTENSION**
>
> Ask Ss to select something from their bag, wallet or pencil case. Collect the items in a bag so the Ss cannot see who is giving what. Put all the items on the desk. Ask: *Who does this belong to?* Ss guess whose it is.

Pronunciation

5a ▶ Write *brother* and *bathroom* on the board. Underline the *th* in both words. Say the two words. Ask: *Is the th sound the same?* (No, brother is /ð/ and bathroom is /θ/). Write the two phonetic symbols on the board.

▶ Write *birthday* on the board. Do not pronounce it yet. Ask: *Which sound is in this word?* Play recording 7.4. Ss listen and identify the /θ/ sound. Ss practise saying the words birthday and bathroom.

b ▶ Ss look at the words. Play recording 7.5. Ss listen and identify which word they hear. Check answers in pairs, then as a whole class.

> Answers: 1 b   2 b   3 a   4 b   5 b

c ▶ Play recording 7.6. Ss listen and tick or cross the numbers.

> Answers: 1 (✓)   2 (✓)   3 (✗)   4 (✗)   5 (✓)
> 6 (✓)   7 (✗)   8 (✓)

Vocabulary

6a ▶ Ss read the tapescript for Ex. 2c again. Ss write down the birthdays of Davy and Tara as given in the tapescript. Gordon's birthday has been done as an example.

> Answers: Davy – the twentieth of this month
> Tara – the first of next month

▶ Ask Ss *What is this month?* Write Davy's birthday on the board. (E.g. November 20) Point at the number. *What number is this?* (twenty) Explain we say the twentieth of November. Remind Ss of the /θ/ sound from Ex. 5.

b ▶ Ss write the numbers from Ex. 6a and then complete the table.

c ▶ Play recording 7.7. Ss listen and check their answers.

> Answers: 1 first   3 third   4 fourth   5 fifth
> 6 sixth   7 seventh   9 ninth   10 tenth
> 11 eleventh   12 twelfth   13 thirteenth
> 15 fifteenth   20 twentieth   30 thirtieth
> 31 thirty-first

7 ▶ Ss complete the exercise by choosing the correct word. Ss check answers in pairs, then as a whole class.

> Answers: 1 first   2 three   3 fourth   4 third
> 5 ninth

8a ▶ Ss find the two months written in Ex. 7.

> Answers: May and July

b ▶ Ss look at the jumbled months and put them in order. January has been numbered 1 for them.

> Answers: February 2   March 3   April 4   May 5
> June 6   July 7   August 8   September 9   October 10
> November 11   December 12

▶ Ss practise saying the months.

c ▶ Ss tell their partner their birthdays and give the dates of national holidays in their country.

9a ▶ Ss mingle and ask each other about their birthdays. (When is your birthday? It's on the first of February, etc.) Ss note down the different dates in their exercise books. When they have found the five Ss, they sit down. Ss call out the answers.

b ▶ Ss work in pairs. They pool information to try and write all the Ss' names in order of their birthdays. The pair who writes all the names in the correct order first wins.

> **OPTIONAL EXTENSION**
>
> Ss work in groups of three or four. Each student writes down five numbers. The numbers selected should correspond to important numbers in the student's life. Demonstrate for Ss first. (E.g. Write 3, 42, 8 ..., etc. *The first number is my brothers. I have 3 brothers. The second number is my age. I am 42.*, etc.)

▶ Ss ask and answer about the numbers in their groups. Encourage Ss to ask further questions about the numbers as well. Do not worry about Ss making mistakes during this activity.

7.3 Finders keepers!

In this lesson Ss read about how two schoolgirls found thousands of pieces of banknotes on their way to school and what they did with the money. Through this context, Ss learn how to understand a narrative text, Past Simple (irregular verbs) and phrasal verbs.

OPTIONAL WARMER

Ss work in small groups. They discuss what they would do in the following situations: (1) they find a large sum of money in a rubbish bin, (2) the shop assistant gives them change for 100 euros instead of 10 euros, (3) they realise outside the shop that they have forgotten to pay for books. Don't worry about Ss making mistakes. They will be able to use only very basic language for this discussion.

Reading

1 ▶ Ss look at the photo and say what kind of game it shows. (It's a jigsaw puzzle.) Explain the difference between games and puzzles, give some examples. Ss discuss whether they like games and puzzles.

2 ▶ Scanning: Explain to Ss that before they read the text properly they will read it very quickly to get an idea of what it is about. Direct them to the question and tell them they have two minutes to find what *the jigsaw* is in the text as quickly as possible. Explain that they do not need to understand the text fully at this point. Stop the activity after two minutes.

> **Answer:** Putting all the pieces of money back together.

3 ▶ Ss focus on new vocabulary in the text. They look at the meanings given and read the lines indicated to find the words in the text. Ss check answers in pairs, then as a whole class.

> **Answers:** 1 tiny pieces   2 banknotes   3 noticed
> 4 stepfather

4 ▶ Ss look at the six statements. They read the text again, this time more slowly to find the correct order of events. The first one is done for them. Ss check answers in pairs, then as a whole class.

> **Answers:** c 2   b 3   a 4   f 5   d 6

5 ▶ Ss find the detailed information in the text. Encourage them not to write full answers to the questions but just to use a few words for the answers, as in the example. Ss check answers in pairs, then as a whole class.

> **Answers:** 1 thousands of pieces of banknotes
> 2 their teachers   3 to the police station   4 six
> months   5 no owner asked for it   6 by matching the
> numbers on the pieces   7 no idea

6 ▶ Ss focus on the types of questions asked in Exs. 3, 4 and 5. Explain that the three exercises help develop different

reading skills. Ss look at the three strategies in the How to box and then match the strategy to the exercises. Ss check answers in pairs, then as a whole class.

> **Answers:** Exercise 4   Exercise 3   Exercise 5

Grammar

7 ▶ Ask Ss to underline the verb in the first sentence of the text (were). They should be familiar with the past simple of the verb to be. Explain this is an irregular past tense. It has no -ed ending.

▶ Ss look at the verbs from the text in the Active grammar box. They match the present to the past forms of each verb.

> **Answers:** 1 d   2 g   3 i   4 h   5 b   6 e   7 c
> 8 a   9 f

Many of the most common verbs in English are irregular. They do not have an -ed ending.

▶ Direct Ss to the reference section on page 73.

OPTIONAL GRAMMAR LEAD-IN

Ss focus on the text. They do not look at Ex. 7. Ask Ss to underline all the verbs in the text. Write the present forms on the board in a jumbled order. Ss match each of the present forms to one of the underlined past forms in the text.

---

8 ▶ Ss make sentences about the text in the Past Simple using the prompts given. An example is given.

> **Answers:** 1 The bag had thousands of pieces of
> banknotes in it.   2 The girls told their teachers.
> 3 The girls took the money to the police station.
> 4 The police kept the money for six months.
> 5 The girls put the pieces of banknotes together.

Person to person

9 ▶ Ask Ss to think about the previous year. Ask them to note down any significant events or achievements which happened. (E.g. passing driving test, meeting a new boyfriend/girlfriend; changing job, etc.) Write the timeframes on the board. Each student writes five sentences about themselves by selecting one activity/ event/achievement which they did at the times referred to. An example is given.

▶ When they are ready, Ss work in pairs and ask each other about the sentences. (E.g. What did you do six months ago? I went to my sister's wedding., etc.) Encourage Ss to ask for further details during the activity.

Vocabulary

10a ▶ Ss scan through the text quickly to find the second part of the verbs.

> **Answers:** 1 look at   2 hand in   3 give back
> 4 put together

b ▶ Ss look at the cartoons and match the correct two-part verbs to the picture. Ss check answers in pairs then as a whole class.

> **Answers:** 1 Look at   2 hand in   3 pick up   4 give back   5 put together

c ▶ Ss use the verbs to complete the sentences about the pictures.

> **Answers:** 1 look at   2 hand in   3 pick up   4 give back   5 put together

Pronunciation

11 ▶ Ss focus on the questions in Ex. 5. Write the question words on the board. *What, who, where, how long, why, how, whose.* Say: *what* and *how.* Elicit the difference in pronunciation of the two words. Write /w/ under *what* and /h/ under *how.*

▶ Play recording 7.8. Ss listen and identify the initial sound for the other question words. Ss check answers in pairs, then as a whole class.

> **Answers:** /w/: what, where, why   /h/: who, how long, how, whose

▶ Ss practise saying the questions.

> **OPTIONAL EXTENSION**
>
> Say one or two answers which relate to the text and ask Ss to call out the questions. (E.g. *£1,200* (How much do they have now?); *Rachel's stepfather* (Who helped them to put the notes together?) etc. Ss work in pairs. Each pair prepares three answers relating to the text. The pairs then take turns to say the answers to another pair who have to call out the questions. Monitor closely, paying particular attention to the pronunciation of the question words.

Speaking

12a ▶ Ss look at the list of Past Simple endings on page 149. They find the endings to the verbs given in their books. Each student writes five *Wh-* questions using the verbs in the box. Examples are given.

b ▶ Ss work in pairs. They ask and answer the questions they have written with their partners.

> **OPTIONAL EXTENSION**
>
> Ss conduct a roleplay in pairs. A is one of the girls who found the money and B is the reporter who wrote the newspaper article. Bs interview As about the incident. Encourage Ss to imagine answers where the information is not given in the text. Don't worry about Ss making mistakes during this activity. Note down any obvious errors to deal with later.

Communication: Identifying people

Ss identify people based on oral descriptions and complete a police report form for missing persons.

1 ▶ Ss focus on the picture. Discuss as a whole class where the man in the picture is and why. (He is in a police station. We don't know why.) Elicit suggestions. Accept all suggestions.

2a ▶ Play recording 7.9. Ss listen to get the general idea of where the man is and why he is there. Ss check answers in pairs, then as a whole class.

> **Answers:** 1 In a police station   2 A woman he met a few days ago has gone missing   her clothes are still in her room and she has his bag

b ▶ Play the recording a second time. Ss listen and note down the details to complete the police report form. Check answers in pairs, then as a whole class.

> **Answers:** Name: Gemma Hunston   Woman   Age: 24   Height: tall, about 1.7 metres   Hair: dark brown hair, quite long   Body type: quite slim   Eyes: green   Skin: very tanned   Other features: glasses   Last seen: yesterday afternoon   Name of person reporting: David Kennedy   Relationship to missing person: friend, met a few days ago

c ▶ Ss decide in pairs which picture shows the missing woman.

> **Answer:** C

3 ▶ Play the recording again. Ss read the tapescript on page 155 while listening. Ss underline the questions as they read. (How old is she? What's her name? etc.) Write the questions on the board so that Ss have a record of them for the next activity.

4a ▶ Ss work in pairs. Student A looks at the pictures on page 127 and chooses one of the people to invent a missing person story about. Student B is the police officer completing a missing persons report form. When the report is complete, Student B looks at the pictures and identifies the person from Student A's description.

b ▶ Ss swap roles. This time student A is the police officer. Student B uses the pictures on page 130 to choose their missing person.

> **OPTIONAL EXTENSION**
>
> Cut out photos of people from magazines. Ss work in pairs. Student A has just witnessed a robbery. Student B is a police artist who draws people based on descriptions of eyewitnesses. Give As one of the photos and tell them to imagine this is the person they saw. They describe the person and student B draws an 'identikit' picture. Ss compare the photo and the picture during feedback. Note: Ss do not have to be good at drawing for this activity.

Review and practice

1 ▶

Answers: the red one? modern ones? those ones in the corner The metal ones? how about this one? I don't like that one a different one

2 ▶

Answers: 2 h 3 b 4 a 5 d 6 c 7 g 8 f

3 ▶

Answers: 1 left 2 spoke 3 came 4 spent
5 became 6 thought 7 had 8 ate 9 wrote
10 bought

4 ▶

Answers: 1 eighth 2 twenty-fifth 3 first
4 eighteenth 5 ninth

5 ▶

Answers: 2 d 3 e 4 a 5 b

6 ▶

Answers: 1 put/together; 2 Pick/up; 3 give back;
4 looked at

Notes for using the Common European Framework (CEF)

CEF References

7.1 Can do: write an informal letter describing family members

CEF A2 descriptor: can write a series of simple phrases and sentences about their family, living conditions, educational background, present or most recent job (CEF page 62)

7.2 Can do: say who objects belong to

CEF A1 descriptor: can produce simple mainly isolated phrases about people and places (CEF page 58)

7.3 Can do: understand an article

CEF A2 descriptor: can understand short, simple texts containing the highest frequency vocabulary, including a proportion of shared international vocabulary items (CEF page 69)

CEF quick brief

Though the reference levels in the Common European Framework suggest that students progress 'vertically', from A1 to A2, etc., the Framework itself says that 'learning a language is a matter of horizontal as well as vertical progression'. This means that some learners might like to move from A2 level in a business context to A2 level in a tourist context. The CEF identifies four basic 'domains' that help to understand this horizontal language development: the public domain, the personal domain, the educational domain and the occupational domain.

Portfolio task

Download the Total English Portfolio free from www.longman.com/totalenglish.

Objective: to help Ss complete the 'significant linguistic and intercultural experiences' section of their Portfolio Biography.

This task can be done in Ss' own language.

▶ Ss can further improve their language learning skills by reflecting on significant experiences that have helped them to learn another language or about another culture.

1 ▶ Refer Ss back to the section of their Passport where they listed their language learning and intercultural experiences.

2 ▶ Ask Ss to choose the most important experiences that have helped them learn a language or learn about a culture. It can help to give examples of your own.

3 ▶ Ask Ss to compare with each other and explain why they were important.

Day to day

Overview

Lead-in	**Vocabulary:** clothes
8.1	**Grammar:** Present Simple; adverbs of frequency
	Vocabulary: clothes
	Can do: write a request to a colleague
8.2	**Grammar:** Present Continuous; adverbs of manner
	Vocabulary: activities, revision of rooms and clothes
	Can do: describe what you are doing now
8.3	**Grammar:** Present Simple and Present Continuous
	Vocabulary: the weather; health
	Can do: take part in a factual conversation on a simple topic
Com. Focus	Making a complaint
Reference	
Practice	

Summary

Lesson 1: Ss read about three problems concerning what clothes to wear and the response of a fashion expert to the three problems.

Lesson 2: Ss listen to part of a Big Brother type reality TV programme.

Lesson 3: Ss listen first to a Europe-wide weather forecast and then to two people discussing how the weather affects their mood and health. They also read three emails sent to a "Your health and the Weather" website.

Communication: Ss complain about faulty goods to a shop assistant.

Film bank: The Notting Hill Carnival (3'39")
A short film about this famous carnival.

Over one million people attend the Notting Hill Carnival every year. This short film interviews some of the participants and gives a flavour of what it's like to prepare for and attend the largest street carnival in Europe.

Possible places to use this short film are:

▶ after lesson 1 to extend the work on clothes

▶ after lesson 2 to practise the Present Continuous

▶ at the end of the unit to round up the topic and language

For ways to use this short film in class, see Students' Book page 138 and Teacher's Book page 192.

Lead-in

OPTIONAL WARMER

Ss discuss the following questions in small groups of three or four: *Do you like shopping for clothes? How often do you do it? Do you bring someone with you to help you choose? Which clothes item do you have the most of?* (E.g. shoes, coats, jeans, etc.)

---

1 ▶ Ss look at photos A and B. Elicit where the people are and what the seasons are in each photo.

Answers: A summer, at the beach; B winter, in a park

2a ▶ Ss focus on the clothes in the photos. They match the clothes in the box to the pictures. Ss check answers in pairs, then as a whole class.

Answers: hat B jacket C jeans A pullover D scarf B shorts A skirt E suit C T-shirt A trainers A

---

b ▶ Ss work in pairs and name other clothes in the pictures. They can use their dictionaries.

3a ▶ Ss match the adjectives to their meanings. Ss check answers in pairs, then as a whole class.

Answers: 1 d 2 e 3 f 4 b 5 a 6 c

---

b ▶ Ss work in pairs. They use the adjectives to describe the clothes in photos C–E. Play recording 8.1. Ss listen to check their answers. The first one is done for them.

Answers: C a smart suit, a formal suit, a light shirt D a loose pullover; a casual pullover E a tight jacket, a smart suit

---

c ▶ Ss work in pairs. They give their opinions on the four statements.

EXTEND THE LEAD-IN

Write different historical periods on the board. E.g. the 1960s/the 18th century/the Roman empire. (Note: Choose historical periods which are familiar to Ss in your class.) Elicit a few examples of the types of clothes people wore then. (E.g. women: long dresses, men: tall hats, etc.) Ss discuss in pairs which of the eras had the best fashions and why. (I like the 18th century because the dresses were beautiful and big and feminine. I don't like the Roman Empire because the men wore light dresses and ugly shoes, etc.)

8.1 Clothes for all seasons

In this lesson Ss read about three problems concerning what clothes to wear and the response of a fashion expert to the problems. Through this context Ss learn adverbs of frequency and how to write a request to a colleague.

Reading

1 ▶ Discuss the questions as a whole class.

> **OPTIONAL WARMER**
>
> Ss work in pairs. They tell each other the kind of clothes they would choose to wear on the following occasions: (1) a wedding; (2) going out to dinner in a restaurant with friends; (3) going to the cinema on a date; (4) special family celebrations (e.g. birthdays, Christmas, etc.); (5) a job interview; (6) a long plane journey. Write the occasions on the board. Explain *wedding* (marriage party) and *date* (romantic appointment, when the two people don't know each other very well).

2a ▶ Scanning. Explain to Ss that they will read the letters twice, the first time very quickly and the second time much more slowly. Direct them to the exercise and tell them they have two minutes to match the letters to the answers as quickly as possible. Explain that they do not need to understand the text fully at this point. Stop the activity after two minutes. Ss compare answers in pairs and then as a whole class.

> **Answers:** 1 C   2 A   3 B

b ▶ Ss read the texts more slowly, this time focusing on the letters 1–3. Teach *cool* (a little bit cold) and *travel for business* (for your job). Ss read through the situations and then match the writer to the situation. Ss read at their own pace. Ss check answers in pairs, then as a whole class.

> **Answers:** 1 Mr and Mrs Jackson   2 Sindy
> 3 Geoffrey   4 Sindy   5 Geoffrey

> **OPTIONAL VARIATION TO READING**
>
> Ss cover Alison's answers to the three letters. They read the three problem letters 1–3 and identify the problem in each one. Check answers. Then Ss work in pairs and imagine they are Alison. Together they decide on advice to give the three writers. They compare answers with another pair. Ss then read and match the answers A–C to the three problem letters. They see if their suggestions are similar to Alison's.

Vocabulary

3a ▶ Ss focus on the vocabulary in the text. They find words with opposite meanings to those listed. Ss check answers in pairs, then as a whole class.

> **Answers:** 1 comfortable   2 formal   3 take off
> 4 loose

▶ Draw Ss' attention to the prefixes *un-* and *in-* but do not spend too long on this.

b ▶ Ss match the four words from the text to their meanings. Ss check answers in pairs, then as a whole class. The first one has been done for them.

> **Answers:** 2 d   3 a   4 b

▶ Focus on the pronunciation of these words, especially *wool* and *layers*.

4 ▶ All the items of clothing in the picture are mentioned in the problem letters text. In pairs, Ss look at the picture and identify the clothing. The first one has been done for them.

> **Answers:** B trousers   C a pullover   D a T-shirt
> E a belt   F jeans   G a jacket   H top   I a skirt
> J trainers   K shoes   L scarves   M gloves
> N a tie   O a suit   P coats

▶ Focus on the pronunciation of these words, especially the initial /dʒ/ in jacket and jeans and the /uː/ sound in suit.

> **OPTIONAL EXTENSION**
>
> In pairs, Ss categorise the vocabulary into (1) clothes worn on the top half of the body and (2) clothes worn on the lower part of the body.

Grammar

5 ▶ Ss scan through the three problem letters quickly to find the six adverbs of frequency. They write the verb and the adverb in the Active grammar box. Ss check answers in pairs.

> **Answers:** Letter 1: is always, usually go   Letter 2:
> often travel, am never   Letter 3: usually wear, hardly
> ever wear, sometimes go

▶ Ss choose the correct word to complete the rule. Check answers in pairs, then as a whole class.

> **Answers:** after the verb to be   before other verbs

▶ Review the meaning of the adverbs of frequency in the Active grammar box. Teach *hardly ever*. The other vocabulary should be familiar to Ss. Direct Ss to the scale on the left hand column of the box. Direct Ss to the Reference section on page 83.

6 ▶ Review the use of the indefinite article in *once a week, twice a month*, etc. Ss work in pairs. They choose the most appropriate adverb of frequency and rewrite the sentences. The first one has been done for them.

> **Answers:** 1 We sometimes go to the cinema
> 2 He never drinks coffee   3 He always drinks coffee
> 4 I usually take the dog for a walk   5 I hardly ever
> see my parents

7a ▶ Ss look at the sentences about David and rewrite them using the appropriate adverb of frequency from the box. The first one has been done for them. Ss check answers in pairs, then as a whole class.

> **Answers:** David never smokes   David sometimes eats pasta   David hardly ever sees his brother   David usually wears a suit   David often goes to the gym

b ▶ Ss write sentences about themselves using the adverbs of frequency. Ss compare answers with a partner.

> **OPTIONAL EXTENSION**
>
> Ss practise using the adverbs of frequency in pairs. Write *suit, hat, tracksuit, tie, dress, gloves, smart shoes* on the board. Ss say true sentences to each other about how often they wear these clothes. (E.g. I never wear a hat, I always wear smart shoes, etc.)

Person to person

8 ▶ Ss ask each other the three questions about their clothes: what they wear, where they buy their clothes and their favourite clothes. Don't worry about Ss making mistakes during this activity.

Writing

9a ▶ Ss look at the letter from Mr and Mrs Jackson again. They underline the phrases used to request advice. Ss call out the answers.

> **Answers:** Can you give us some advice? So, what clothes can we all wear?

b ▶ Ss work in pairs. They imagine they are colleagues, about to begin a three month job in a new city. As read the information on page 127 and Bs read the information on page 130, Each student writes a letter to the other requesting advice about what clothes to bring. When Ss have finished, they exchange letters and write the reply.

▶ When Ss have finished writing, they give the reply to their partner to read. Direct Ss to the writing bank on page 144 for a quick review of the format for an informal letter.

8.2 We're watching you!

Reality TV shows have become extremely popular in recent years. The most well-known is Big Brother where twelve contestants enter the Big Brother house at the beginning of the series. They stay in the house for several weeks but are allowed no contact with the outside world while they are inside the house. Each week the contestants nominate two of their housemates to be voted off the programme and the public chooses which one will leave. Eventually there is only one contestant left who wins the prize money.

Listening

1 ▶ Ss look at the picture and at the six screens showing scenes from a Big Brother type TV series. Ask Ss if they are familiar with this type of reality TV show and explain the basic format to them. Ss discuss the four questions in their books as a whole class. Teach 'screen' (the front part of a TV or computer).

> **Possible Answers:** 1 In the TV studio of a Big Brother type programme.   2 the people on the TV screens are the contestants inside the house.   3 Ss give their opinions on this type of programme.

> **OPTIONAL WARMER**
>
> Ss look at the six screens. In pairs they decide (1) where each person is, (2) how the people on the different screens are feeling, and (3) what they are doing. (E.g. The woman in number two is in a bedroom. I think she is sad. Maybe the other people in the house said something unkind to her., etc.) Some Ss may use the Present Continuous during this activity. Accept all suggestions from Ss but do not highlight this language at this point.

2a ▶ Teach *to have an argument with someone* (to disagree with, shout at someone). Play recording 8.2. Ss listen and match the person to the screen. Ss check answers in pairs.

> **Answers:** Adam and Rosa 5   Cara 2   Erica 4   Gary 6   Greg 1   Jason 3

b ▶ Play the recording again. Ss listen and complete the sentences with the correct name. Ss check answers in pairs.

> **Answers:** 1 Erica   2 Adam and Rosa   3 Jason   4 Greg   5 Gary   6 Cara

> **OPTIONAL EXTENSION**
>
> Ss talk about being a contestant on the Big Brother programme. In pairs they list (1) good things and (2) difficult things about being inside the house. (E.g. Good: In the Big Brother house you don't go to work. Difficult: I don't like to meet the same people every day, etc.) In feedback, ask Ss: *Would you like to be on the Big Brother TV programme?*

Grammar

▶ Ss focus on the photo of the presenters and the six screens behind them. Establish that the screens show what the people are doing at the same time that the presenters are talking to the TV audience. Ask: *Is Greg in the kitchen now?* (Yes). Ask: *Why is he in the kitchen?* (cooking, preparing dinner). Say: *He is preparing dinner.*

3a ▶ Ss look at the sentences in Ex. 2b and the sentences from the listening text in Ex. 2a. They use them to complete the Active grammar box. Ss check answers in pairs, then as a whole class.

> **Answers:**   's digging   're shouting   isn't digging   Is   Are   are   isn't

b ▶ Ss complete the rules for the Present Continuous by choosing the correct answers.

> **Answers:**   1 b   2 to be

▶ Emphasise the difference between the TV presenters saying: *Greg prepares dinner every day* and *He is preparing dinner now* (at the moment of speaking). Focus on the *-ing* form of the verb. Direct Ss to the reference section on page 83.

c ▶ Ss focus on the spelling of the *-ing* form. Ss check answers in pairs, then as a whole class.

> **Answers:**   1 talking, crying   2 cycling, preparing   3 digging

4a ▶ Ss write sentences about the people in the house using the present continuous. The first one is done for them. Ss check answers in pairs, then as a whole class.

> **Answers:**   1 Greg isn't preparing breakfast.   2 Cara isn't sleeping.   3 Jason is digging up flowers.   4 Erica isn't jogging.   5 Erica is singing.   6 Adam and Rosa aren't writing.

b ▶ Ss work in pairs. Student A describes one of the scenes on the screen and student B guesses the name of the person being described.

Grammar

5 ▶ Ss focus on Adam and Rosa in screen five. Ask: *What are they doing?* (talking) Ask: *Are they talking like this* (indicate whispering, talking quietly) *or like this?* (indicate speaking loudly, raise your voice). Say: *They are talking quietly.*

▶ Ss look at the three excerpts from the recording. Elicit who the sentences refer to. (Erika is cycling fast; Adam and Rosa are talking quietly and Gary is looking carefully.) Ss focus on the underlined adverbs. Ask: *Which of the three words is irregular, do you think? How do you know?* (fast, no *-ly* ending) *Which are the regular adverbs?* (carefully, quietly). Ss choose the correct answers to complete the rules.

> **Answers:**   1 the activity   2 after the verb

▶ Direct Ss to the reference section on page 83.

6 ▶ Ss choose the correct explanation for each adverb. Check answers in pairs, then as a whole class.

> **Answers:**   1 a   2 b   3 a

7 ▶ Ss use the adverbs in the box to complete the sentences. Check answers in pairs, then as a whole class.

> **Answers:**   1 healthily   2 quietly   3 well   4 happily   5 carefully

▶ Ss focus on healthily and happily. Ask: *What do you notice about the spelling of these adverbs?* (no *-y*, add *-ily* instead of *-ly*)

OPTIONAL EXTENSION

Write the following on the board *I'd like to be in the Big Brother house with someone who ... | I wouldn't like to be in the Big Brother house with someone who ...*

Ss choose a verb and an adverb to complete each sentence. (E.g. sings loudly in the morning/cooks badly/acts rudely/works hard, etc.)

Ss compare sentence endings. In feedback, elicit examples of the worst/best type of person to share the Big Brother house with.

Pronunciation

8a ▶ Play recording 8.3. Ss listen and underline the strong syllables they hear. Ss check answers in pairs, then listen again and repeat. The first one has been done for them.

> **Answers:**   1 They're <u>talk</u>ing <u>qui</u>etly.   2 He's <u>look</u>ing very <u>care</u>fully.   3 You're <u>speak</u>ing <u>loud</u>ly.   4 We're <u>liv</u>ing <u>heal</u>thily.

b ▶ Ss mime one of the verb and adverb combinations from the box and the other Ss try to guess the activity. Model an example first for Ss.

Speaking

9 ▶ Ss work in pairs. Student A looks at the picture on page 127. Student B looks at the picture on page 130. The scenes are the same but the names of different people are included/not included in each picture. Ss ask and answer to find the names of the unidentified people in their pictures.

8.3 Under the weather

In this lesson, Ss listen first to a Europe-wide weather forecast and then to two people discussing how the weather affects their mood and health. They also read three emails sent to a 'Your health and the Weather' website. Through this context Ss learn the Present Simple contrasted with the Present Continuous and how to take part in a factual conversation on a simple topic.

> **OPTIONAL WARMER**
>
> Ss think of three reasons to like each of the four seasons. E.g. Spring: flowers grow in the gardens; the weather begins to get warmer; people put their winter coats away, etc. In feedback, establish which season Ss like best.

Vocabulary

1a ▶ Ss match the weather symbols to the weather words. The first one has been done for them. Ss check answers in pairs. Do not give the answers yet.

> Answers: 2 H   3 A   4 D   5 F   6 G   7 E   8 C

b ▶ Play recording 8.4. Ss listen to check their answers.

c ▶ Play the recording again. Ss listen and complete the gaps in the text. Check answers as a whole class.

> Answers: 1 foggy   2 raining   3 cold   4 cloudy
> 5 sunny   6 warm   7 windy

▶ Highlight that *It's snowing* and *It's raining* are Present Continuous verbs here and the other weather words are adjectives.

Pronunciation

2a ▶ Direct Ss to the letter *o* in each word. Play recording 8.5. Ss listen to identify the two sounds /əʊ/ and /ɒ/. Ss check answers in pairs, then as a whole class. Write the phonetic symbols on the board.

> Answers: cold and snowing are /əʊ/ sounds and hot and foggy are /ɒ/ sounds.

b ▶ Play recording 8.6. Ss listen and list the words they hear under the two columns. Check answers in pairs, then as a whole class.

> Answers: /ɒ/: clock, cost, not, on, bottle   /əʊ/: old, note, hotel, wrote, own.

c ▶ Ss look at the three sentences. Play recording 8.7. Ss listen and underline the words which contain the sounds. Check answers in pairs, then as a whole class.

> Answers: 1 It often snows a lot in Poland   2 The doctor told me not to get cold   3 She wears tops and coats in orange and gold

Reading

3a ▶ Scanning. Explain to Ss that they will read the text twice, the first time very quickly and the second time much more slowly. Direct them to the heading and tell them they have one minute to complete the title for the text as quickly as possible. Explain that they do not need to understand the text fully at this point. Stop the activity after a minute. Ss check answers in pairs, then as a whole class.

> Answer: weather

b ▶ Ss read the texts again, completing the table as they read. Before they start, write the words from Ex. 5 on the board and ask Ss to find them in the text. Ask Ss not to use dictionaries but to try to guess the meanings of the words.

> Answers: Pablo/Argentina, headaches   rain, aches in arms and legs   Lars/Norway, cold and dark

4 ▶ Ss focus on the new vocabulary in the text. They match the words to the correct meaning. Check answers in pairs, then as a whole class.

> Answers: 1 e   2 c   3 a   4 f   5 b   6 d

Lifelong learning

▶ Ss focus on the suffix *-ness*. Write *dark/darkness* on the board. Ask: *Which word is the noun?* (darkness) *What type of word is dark?* (an adjective) Explain that the suffix *-ness* is added to adjectives to make them nouns. Encourage Ss to look out for different word endings and note the different forms in their vocabulary journals.

5 ▶ Ss look at the nouns with the suffix *-ness* and say which adjectives they come from. Ss check answers in pairs, then as a whole class.

> Answers: 1 tired   2 happy   3 fit   4 sick   5 bald
> 6 crazy

▶ Ask Ss: *What do you notice about happiness and craziness?* (No *-y* at the end and *-iness* instead.)

Speaking

▶ Teach *(high) temperature* (how hot it is) and *that's a shame* (that's a pity).

> **OPTIONAL LISTENING LEAD-IN**
>
> Write *high temperatures/hot weather* on the board. Ss work in pairs. They list three good and three bad things about really hot weather. (E.g. go to the beach, wear T-shirts; hard to go to the office; sunburn, etc.) Elicit if Ss like really hot weather and how it affects their health.

6a ▶ Ss look at the How to box. Explain *agree* and *disagree* (when two people have the same/different opinions). Play recording 8.8. Ss listen and find the expressions to complete the How to box.

Answers: think agree sure

b▶ Ss look at the tapescript on page 156 and find a second expression for each strategy. Ss check answers in pairs, then as a whole class.

Answers: I believe that the sun is good for us. Yes, you're right. I don't think so.

c▶ Ss work in pairs. They discuss the weather in their country and how it affects their health. Write *Winter/ Summer/Spring/Autumn* on the board to guide the discussion.) Encourage Ss to agree and disagree with each other.

Grammar

7a▶ Direct Ss to the first email in Ex. 4. Explain that some of the verbs are circled and some are underlined. Ask: *Which are circled?* (Present Simple) *and which are underlined?* (Present Continuous).

▶ Ss look at the other emails. They circle the Present Simple verbs and underline the Present Continuous verbs. Ss check answers in pairs, then as a whole class.

Answers: Email 2: Circled: live, rains, aches, rains. Underlined: 'm aching, 's raining   Email 3: Circled: affects, get, stays, 's, 's. Underlined: 're feeling

b▶ Ss complete the rules by filling in the correct tense.

Answers: 1 Present Continuous   2 Present Simple

▶ We use the Present Simple to talk about routines and facts. We use the Present Continuous to talk about actions happening now. Direct Ss to the reference section on page 83.

8▶ Ss choose the correct form of the verb in each sentence.

Answers: 1 am working   2 take   3 carry
4 isn't wearing   5 are studying   6 don't drink

9a▶ Ss write sentences about the people in the pictures, using the prompts. The first one is done for them. Ss check answers in pairs, then as a whole class.

Answers: 2 Laura usually walks to work but today she is driving her new car.   3 Sally usually cleans the house every day but today she is playing football.   4 Anna usually wears jeans but today she is wearing a dress.

b▶ Ss practise the two tenses by asking each other questions about the people in the pictures. An example is given.

Communication: Making a complaint

OPTIONAL WARMER

Ss work in pairs. Write the following situations on the board. (People talking in the cinema; cold food in a restaurant; a mark on a shirt you have bought; noisy neighbours; the bus is late.) Ss discuss whether they would complain in these situations or not. Ss will only be able to express their views in very basic English.

1▶ Ss look at the pictures. Elicit what is happening in each picture without focusing on the phrases. Ss then match the phrases to the pictures.

Answers: it doesn't work – it's broken E
a receipt B   a refund C   an exchange D

2a▶ Play recording 8.9. Ss listen and identify which pictures correspond to which dialogue.

Answers: Dialogue 1: A, C   Dialogue 2: B, D, E

b▶ Ss listen again and tick the phrases they hear. Ss check answers in pairs, then as a whole class.

Answers: it doesn't work – it's broken 2   it doesn't fit 1   a receipt 1 and 2   a refund 1   an exchange 2

3a▶ Elicit the stages in making a complaint. *What do you do first/second?*, etc. (Explain the problem, ask for money/exchange, etc.). Ss look at the stages in the How to box. They read the tapescript on page 156 and complete the gaps in the box. Check answers.

Answers: can   bought   doesn't   exchange/like

b▶ Ss practise saying the dialogue to each other. Monitor closely, correcting any pronunciation errors.

4▶ Ss work in pairs. One student is a customer and the other is a shop assistant. Student A's card is on page 82 and student B's is on page 127. Give Ss a minute or two to read through the information on their cards. They can use their dictionaries for words they don't understand. When they have finished they exchange roles and read the information for Roleplay 2. They conduct the second roleplay in pairs.

5a▶ Ss read the letter and answer the questions in pairs.

Answers: 1 To complain about faulty goods.   2 Formal
3 Dear Sir/ Dear Madam   4 Yours faithfully   5 included

b▶ Ss read the letter again and match the underlined phrases to the descriptions. Check answers.

Answers: B Toshiba RX90 cooker   C 20th June
D Heaton Shopping Centre   E the clock is broken

6▶ Ss use the information from Roleplay 1 to write a letter of complaint.

Review and practice

1 ▶

> **Answers:** 1 usually 2 hardly ever 3 always
> 4 never 5 sometimes

2a ▶

> **Answers:** 1 digging 2 making 3 planning
> 4 reading 5 riding 6 sitting 7 studying
> 8 swimming 9 using 10 waiting 11 writing
> 12 carrying

b ▶

> **Answers:** 1 'm writing 2 'm waiting
> 3 is studying 4 is using 5 is making
> 6 'm reading 7 are planning

3 ▶

> **Answers:** 1 Are you reading a good book? Yes, I am.
> 2 Are you studying German? No, I'm not studying
> German. I'm studying English. 3 Is she cooking
> dinner? No, she isn't cooking dinner. She's preparing
> tomorrow's lunch. 4 Is he working at home today?
> Yes, he is. 5 Are they playing tennis? No, they aren't
> playing tennis. They're playing badminton.

4 ▶

> **Answers:** 1 She usually wears formal business suits.
> 2 Today she's wearing jeans and a T-shirt. 3 She
> usually talks to people in the office. 4 Today she's
> talking to clients at the match. 5 She usually has a
> sandwich for lunch in the office. 6 Today she's having
> a big meal in a restaurant.

5a ▶

> **Answers:** 2 f 3 a 4 c 5 b 6 d

b ▶

> **Answers:** 2 loudly 3 comfortably/uncomfortably
> 4 quietly 5 carefully/carelessly, badly/well, slowly/
> fast

6 ▶

> **Possible Answers:** 1 a coat 2 a hat 3 trainers
> 4 a dress 5 a suit 6 a jacket

Notes for using the Common European Framework (CEF)

CEF References

8.1 Can do: write a request to a colleague

CEF A1 descriptor: can ask people for things and give people things (CEF page 80)

8.2 Can do: describe what you are doing now

CEF A2 descriptor: can give short, basic descriptions of events and activities (CEF page 59)

8.3 Can do: take part in a factual conversation on a simple topic

CEF A2 descriptor: can participate in short conversations in routine contexts on topics of interest (CEF page 76)

CEF quick brief

The reference levels in the Common European Framework (A1–C2) allow a correlation with common international exams as well as exams within a country or institution. This means that employers can have a more accurate idea of what a student with a particular qualification can actually do. For more information see the introduction at the start of this Teacher's Book.

Portfolio task

Download the Total English Portfolio free from www.longman.com/totalenglish.

Objective: to help Ss start using the Portfolio to assess their progress and priorities in English.

This task can be done in Ss' own language.

▶ The Biography section of the Portfolio contains the Can do statements from each lesson in the book. Ss can use this section to review and keep track of their progress. It is helpful to remind students to complete the tick boxes in this section at a regular intervals, perhaps at the end of every unit or at the end of semester.

1 ▶ Ask Ss to look at the Can do statements in the Biography section of their Portfolio. Show how the statements relate to the work they have completed in their coursebooks.

2 ▶ Ask Ss to look through the statements at A1 level and complete the tick boxes.

3 ▶ Explain that as they progress through the course, they will be able to achieve more Can do goals at A1 and will also start to complete goals at A2 level.

Overview

Lead-in	**Vocabulary:** the arts
9.1	**Grammar:** comparison of adjectives
	Vocabulary: news media
	Can do: make comparisons between things and people
9.2	**Grammar:** superlative adjectives
	Vocabulary: films
	Can do: write a short film review
9.3	**Grammar:** *prefer* + noun/-*ing* form; *will* for spontaneous decisions and offers
	Vocabulary: art
	Can do: talk about personal preferences
Com. Focus Reference Practice	An evening out

Summary

Lesson 1: Ss read about the features of different news sources and listen to two people discussing their preferred news source.

Lesson 2: Ss listen to a film critic giving her opinions on various films of the last 10 years and then read questions and answers from a film quiz.

Lesson 3: Ss read a text about modern art and then listen to two people selecting which postcards depicting various works of art to buy.

Communication: Ss plan an evening out together.

Film bank: Spirit of the City (6'02")
A short film about a painter and the huge cityscapes that he paints.

This independently-made film about Richard Tate, an artist who lives and works in London, tells us about the man and his reasons for paintings. We also see stunning shots of London and the huge paintings that Richard produces of this city.

Possible places to use this short film are:

▶ before lesson 3 to introduce the topic of art and artists

▶ after lesson 3 to prompt a discussion about what art students like

▶ at the end of the unit to round up the topic and language

For ways to use this short film in class, see Students' Book page 139 and Teacher's Book page 193.

Lead-in

OPTIONAL WARMER

Ss imagine they have won a prize to go to any show in London. Write the following on the board *ballet/ theatre/musical/film premiere/art exhibition/opera/ concert/poetry reading*. Ss discuss in pairs which type of show they would like best.

1a ▶ Ss look at the jumbled letters and reorder them to match the four pictures.

Answers: 1 music B   2 film A   3 theatre D
4 painting C

---

b ▶ Ss work in pairs. They name one example of each of the art forms in the box. E.g. ballet – Swan Lake; cartoon – the Simpsons, etc.

2a ▶ Ss look at the picture of the incomplete word map. The head word is *the arts*. Explain there are five subheadings. Ss use the words from Exs. 1a and 1b to complete the word map. Tell Ss they can put words in more than one category if they wish. Ss compare answers with a partner.

b ▶ Play recording 9.1. Ss listen and compare their word map to that of the two people on the recording.

Answers: (This is the word map from the recording but there are several possible variations.)
Theatre: ballet, dance, plays, opera
Music: ballet, opera, dance, classical music, rock music
Film: cartoon, comedy, horror
Literature: novels, plays, poetry
Painting: modern art

---

c ▶ Ss think of more words to add to the word map. (E.g. architecture, modern dance, etc.)

3 ▶ Ss work in groups and answer the questions. Encourage Ss to explain why they like a particular novel or film. (E.g. My favourite book is *War and Peace* by Leo Tolstoy. I love long historical novels. It is about life, etc.) Ss will only be able to express very basic opinions about the various works of art.

EXTEND THE LEAD-IN

Ss imagine they are going to visit a famous capital city for the weekend. (E.g. New York, Paris, Beijing, etc.) Write the following things to do on the board *go shopping/visit an art gallery/visit a museum/go to an expensive restaurant/go to local bars and clubs/ go to the theatre/travel around the city on foot/by bus, etc./visit famous historical buildings/go to the zoo*. Ss rank the activities in order of preference. They discuss the various activities and compare preferences.

9.1 Making news

In this lesson Ss read about the features of different news sources and listen to two people discussing their preferred news source. Through this context Ss learn comparison of adjectives and how to make comparisons between things and people.

OPTIONAL WARMER

Bring a newspaper to class if you can. Elicit from Ss the different sections of the newspaper and write them on the board. (E.g. TV pages, international news, national news, sports section, horoscope, etc.) Ss work in pairs. They tell each other which parts of the newspaper they (1) usually read first and which parts they (2) hardly ever read.

Reading

1a ▶ Elicit the big news stories at the moment. Discuss the different ways of finding out about the news with Ss. Elicit different news sources (radio, TV, newspaper, etc.).

b ▶ Ss look at the list of news sources in Ex. 2a and match the words to the pictures. Check answers in pairs, then as a whole class.

Answers: 1 text message   2 the TV   3 newspaper
4 Teletext   5 radio   6 Internet

Vocabulary

2a ▶ Scanning. Explain to Ss that they will read the text twice, the first time very quickly and the second time much more slowly. Direct Ss to the chart. Teach *detailed* (a lot of information) and *versatile* (you can do it in different ways and in different places). Tell Ss they have one minute to find the adjectives in the text and complete the chart. Explain that they do not need to understand the text fully at this point. Stop the activity after a minute. Ss call out the answers.

Answers:

	fast	easy	detailed	cheap	new	exciting	versatile
Newspapers			✓	✓			✓
The radio		✓					
The TV						✓	
Teletext	✓						
The Internet	✓		✓				
Text messages	✓				✓		

b ▶ Ss look at the question. Explain *old-fashioned* (not modern) and *visual* (you look at it). Ss read the text again. Explain they do not need to understand every word. They list the advantages and disadvantages mentioned about the different news sources.

Answers: Newspapers: + cheap, detailed and versatile, you can read them anywhere, – none mentioned
The radio: + easy, you can listen while you are doing something else, – old-fashioned   The TV: + interesting, exciting, visual, lots of different types of programmes, – none mentioned   Teletext: + fast, – not very detailed
The Internet: + detailed, very fast, – expensive   Text messages: fast, very new, messages on mobile phone, – expensive

▶ Ss compare answers in pairs and add to the list of advantages and disadvantages.

c ▶ Ss discuss the opinions in the text.

Grammar

3a ▶ Direct Ss to the chart in Ex. 2a. Ask: *Which news sources are fast?* (the Internet, teletext, text messages). Ask: *Are newspapers fast?* (no). Say and write on the board *The Internet is faster than newspapers*.

▶ Ss focus on the six sentences. Play recording 9.2. Ss listen and write the correct news source in the space provided. Ss check answers in pairs, then as a whole class.

Answers: 1 newspapers   2 text messaging
3 the Internet   4 TV   5 the radio   6 TV

b ▶ Ss use the underlined words in Ex. 3a to complete the Active grammar box. Ss check answers in pairs.

Answers: cheaper than   easier than
more detailed than   more exciting than   better than

▶ Ss read through the four rules. They find examples of each rule from the list. Ss check answers in pairs. Direct Ss to the Reference section on page 93.

Answers: 1 cheap   2 easy   3 detailed, exciting
4 good, bad

▶ Focus on the sentence stress of comparative sentences, especially the weak vowel sound /ə/ in fast<u>er</u> th<u>a</u>n. Explain that only two syllable adjectives which end in *-y* take *-er*. (easier/funnier than). Other two-syllable adjectives take more ... than (e.g. modern, polite).

4 ▶ Ss complete the sentences by using the correct comparative form of the adjective and another news source. Ss check answers in pairs, then as a whole class.

Answers: 1 more immediate than (newspapers)
2 more detailed than (text messaging)   3 more modern than (the radio)   4 better than (the Internet). The sources in brackets are suggested answers only.

5 ▶ Ss identify the pairs of things in the pictures. They then make sentences comparing the two. An example is done for them. Ss can do this exercise in pairs. Compare the different suggestions in feedback.

OPTIONAL VARIATION

Elicit the names of ten people and things from Ss. They call out the first ones that come into their heads. (E.g. Colin Farrell, eggs, football, apples, etc.) The less obvious connection between the nouns the better. Ss work in small teams of three or four. They make as many sentences as they can comparing two of the nouns on the board. They cannot compare the same two things with each other twice and they cannot use the same adjective twice. Monitor closely, correcting any errors you hear. At the end, the team with the most sentences wins.

Pronunciation

6a▶ Write *The radio is easier than newspapers* on the board. Underline the /ə/ sounds. Say the sentence for Ss. Play recording 9.3. Ss listen to the phrases and underline the /ə/ sounds. Ss check answers in pairs, then as a whole class. Ss practise saying the phrases.

> **Answers:**   1 fast<u>e</u>r th<u>a</u>n   2 cold<u>e</u>r th<u>a</u>n   3 healthi<u>e</u>r th<u>a</u>n

b▶ Ss write the sentences and practise saying them with a partner. Monitor closely, correcting any pronunciation errors you hear.

> **Answers:**   1 Iceland is colder than Egypt.   2 Spanish is easier than English.   3 Fruit is healthier than chocolate.   4 A Ferrari is faster than a Fiat.

Writing and speaking

7a▶ Ss complete the table by filling in the names of things they like and don't like in the given categories. An example has been done for them.

b▶ Ss write sentences explaining why they like one thing more than another.

c▶ Ss compare sentences in pairs.

8▶ Ss work in small groups of three or four. They compare each others' choices from the table in Ex. 7a and explain their preferences.

OPTIONAL EXTENSION

Direct Ss to Ex. 5. Focus on the first sentence: *'The Washington Post' is more serious than 'Hello!'* magazine. Elicit other serious type newspapers or magazines (e.g. 'The Guardian', the 'New York Times', 'Time' magazine, etc.). Elicit other tabloid-type magazines and newspapers (e.g. 'The Daily Mirror', 'USA Today', etc.). Ss work in pairs and compare the two types of print media. Put the headings *types of stories/the truth/photos/style of writing* on the board to guide the discussion. Don't worry about Ss making mistakes as they try to express their opinions during this activity.

9.2 Movie magic

In this lesson Ss listen to a film critic giving her opinions on various films of the last ten years and then read questions and answers from a film quiz. Through this context Ss learn superlative adjectives and how to write a short film review.

OPTIONAL WARMER

Teach *ingredients* (the different things you need to make a particular recipe or dish). Elicit the ingredients of pizza or some other well-known dish. Write *horror film/a love story/a science fiction film* on the board. Ss work in pairs and list the typical *ingredients* of these type of films. (E.g. horror film: blood, an evil person or monster, a beautiful girl alone, etc.) Write the suggestions on the board during feedback.

Vocabulary

1a▶ Ss look at the four photos of different films. Elicit the names of the four films. (A = LA Confidential; B = Casablanca; C= Rugrats D =I, Robot) Ss match the film genre to the film. Check answers in pairs, then as a whole class.

> **Answers:**   A = thriller   B = cartoon   C = love story   D = science fiction

b▶ In pairs, Ss think of one film for each of the genres in the box. An example has been done for them.

c▶ Ss use the adjectives to describe the different film genres. Teach *scary* (makes you afraid) *romantic* (about love) and *violent* (a lot of killing and fighting in the film). A great deal of overlap is possible here. Focus on the pronunciation of these words.

> **Possible Answers:**   sad: a love story   exciting: an action/adventure film, a horror film, a thriller, a science fiction film   violent: horror, thriller, action/adventure   clever: science fiction, comedy and thriller   funny: comedy, a cartoon but other genres also   scary: a horror film, thriller, a science fiction   romantic: a love story, a musical   happy: comedy, love story, musical, a cartoon   interesting: any of the films

2▶ Ss discuss the types of film they like and dislike and explain why.

Listening

OPTIONAL LISTENING LEAD-IN

Ss look at film titles in the box. Ss discuss what they know about the six films and which of the opinions in Ex. 3 they feel most applies to which film.

3 ▶ Go through the list of opinions first to ensure Ss understand the vocabulary. Teach *foreign language film* (in Hollywood, this means not in English), *unusual* (different to usual, new ideas) a *fresh* musical (new, modern, different), a *mixture of* action and comedy (both action and comedy are in it). Explain the difference between *the actors* (the people in the film) and *the acting* (the performance of the people in the film). Avoid any overt focus on the superlatives yet. Play recording 9.4. Ss listen and match the film to the opinion of Mariela. More than one opinion can apply to a film. Ss check answers in pairs, then as a whole class.

> **Answers:** American Beauty: 1, 6, 10   Gladiator: 3
> The Sixth Sense: 2, 4   All About My Mother: 5
> Pulp Fiction: 7, 9   Chicago: 8

▶ Ask: *Do you agree with Mariela?*

Grammar

4a ▶ Ss look at the example sentence and then match it to the correct meaning. Ss check answers in pairs, then as a whole class.

> **Answer:**   2

b ▶ Ss use the superlative adjectives from Ex. 3 to complete the Active grammar box. The first two have been done for them.

> **Answers:**   the most exciting   the freshest
> the scariest   the best   the most interesting
> the most unusual   the most violent

▶ Ss choose the correct option to complete the rules. Ss check answers in pairs, then as a whole class.

> **Answers:**   -est   most

▶ Ask Ss: *What about two-syllable adjectives?* When they end in *-y*, we drop the *-y* and add *-iest*, e.g. funny – funniest, scary – scariest. For other two syllable adjectives we use the most, e.g. famous – the most famous; polite – the most polite. Emphasise the use of the definite article in superlatives. (American Beauty <u>is best</u> film is incorrect.)

▶ Focus on the typical sentence stress used in superlative sentences. It's the most <u>unusual film</u>.; It's the <u>freshest musical</u>. Direct Ss to the reference section on page 93.

5 ▶ Ss write superlative sentences using the prompts. Check answers in pairs, then as a whole class. The first one has been done for them.

> **Answers:**   1 Asia is the largest continent (in the world).
> 2 The Pacific Ocean is the deepest ocean (in the world).
> 3 Heathrow is the busiest international airport (in the world).   4 A Rolls Royce is the most comfortable car.

Reading and speaking

6a ▶ Ss complete the questions in the quiz questions by inserting the superlative forms.

> **Answers:**   2 the earliest   3 the longest   4 the most successful   5 the richest   6 the youngest   7 the most romantic   8 the scariest   9 the worst

b ▶ Ss do the quiz in groups of three. Each student is given three of the answers but not the questions they correspond to. Ss discuss the questions and match the answers to the questions. Ss turn to page 127 to check their answers.

Person to person

7 ▶ Ss discuss the three questions in pairs. Compare Ss' suggestions for questions two and three in feedback.

> **OPTIONAL EXTENSION**
>
> Conduct an *Academy Awards of all time* in class. Elicit nominations for different categories. Limit the nominations to about four or five names. Suggested categories are: Best Film ever, Best Actor; Best Actress. (You can elicit suggestions from Ss for other categories.) Write the nominations for each category on the board and ask Ss to vote. Collect the votes and ask two Ss to count the votes for each category and to announce the winner. (E.g. The nominations for Best Film ever were … And the winner is …)

Writing

8a ▶ Ask: *What makes you decide to go and see a film?* (friends say it is good, newspaper, etc.) Teach *film review* (an opinion about a film written in a magazine or newspaper) and *film critic* (job where you watch films and write about them in a magazine or newspaper).

▶ Ss look at the headings and then read the film review to find the sentences/phrases with the information. Ss put the headings in order. Check answers in pairs.

> **Answers:**   1 the writer's choice of film – In my opinion the best film of the last ten years is LA Confidential   2 the type of film – It's a thriller   3 the stars – It stars Russell Crowe, Guy Pearce, Kim Bassinger, Kevin Spacey   4 the film's location – The film is set in Los Angeles in the 1950s   5 the story of the film – It's about problems in the police department   6 what the writer thinks is good about the film – It's very exciting and the acting is excellent   7 a recommendation – Go and see it!

b ▶ Ss work in pairs. They choose a film and make notes for the headings given in Ex.8a. They decide why they like the film and then write a review of the film.

> **OPTIONAL EXTENSION**
>
> Ss block out the name of the film in their review. Put the film reviews around the wall. Ss circulate and read the different reviews and note down which film they think is being reviewed. Check answers in feedback.

9.3 Is it art?

In this lesson Ss read a text about modern art and listen to two people discussing which postcards depicting various works of art to buy. Through this context Ss learn *prefer* + noun/*-ing* form, *will* for spontaneous decisions and offers, and how to talk about personal preferences.

OPTIONAL WARMER

Elicit the name of some famous artists and sculptors and some of their works. Write the suggestions on the board. Ss work in pairs. Ask: *What is your favourite work of art?* Ss discuss in pairs.

Reading

1 ▶ Ss look at the pictures and discuss the questions. Elicit their opinions on the pictures as works of art.

2a ▶ Scanning. Explain to Ss that they will read the text twice, the first time very quickly and the second time much more slowly. Direct them to the heading and tell them they have one minute to match the art described in the text to one of the pictures. Explain that they do not need to understand the text fully at this point. Stop the activity after one minute.

Answer: Picture D

b ▶ Ss read the text more slowly, focusing on the questions. Teach *main aim* (the main reason for or purpose of something). Ss read the text and answer the questions. Ss check answers in pairs, then as a whole class.

Answers: 1 It is difficult to understand 2 American 3 To see everyday things in a new way

c ▶ Ss look up words they don't understand in a dictionary and compare meanings with a partner. Focus on *abstract* painting (when the physical appearance of something is not clear), *wrap/wrapped* (cover up something). Review *wrapping paper* and *shark* (draw one) as Ss will need this vocabulary for the listening.

Listening

3a ▶ Ask Ss: *Do you buy postcards or posters of your favourite paintings? Why?* Play recording 9.5. Ss listen and match the artists to the postcards. The first one is done for them. Ss check answers in pairs, then as a whole class.

Answers: Christo D Damien Hirst A Antony Gormley B Kazimir Malevich E Claude Monet C

b ▶ Play the recording a second time. Ss listen and write the name of the speaker beside the art they like. They then match the types of art to the pictures. Ss check answers in pairs, then as a whole class.

Answers: 1 S, B 2 S, C 3 J, D 4 J, E

Grammar

4 ▶ Play recording 9.5 again. Ss listen and focus on how *prefer* is used, what it means and choose the correct statements to complete the Active grammar box. Ss check answers in pairs, then as a whole class.

Answers: 1 a and c 2 a to buying

▶ Write *I prefer buying postcards to posters* and *I prefer sculpture to paintings* on the board. Focus on the underlined words. Ss repeat the sentences from the recording. Direct Ss to the reference section on page 93.

5a ▶ Ss work in pairs. They take turns to ask each other about their preferences using the prompts. An example is given.

b ▶ Ss look at the tapescript on page 157 and complete the How to box. Ss check answers in pairs, than as a whole class.

Answers: like, more prefer

Person to person

6a ▶ Ss work in pairs. They discuss whether they agree with the speakers in the recording and which of the postcards they prefer themselves. Encourage them to use both *prefer ... to* and *like ... more than ...* in their answers.

b ▶ Ss talk to other Ss in the class asking them about their preferences based on the five questions.

Grammar

OPTIONAL LISTENING LEAD-IN

Elicit all the places of interest in London. (Buckingham Palace, Oxford St, Tate Gallery, Big Ben, etc.) Ss decide in pairs which place they would find most interesting/least interesting to visit in London.

7a ▶ Direct Ss to the three art galleries which Jenny and Serge might visit while they are in London. Play recording 9.6. Ss listen and tick the two places they plan to visit. Ss check answers in pairs, then as a whole class.

Answers: Tate Modern and the Hayward Gallery

b ▶ Play the recording again. Ss listen and complete the sentences in the Active grammar box. Ss compare answers in pairs, then by looking at the tapescript on page 157.

Answers: guidebook map lunch

▶ Ss focus on the three sentences in the tapescript. Ask: *Which of the three sentences are offers?* (I'll get the guidebook. and I'll look at the map.) *Which is a decision?* (We'll go this afternoon.) Ss complete the rule in their books. Ss check answers in pairs, then as a whole class.

Answer: at the time of

▶ Write *I + will + get* on the board. Explain that *get* is the infinitive form of the verb without *to*. Write *I'll get the guidebook* on the board. Underline the contraction. Explain this is *I will* but we always use the contractions in spoken English.

▶ Focus on the pronunciation of *I'll* and *We'll*. Explain to Ss that we don't use present tenses in this situation even though the offer and decision are made at the time of speaking. *I get the guidebook* and *I'm getting the guidebook* are both incorrect in this situation.

8 ▶ Ss look at the situations in the pictures. Elicit what the problem is in each picture. Ss practise making offers using words from the box.

> **Suggested Answers:** 1 I'll open the door for you.
> 2 I'll answer the phone for you/look after the baby for you. 3 I'll find your mother. 4 I'll phone an ambulance.

Pronunciation

9a ▶ Ss focus on the two questions from the recording in Ex. 7. Ss find the two questions in the tapescript on page 157, then turn back to page 91. Play recording 9.7. Ss listen and note whether the voice goes up or down at the end in each sentence. Ss check answers in pairs, then as a whole class.

> **Answer:** The voice goes up at the end in both questions.

b ▶ Ss look at the six sentences. Establish that some are questions and some are answers. Play recording 9.8. Ss listen and note whether the voice goes up or down at the end. Ss check answers in pairs, then as a whole class.

> **Answers:** The voice goes up in the questions (1, 3, 5, 6) and down in the answers (2, 4).

▶ Play the recording again and Ss repeat the sentences. Ask: *What kind of questions are these?* (Yes/No questions, not Question word questions.)

10a ▶ Ss make sentences using the prompts and practise saying them in pairs. The first two are done for them.

> **Answers:** 3 Is it cheap? 4 Is it new? 5 Does she smoke? 6 Do they work?

b ▶ Now Ss write the answers to the questions and practice them in pairs.

> **Answers:** 1 Yes, it is./No, it isn't. 2 Yes, he does./No, he doesn't. 3 Yes, it is./No, it isn't. 4 Yes, it is./No, it isn't. 5 Yes, she does./No, she doesn't. 6 Yes, they do./No, they don't.

Communication: An evening out

> **OPTIONAL WARMER**
>
> Write up a list of things to do in your free time. *Shopping/the cinema/a restaurant/the pub/a nightclub/the swimming pool/a sports event/a concert.* Ss categorise the activities into things you usually do during the day and things you usually do in the evening. Some things, e.g. the cinema, can be both. Ask Ss about their preferred times for these activities.

1a ▶ Ss make a list of things they usually do on Saturdays with a partner.

b ▶ Teach *very crowded* (a lot of people there). Play recording 9.9. Ss listen and tick the things the friends decide to do on Saturday. Ss check answers in pairs, then as a whole class.

> **Answers:** have lunch   go shopping

c ▶ Play the recording again. Ss listen and complete the How to box. Ss check answers in pairs, then as a whole class.

> **Answers:** don't, go   Let's   prefer   than   more   We'll

▶ Review the different ways of making suggestions and the appropriate responses. (E.g. *That sounds like fun* and *I prefer …* are both used in the tapescript.)

2a ▶ Ss focus on the list of activities. Ss match three of the activities to the pictures.

> **Answers:** 1 i   2 g   3 c

b ▶ Ss rank the list according to which activity they prefer.

c ▶ Ss compare lists in pairs and discuss their preferences.

3a ▶ Ss work in small groups of four or five. They organise an evening out together, which all members of the group will enjoy. They first agree on an activity and then choose a location in the area. Finally, they agree on a time and place to meet.

b ▶ Ss write a text message to a friend with information about the arrangement for tomorrow evening.

> **OPTIONAL EXTENSION**
>
> Ss work in pairs. They must work with a student from another group. Assign roles A and B. A calls B and makes a suggestion to join his/her group for the evening out tomorrow night. B explains he/she has already made an arrangement with another group of friends.

Review and practice

1 ▶

> Answers: 1 taller   2 more handsome   3 fitter
> 4 fatter   5 happier   6 darker   7 shorter

2 ▶

> Answers: 2 worse/worst   3 more beautiful/most
> beautiful   4 crazier/craziest   5 drier/driest
> 6 fitter/fittest   7 better/best   8 more informal/most
> informal   9 noisier/noisiest   10 more private/most
> private

3a ▶

> Answers: 2 a   3 e   4 g   5 b   6 c   7 h   8 d

b ▶

> Answers: Kilimanjaro is the highest mountain in
> Africa.   The Great Wall of China is the biggest structure
> in the world.   Edvard Grieg is the most famous
> Norwegian composer.   William Shakespeare is the
> most translated British writer.   The Louvre is the
> largest museum in the world.   Denmark's is the oldest
> national flag.   Psycho is the scariest film.

4 ▶

> Answers: 1 to watch   2 prefer reading books
> 3 to science fiction ones   4 prefer   5 to drive
> 6 to listening to CDs   7 prefers swimming

5 ▶

> Answers: 2 e   3 d   4 a   5 b   6 g   7 f

6 ▶

> Answers: 1 a play   2 a painting   3 classical
> music   4 an opera   5 a film   6 a novel
> 7 a sculpture   8 rock music

Notes for using the Common European Framework (CEF)

CEF References

9.1 Can do: make comparisons between things and people

CEF A2 descriptor: can use simple descriptive language to make brief statements about and compare objects and possessions (CEF page 59)

9.2 Can do: write a short film review

CEF A2 descriptor: can use the most frequently occurring connectors to link simple sentences in order to tell a story or describe something as a simple list of points (CEF page 125)

9.3 Can do: talk about personal preferences

CEF A2 descriptor: can produce brief everyday expressions in order to satisfy simple needs of a concrete type: personal details, daily routines, wants and needs, requests for information (CEF page 110)

CEF quick brief

One of the key ideas within the Common European Framework is that learning a language is a lifelong task; it requires 'lifelong learning' skills. Like all skills, we can improve how we learn and one of the teacher's responsibilities is to show Ss how to do this. The Lifelong learning boxes in Total English offer help in this task and showing Ss how to use their Portfolio is another way that teachers can help.

Portfolio task

Download the Total English Portfolio free from www.longman.com/totalenglish.

Objective: to introduce Ss to the Dossier section of their Portfolio.

This task can be done in Ss' own language.

▶ The Dossier section of the Portfolio allows Ss to record and store examples of good work in English to show other people. It can include anything from stories to recorded interviews to videos.

1 ▶ Explain the purpose of the Dossier section of the Portfolio to Ss.

2 ▶ Ask Ss to look back at their work over the last few months and choose one or two pieces of work which they feel proud of.

3 ▶ Ask Ss to compare the work in groups and explain why they feel proud.

4 ▶ Ask Ss to record details of the work relevant section of their Dossier and store the work separately in a Dossier folder. If necessary, learners might like to redo the work, correcting mistakes from the original version.

10 Journeys

Overview

Lead-in	**Vocabulary:** transport
10.1	**Grammar:** Present Perfect (*been* with *ever/never*): *I/you/we/they*
	Vocabulary: travel, holiday activities, sports
	Can do: talk about personal experiences
10.2	**Grammar:** Present Perfect with regular and irregular verbs (*he/she/it*)
	Vocabulary: holidays
	Can do: understand key points in a brochure; write a holiday postcard to a friend
10.3	**Grammar:** *-ing* form as a noun (subject only)
	Vocabulary: types of transport
	Can do: book a travel ticket
Com. Focus	Booking a hotel room
Reference	
Practice	

Summary

Lesson 1: In this lesson Ss read part of a TV guide. Ss then listen to an extract from one of the programmes where a family are interviewed before going on an adventure holiday to Australia.

Lesson 2: Ss read a brochure for Seagaia, a luxurious holiday resort in Japan. They then read a postcard which Lara has sent from Seagaia, describing what she has done on her holiday so far.

Lesson 3: Ss read about two commuters and their mode of transport going to and from work. They then listen to two other commuters describe their journey to and from work. Later in the lesson Ss listen to one of the commuters book a return ticket to New Zealand for his family.

Communication: Ss practise booking a room in a hotel and making complaints to the receptionist in the hotel.

Film bank: Commuting (6'00")
Six people talk about their commute to work.

Commuters from Tokyo to London explain what their commute to work is like, what they do while they are commuting and what they like/dislike about their journey.

Possible places to use this short film are:

▶ before lesson 3 to introduce the topic of journeys to work

▶ after lesson 3 to provide a model for Ss to talk about their own journeys to work

▶ at the end of the unit to round up the topic and language

For ways to use this short film in class, see Students' Book page 140 and Teacher's Book page 193.

Lead-in

OPTIONAL WARMER
Write *air travel/rail travel/road travel/sea travel* on the board. Elicit the different modes of transport associated with each. (E.g. car, bicycle, walking; train, underground, tram; airplane, helicopter; boat, ferry, etc.)

▶ Ss work in pairs. They tell their partner about (1) their journey to work and (2) journey to visit their parents/ grandparents. Write the following questions on the board to guide their discussion. *Which mode of transport do you take?, How long does it take?, How often do you take this journey?*

1 ▶ Ss look at the four pictures and then match the captions to the photos in pairs. Ss will focus on the vocabulary in Ex. 3a.

> **Answers:** 1 C 2 A 3 D 4 B

▶ Ask: *Which commuter has the most pleasant journey do you think?* Ss give their opinions.

2 ▶ Ss find the forms of transport in the photos. Ss check answers in pairs, then as a whole class.

> **Answers:** A: car, bus, motorbike B: underground train C: plane D: bicycle

3 ▶ Ss focus on vocabulary. They match the words 1–6 to their meanings a–f. Ss check answers in pairs, then as a whole class. The first one has been done for them.

> **Answers:** 2 f 3 e 4 c 5 a 6 d

▶ Say the words and Ss note the word stress in each word. Focus on the /ʌ/ sound in s<u>u</u>burbs and r<u>u</u>sh hour.

4 ▶ Ss look at the three headings in the table. They put the words in the box into the correct columns. Some words can go into more than one column.

> **Answer:** Air: airport, flight, journey, passenger, plane, ticket Rail: journey, passenger, platform, station, ticket, train Road: car, drive, garage, journey, park, passenger, traffic

---

EXTEND THE LEAD-IN
Ss work in groups of three or four. They choose four ways to improve the traffic situation in their local town/city or the city they are studying in. If traffic is not a problem Ss can focus on a city like Delhi or Tokyo. (E.g. more bus lanes, pay more to park in the city centre, etc.) Each group presents their 'solutions' to the rest of the class. Write all the solutions on the board and the class vote on what they consider to be the two most effective solutions. Don't worry about Ss making mistakes during this activity. Note down any obvious errors to deal with later.

10.1 Experiences

In this lesson Ss read part of a TV guide. Ss then listen to an extract from one of the programmes. This is an interview with the Garfield family who are about to go on an adventure holiday to Australia for the first time. Through this context Ss learn the Present Perfect (*been* with *ever/never*) and how to talk about personal experiences.

OPTIONAL WARMER

Ss work in pairs. They decide which is: (1) the most exciting sport, (2) the most disgusting food, (3) the most interesting country to visit and (4) the most beautiful place in the world.

Reading and listening

1a▶ Ss scan through the text to find words or phrases which describe the activities in the photos. Ss check answers in pairs, then as a whole class.

Answers: A bungee-jumping (Extreme Sports Challenge) B long-haul flight (The Holiday Show) C horse-riding (The Countryside Today) D hiking (the Countryside Today)

b▶ Elicit Ss' experiences of the four activities. Ensure Ss know what *a long-haul flight* means.

OPTIONAL EXTENSION

Write *negative results/experience of a lifetime/afraid of heights* on the board. Ss read the TV guide again and try to guess what these words mean in the text.

Answers: Negative results: bad consequences; experience of a lifetime: something good that will only happen once or twice in your life; afraid of heights: when you find it scary to be high up

▶ Elicit which of the three programmes Ss would like to watch.

2a▶ Play recording 10.1. Explain that it is part of one of the programmes. Ss listen and decide which one. Check answers in pairs, then as a whole class.

Answer: The Holiday Show

b▶ Ask: *What words describes how the family are feeling about the trip to Australia?* (Excited, nervous, etc.) *Why?* (It is new for them. It is the first time for them.) Ss read the sentence and answer the question.

Answer: Yes

▶ Explain that *I've never been ... before* means that this is his first time.

c▶ Ss look at the table. Establish that Moira and Derek are the parents and Todd and Alicia their children. Play the recording again. Ss listen and complete the table. Check answers in pairs, then as a whole class.

Answers: Moira and Derek: Visit Australia 1st, Horse riding 1st, Hiking 2nd, Bungee jumping 1st   Todd and Alicia: Long-haul flight 2nd, Visit Australia 1st, Horse riding 2nd, Hiking 2nd, Bungee jumping 1st

Grammar

3a▶ Ss focus on the four sentences from the recording. Ask: *Who said each sentence?* (a Derek; b the interviewer; c Derek; d. Todd). Ss look at the three questions about the sentences and answer them in pairs. Write the answers on the board during feedback and underline the Present Perfect in each one.

Answers: 1 d, two years ago   2 a, b, c   3 Present Perfect

b▶ Ss turn to the tapescript on page 158. Play the recording again. Ss read as they listen and then complete the Active grammar box. Ss check answers in pairs.

Answers: been   haven't been   've, been   you, been   haven't

▶ Ss choose the correct words to complete the rules. Ss check answers in pairs.

Answers: 1 any time up to now   2 past participle

▶ Focus on the first sentence *We've been to America.* Ask: *Did they go to America in the past?* (Yes). *In this sentence do we know <u>when</u> they went to America?* (No) *Can they go to America again?* (Yes). Explain that we use the Present Perfect to talk about actions that happened at some point in the past. We don't specify exactly when. *He has been to America <u>last year</u>* is incorrect in English because <u>last year</u> tells us exactly when he went to America.

▶ Stress that it doesn't matter how long ago the action happened (it is <u>not</u> necessarily the recent past), but there must be the possibility of doing it again.

The Past Participle (e.g. *been*) never changes. The auxiliary verb (*to have*) can be <u>have</u> (*I/We/you/They*) or <u>has</u> (*he/she/it*).

▶ Direct Ss to the reference section on page 103.

OPTIONAL EXTENSION

Write the following time expressions on the board *two years ago/in my life/when I was 16/ever/ yesterday/ before.* Ss work in pairs and categorise the expressions into (1) ones we use with the Past Simple and (2) ones we use with the Present Perfect. Ask: *Why?*

Answers: (1) Past Simple: two years ago, when I was 16, yesterday; (2) Present Perfect: in my life, ever, before. The time expressions in (1) tell us <u>an exact time</u> in the past. The time expressions in (2) do not specify a time in the past but encompass <u>all past time up to now</u>.

4a ▶ Ss complete the questions and answers using the Present Perfect. Ss check answers in pairs, then as a whole class.

> **Answers:**   1 ever, have   2 Has, hasn't   3 been, went

b ▶ Ss find and correct the mistakes with a partner. An example is given. Check answers.

> **Answers:**   1 I have never been bungee jumping.
> 2 They have never been to Scotland.   3 Have you ever been to a classical concert?   4 Have you ever been on an adventure holiday?

Pronunciation

5a ▶ Write *India* and *Greece* on the board. Say the words and write the phonetic symbol /ɪ/ under *India* and the symbol /iː/ under *Greece*. Say the two sounds. Ss look at the two sentences. Play recording 10.2. Ss listen and identify the sound of the underlined words. Ss check answers in pairs, then as a whole class.

> **Answer:**   /ɪ/

b ▶ Ss look at the four sentences. First they predict where the four /ɪ/ sounds will be in each sentence with a partner. Play recording 10.3. Ss listen and identify the four /ɪ/ sounds in each sentence. Check in pairs, then as a whole class.

> **Answers:**   1 Have you been to the cinema in Italy?
> 2 I've never been on a ship with him.   3 Has she ever been to dinner in Finland?   4 We've never been to Paris in spring.

6 ▶ Ss look at the pictures in Ex. 1 again and write sentences using *ever*. Then they take turns to practise asking and answering the questions with a partner. Monitor closely, correcting any errors you hear.

> **Answers:**   Have you ever been on a long-haul flight?
> Have you ever been horse-riding?   Have you ever been bungee jumping?   Have you ever been hiking?

Speaking

7 ▶ Divide the class into As, Bs and Cs. As look at page 128, Bs look at page 130 and Cs look at page 97. Each group has a different list of activities. Give Ss time to check the meaning of the activities on their list with other members of their group.

▶ When they are ready, Ss mingle asking the other Ss if they have ever been to the places on their list. If the answer is *No*, they move on to the next student but if the answer is *Yes*, they must ask a follow-on question *Did you like it?* Stop the activity when each student has spoken to about five other Ss in the class.

10.2 Holiday heaven

In this lesson Ss read a brochure for Seagaia, a luxurious holiday resort in Japan. They then read a postcard which Lara has sent from Seagaia, describing what she has done on her holiday so far. Through this context Ss learn the Present Perfect with regular and irregular verbs and how to write a holiday postcard to a friend.

> **OPTIONAL WARMER**
> Ss work in pairs. They tell each other about (1) the best holiday and (2) the worst holiday they have ever been on. Write *where/when/who with/why good/bad* on the board to guide the discussion.

Vocabulary

1a ▶ Ss look at the pictures of different types of holidays. Ss match the words in the box to the pictures. The first one has been done for them. Ss check answers in pairs, then as a whole class.

> **Answers:**   B winter sports   C activity
> D sightseeing   E water sports   F cultural

b ▶ Ss discuss their experiences of the different types of holidays in pairs. Elicit the most popular type of holiday.

Reading

2a ▶ Ss focus on the pictures of the Seagaia resort in Japan. This resort is in Miyazaki, south west of Tokyo. Teach *resort* (a village or small town which caters for people on holiday), *dome* (draw a dome shape) and *roof* (draw a roof on a house). Ss then read the text to find out what people can do at the Seagaia resort. Ask Ss not to use dictionaries for this as they will focus on vocabulary from the text in the next exercise. Explain that they do not need to understand everything in the text to answer the questions.

> **Answers:**   sunbathe, swim, play golf, surf, sail, play tennis, go horse-riding, visit the zoo, theme park and gardens

b ▶ Ss look at the words 1–5 and find them in the text. They try to guess what the words mean. Then Ss match the words to the definitions. The first one has been done for them. Ss check answers in pairs, then as a whole class.

> **Answers:**   2 b   3 a   4 e   5 c

▶ Focus on the pronunciation of these words, especially on the word stress of the longer words *luxurious*, *exclusive* and *artificial*.

3a ▶ Ss read the text again and write questions to match the answers given. The first one has been done for them. Ss check answers in pairs, then as a whole class.

> **Answers:**   2 Where is Seagaia?   3 What is the Ocean Dome?   4 Where can you stay in Seagaia?   5 What can you visit?

b ▶ Ss give their opinions about having a holiday in Seagaia and explain why they would/would not like to go there on holiday.

OPTIONAL EXTENSION

Teach *brochure* (an advertisement for a holiday, similar to the text). Ask: *Does a brochure say anything bad about a place?* (No) *Why not?* (Because they want to sell the holiday.) Divide the class into teams. Each team thinks of a positive adjective to describe a resort in a holiday brochure. (E.g. beautiful, clean, luxurious, etc.). Each team calls out an adjective in turn, until one team cannot think of another adjective and drops out of the game. The winning team is the one which can think of the most adjectives to describe a resort. Write up the adjectives as the Ss call them out. These can be used later in Ex. 9b.

Grammar

4a ▶ Ss look at the postcard and answer the questions. Check answers in pairs, then as a whole class.

> **Answers:** from Lara   at Seagaia

b ▶ Ss focus on the two underlined verb forms in the postcard. Ask: *What tense is this?* (Present Perfect) *Which verb is regular?* (we've arrived, -ed ending) *Which is irregular?* (has been, no -ed ending) Direct Ss to the table. Ss read the postcard again and underline all the Present Perfect verbs. They decide whether the verbs are regular or irregular and add them to the table. Ss check answers in pairs, then as a whole class.

> **Answers:** Regular verb: have arrived, haven't played, she's visited   Irregular verb: has been, I've spent, I've seen, has had, she's taken

5 ▶ Ss choose the correct phrases to complete the Active grammar box. Ss check answers in pairs, then as a whole class.

> **Answers:** 1 she is still on holiday   2 have, has   3 Regular

▶ The Present Perfect is used in these examples to talk about a holiday that is still continuing. When the holiday is over and Lara is at home again, the Past Simple is used to describe her experiences on this holiday.

▶ Most verbs are regular but many commonly used verbs (*eat, sleep, drink,* etc.) are irregular. Some irregular Past Participles (e.g. *bought, slept*) are the same as the past simple but others (e.g. *drunk, seen*) are different. Direct Ss to the reference section on page 103.

6 ▶ Ss write the correct form of the verbs in brackets to complete the text. The first one has been done for them. Ss check answers in pairs, then as a whole class.

> **Answers:** 1 have been   2 haven't spent   3 've played   4 've also spent   5 has visited   6 has seen   7 hasn't taken

Lifelong learning

7 ▶ Encourage Ss to note down Past Simple and Past Participle forms of verbs as they learn them. A good idea is to keep a similar table to the one in the Lifelong learning box in their vocabulary journal. Dictionaries give Past Simple and Past Participle forms and grammar books usually have lists of irregular verbs. Ss make a table like the example and add the irregular Past Participles from Ex. 4b and the ones in the box to it.

> **Answers:** see–seen   have–had   take–taken   buy–bought   eat–eaten   get–got   write–written

---

OPTIONAL EXTENSION

Ss stand up to form a circle. Call out the base form of verbs, both regular and irregular, to Ss in turn. The student immediately responds with the Past Participle form of the verb (e.g. T: *make* St: *made*). This should be done in a quick and snappy way. When a student doesn't know the Past Participle form, he or she sits down and the next student answers. The last student left standing is the Past Participle Champion!

Pronunciation

8a ▶ Write *ship* and *sheep* on the board. Say the two words and ask Ss *Which sound is longer?* (the /iː/ in sheep). Write the short /ɪ/ sound under ship and the long /iː/ sound under sheep and explain that /ː/ tells us that the sound is a long sound.

▶ Ss focus on the table. Play recording 10.4. Ss listen and repeat the words.

b ▶ Ss look at the six pairs of words. They decide which word has a long vowel sound and which a short vowel sound. Play recording 10.5. Ss listen and circle the word they hear from each pair. Ss check answers in pairs, then as a whole class.

> **Answers:** 1 have   2 fit   3 short   4 park   5 bald   6 sleep

Speaking and writing

9 ▶ Ss work in pairs. They imagine they are on a weekend break. Note: It is Sunday so the weekend is not over yet. Ss decide on the details of the weekend by answering the four questions. They note down their answers.

10a ▶ Elicit which tense Lara used in the postcard to describe what she has done (Present Perfect). Ss look at the paragraph headings in question 2 and match them to paragraphs in Lara's postcard. Ss check answers in pairs, then as a whole class.

> **Answers:** describes the writer's activities 2   describes her family's activities 3   gives a reason for ending the postcard 4   describes the hotel 1

b ▶ Ss write a postcard based on the notes they made for the weekend away in Ex. 9. They use a similar paragraph structure to Lara's postcard. Remind Ss that it is Sunday so the weekend is not over yet.

10.3 Cycle city

In this lesson Ss read about two commuters and their mode of transport going to and from work. They then listen to two other commuters describe their journey to and from work. Later in the lesson Ss listen to one of the commuters book a return ticket to New Zealand for his family. Through this context Ss learn the -ing form as noun (subject only) and how to book a travel ticket.

> **OPTIONAL WARMER**
>
> Write *public transport* on the board. Elicit different types of public transport – bus, taxi, tram, etc. Ask Ss: *Do most people use public transport in your country? Why/Why not?* Ss work in pairs and list three reasons why people choose to use public transport and three reasons why they don't. (E.g. Public transport is cheaper; It is better for the environment; It can be very slow, etc.)

Reading and listening

1 ▶ Ss focus on photo A and discuss the questions.

2a ▶ Scanning. Explain to Ss that they will read the text twice, the first time very quickly and the second time much more slowly. Direct them to the heading and tell them they have one minute to match the text to two of the photos as quickly as possible. Explain that they do not need to understand the text fully at this point. Stop the activity after one minute and Ss call out the answers.

> **Answers:** B (underground in São Paulo) and D (cycling in Amsterdam)

b ▶ Ss read the texts more slowly, this time focusing on the table. Teach *convenient* (easy to use or do) and *flat* (no hills or mountains). Ss read through the text and complete the first half of the table. Ss check answers in pairs.

3 ▶ Teach *Miami* (the pronunciation of this American city might be difficult for Ss) and *rollerblading* (special shoes with wheels) Play recording 10.6. Ss listen and complete the second half of the table. Ss check answers in pairs. Draw the table on the board, elicit and write in the answers to Exs. 2b and 3.

> **Answers:** Fatima: B São Paulo underground/metro convenient crowded. Jan: D Amsterdam cycling very cheap horrible when it rains. Julia: E Miami quick, costs nothing, healthy, enjoyable dangerous on busy roads, tiring. Billy: C London bus easier than the car, not expensive sometimes slow, waiting for the bus is boring

Person to person

4 ▶ In pairs Ss discuss the questions about the four modes of transport. Ss decide which one they consider the best way of commuting to work.

> **OPTIONAL EXTENSION**
>
> Ss imagine that the government is trying to encourage people not to take their cars to work because of the traffic problems. They have decided to encourage people to use the bus and metro or to cycle and rollerblade to work instead. Ss work in small groups of three or four. They think of different ways to encourage commuters to use these methods of getting to work. Ss think of ways of making the four modes of transport safer, more comfortable, etc. Encourage Ss to be imaginative in their ideas. Don't worry about Ss making mistakes during this activity.

Grammar

5 ▶ Elicit the four forms of transport and write them on the board in a vertical line. *The bus/The metro/ Rollerblading/Cycling*. Ask: *What kind of words are these, nouns, verbs, adjectives?* (nouns) Use the four words as subject nouns in sentences based on their opinions in Ex. 4. E.g.

The bus is the cheapest way to get to work.
The metro is the most comfortable way to get to work.
Rollerblading is the most enjoyable way to get to work.
Cycling is the quickest way to get to work.

▶ Ss look at the examples in the Active grammar box. They then find and underline two examples in the text. Ss choose the correct word to complete the sentences.

> **Answers:** is Parking

We can use the -ing form of the verb as a noun when it is the subject of a sentence. We don't use the articles (*a/an* or *the*) with this type of noun. *The cycling is the quickest way to get to work* is incorrect in English.

The -ing form as a noun is uncountable and takes a singular verb after it. (*Cycling are dangerous* is incorrect in English.) When pronouncing these nouns, the -ing is always unstressed.

▶ Direct Ss to the reference section on page 103.

6 ▶ Ss use the prompts to make sentences with the -ing form as the subject of the sentences. An example is done for them. Ss check answers in pairs, then as a whole class.

> **Answers:** 1 Eating vegetables is good for your health. 2 Cycling is popular in Amsterdam. 3 Waiting for a bus is boring. 4 Living in a big city is exciting. 5 Taking taxis is expensive.

Listening

> **OPTIONAL LISTENING LEAD-IN**
>
> Teach *economy class* (cheapest seats) and *business class* (more expensive seats) on an airplane. Ask: *Which way do you travel?* Ss work in pairs. They use comparative adjectives to compare the two types of airline ticket. Write *food/service/seats/entertainment/ legroom* on the board to prompt points of comparison.

7a ▶ Ss look at the questions. Play recording 10.7. Ss listen and answer the questions. Ss check answers in pairs, then as a whole class.

> **Answers:** 1 New Zealand 2 Friday the fifth of next month 3 Air New Zealand is six thousand NZ dollars (about 2000 pounds) or Qantas is 2,300 pounds

b ▶ Ss look at the vocabulary from the listening text and match the words to their meanings. The first one has been done for them. Check answers as a whole class.

> **Answers:** 2 f 3 a 4 g 5 b 6 d 7 e

▶ Ask Ss to identify the word stress in each word/phrase. Note: The stress falls on the second syllable in both dir<u>ect</u> and re<u>turn</u>. Desti<u>na</u>tion and e<u>co</u>nomy are both four syllable words but the word stress is different in each.

c ▶ Teach to book. (to ask someone to keep something for you, e.g. a table in a restaurant, tickets to the theatre.) Ss read the tapescript on page 158. Play the recording as they read. Ss read and complete the How to box. Ss check answers in pairs, then as a whole class.

> **Answers:** tickets go want time direct much four

▶ Ss practise saying the sentences.

▶ Review the use of would in I'd like to go/I'd like four tickets. I <u>like</u> four tickets is incorrect in this context.

8 ▶ Ss work in pairs. They complete the dialogue by using the vocabulary from Exs. 7b and 7c. Check answers as a whole class.

> **Answers:** 1 tickets 2 like 3 return 4 class 5 How 6 direct

▶ Ss practise the dialogue in pairs.

9 ▶ Ss conduct the roleplay in pairs. Student A works in a travel agency and student B is a customer. Student A looks at the information on page 128 and student B looks at the information on page 101. Give Ss time to read the information and find out what they have to do.

▶ Ss work in pairs. Student B finds out about the different flight options from Student A and decides which airline to fly with. In feedback, establish which was the most popular airline and why.

> **OPTIONAL EXTENSION**
>
> Ask Ss to use the Internet to find the cheapest fare from Dublin to London return next weekend. You want to fly to London on Friday afternoon (after 1 p.m.) and return to Dublin on Sunday evening (before 10 p.m.). www.ryanair.com and www.airlingus.com are two websites to check out.

Communication: Booking a hotel room

> **OPTIONAL WARMER**
>
> Elicit the different types of accommodation where people stay on holiday. Write Ss' suggestions on the board. Teach any new vocabulary as it arises. Ss discuss their preferences in pairs.

1 ▶ Ss identify the type of accommodation in the photo (hotel). Ask: *What part of the hotel is this?* (the reception desk) Ss discuss the best hotel they have ever stayed in.

2 ▶ Ss look at the six questions and scan the information board to find the answers. Ss check answers in pairs, then as a whole class.

> **Answers:** 1 85 euros/120 euros 2 Double room 3 No 4 No, the beauty salon doesn't open until 10 a.m. and breakfast finishes at 10 a.m. 5 free to guests 6 at reception

3a ▶ Explain to Ss that they are going to listen to someone book a room in Hotel Europa. Play recording 10.8. Ss listen and answer the questions. Check answers.

> **Answers:** a twin room with bathroom; for the 15th and 16th of May they want to book a beauty treatment in advance

b ▶ Ss read the tapescript on page 158. Play the recording again as they read. Ss complete the How to box. Ss check answers in pairs, then as a whole class.

> **Answers:** book a room, please twin room a private bathroom much is that

4 ▶ Ss work in A/B pairs. As close their books. Bs look at the information board for Hotel Europa. Ss practise booking hotel rooms. Ss swap roles when they have finished.

5a ▶ Teach *We can fit you in* (book a time for you) and *sort out* the problem. Play recording 10.9. Ss listen and identify the three complaints and what happened in each case. Ss check answers.

> **Answers:** 1 a twin room but got a double room; the receptionist changed the room. 2 tea with breakfast but got coffee; the receptionist called the kitchen to get tea. 3 golf in the morning but the golf club say there isn't a booking for him; the receptionist called the golf club to sort it out

Ss conduct the roleplays in A/B pairs. A is the guest and B is the receptionist in the hotel. A's rolecard is on page 102 and B's rolecard is on page 128. Give Ss time to read the information on their card before they start. Student A makes a complaint and student B tries to sort it out for him/her.

▶ In feedback ask what the various solutions to the problems were and if the guests are happy now.

Review and practice

1 ▶

> **Answers:** 1 I've never been on a long-haul flight.
> 2 Have you ever been on an adventure holiday?
> 3 We've been to New York and Boston. 4 She's been horse-riding in Scotland.

2 ▶

> **Answers:** 1 ✗ spent 2 ✓ 3 ✗ taken 4 ✗ played
> 5 ✓ 6 ✗ written

3 ▶

> **Answers:** 1 Lorena's had 2 I've been swimming
> 3 We've taken 4 Lorena's bought 5 I've played golf
> 6 We've gone

4 ▶

> **Answers:** Liz: We went last winter; Sue: I've never been to Switzerland; Liz: we went; Sue: Have you ever been

5 ▶

> **Answers:** 1 Paying 2 Swimming 3 Going
> 4 Driving 5 Taking 6 Commuting

6 ▶

> **Answers:** 1 direct 2 return 3 class 4 platform
> 5 garage 6 passengers

7 ▶

> **Answers:** 1 water sports 2 beach 3 cultural
> 4 winter sports 5 activity

Notes for using the Common European Framework (CEF)

CEF References

10.1 Can do: talk about personal experiences

CEF A2 descriptor: can describe plans and arrangements, habits and routines, past activities and personal experiences (CEF page 59)

10.2 Can do: understand key points in a brochure; write a holiday postcard to a friend

CEF A1 descriptor: can understand short, simple messages on postcards (CEF page 69)

10.3 Can do: book a travel ticket

CEF A2 descriptor: can interact with reasonable ease in structured situations and short conversations, provided the other person helps if necessary (CEF page 74)

CEF quick brief

The Common European Framework suggests that learners need more than language knowledge to communicate successfully in a language. They also need 'communicative competences' which empower the learner to actually use their knowledge. The How to boxes in Total English are designed to develop communicative competences.

Portfolio task

Download the Total English Portfolio free from www.longman.com/totalenglish.

Objective: to reinforce student autonomy in updating the Portfolio.

This task can be done in Ss' L1.

1 ▶ For homework, ask Ss to update the Passport section of their Portfolio. They might like to reassess their abilities in the different skills areas or add to their list of language learning and intercultural experiences.

2 ▶ Ask Ss to bring their Passport sections in and show them to other Ss.

11 Learning

Overview

Lead-in	**Vocabulary:** education
11.1	**Grammar:** *can/can't, have to/don't have to*
	Vocabulary: road rules and signs; traffic offences and penalties
	Can do: understand signs and rules
11.2	**Grammar:** revision of *wh-* questions
	Vocabulary: types of school, education
	Can do: understand and produce a simple explanation
11.3	**Grammar:** Present Continuous for future
	Vocabulary: education
	Can do: talk about future arrangements
Com. Focus	Arrangements and appointments
Reference	
Practice	

Summary

Lesson 1: Ss read about driving in the USA and what happens to people who break the rules of the road. They listen to a tourist information phone line about driving in Britain and also listen to Steve describing other rules in the USA.

Lesson 2: Ss read about the educational system in Japan and listen to a teacher describe her education in New Zealand.

Lesson 3: Ss read an email from Joanna where she writes about her plans to start an Open University degree programme the following month. Ss read four adverts for different courses and listen to representatives from the different organisations describe the courses on offer.

Communication: Ss compare diaries to find a suitable time to meet.

Film bank: Rock climbing (3'50")
A short film about learning to rock climb.

This short film follows two novice climbers on a weekend rock climbing course in Wales. We see them learning to climb on an indoor wall and then watch them make their first climb on a real rock face.

Possible places to use this short film are:

▶ before the Unit Opener to introduce the topic of learning

▶ after lesson 1 to extend the topic of learning physical activities

▶ at the end of the unit to round up the topic and language

For ways to use this short film in class, see Students' Book page 141 and Teacher's Book page 194.

Lead-in

OPTIONAL WARMER

Elicit examples of different types of night class or after-school class people do, E.g. ballet, learn the piano, yoga, etc. Write all the suggestions on the board. Ss divide the classes into (1) really interesting, enjoyable classes (2) uninteresting, boring classes and (3) the other classes. Ss compare lists with a partner and explain the reasons for their choice.

1 ▶ Ss identify the four adult learning situations. They discuss with a partner which courses they have done.

> **Answers:** A Keep fit   B learning English   C learning to drive   D learning to play the guitar

2a ▶ Ss look at the six rules and match them to the learning situation in the photos. Ss check answers in pairs, then as a whole class.

> **Answers:**   1 C   2 B   3 A   4 C   5 D   6 B

b ▶ Ss think about their schooldays. Elicit the types of rules which existed in the schools the Ss went to. (E.g. no smoking; no running in corridors; no eating in class, etc.)

▶ Teach *to obey the rules* (do what you are told) and *punishment* (stay late after school, etc.). Ss work in pairs and discuss whether they usually obeyed the rules at school and what the punishment for breaking the rules was. In feedback, elicit some of the types of punishment. Ask: *What was the worst punishment in school?*

3a ▶ Ss look at the words in the box and categorise them into (1) school subjects and (2) educational institutions. Ss can use their dictionaries for this activity. Ss compare answers in pairs. Do not give feedback yet.

> **Answers:**   School subjects: Biology, Chemistry, Geography, History, Languages, Mathematics, Physics, Science   Educational institutions: college, kindergarten, polytechnic, primary school, secondary school, university

b ▶ Play recording 11.1. Ss check their answers.

▶ Ss look at the vocabulary items again. In pairs they decide how many syllables each word has. Play the recording again. Ss listen to check the number of syllables.

> **Answers:**   (5 syllables) uni<u>ver</u>sity   (4 syllables) bi<u>ol</u>ogy, kinder<u>gar</u>ten, poly<u>tech</u>nic, <u>pri</u>mary school, <u>sec</u>ondary school mathe<u>ma</u>tics   (3 syllables) <u>chem</u>istry, ge<u>og</u>raphy, <u>lan</u>guages,   (2 syllables) <u>his</u>tory, <u>sci</u>ence, <u>coll</u>ege

c ▶ Ss add other school subjects to the list (e.g. art, music, physical education, etc.).

11.1 Rules of the road

In this lesson Ss read about driving in the USA and what happens to people who break the rules of the road. They listen to a tourist information phone line about driving in Britain and also listen to Steve describing other rules in the USA. Through this context, Ss learn *can/can't* and *have to/don't have to* and how to understand signs and rules.

OPTIONAL WARMER

Write the following on the board. *Speeding/Parking on double yellow lines/Drunk Driving/Driving without documents/Careless driving/Talking on the mobile phone while driving.* Ss work in groups of three or four. They look at the list of driving related offences and rank them 1–6 in order of seriousness.

Reading

1 ▶ Direct Ss to the three questions. Teach *speed limit*, *fine* (pay money) and *points on their licence* (a system where drivers get points on their licence when they are caught breaking the rules of the road. After a certain number of points they lose their licence.). Elicit Ss' answers as a whole class.

2a ▶ Scanning. Explain to Ss that they will read the text twice, the first time very quickly and the second time much more slowly. Direct Ss to the question and tell them they have one minute to find which country the text is about. Explain that they do not need to understand the text fully at this point. Stop the activity after a minute. Ss call out the answer.

> **Answer:** the USA

b ▶ Ss read the text more slowly and decide whether the four statements are True or False. Teach *offenders* (people who break the rules). Check answers.

> **Answers:** 1 T   2 F   3 T   4 F

c ▶ Ss discuss the two questions as a whole class.

Grammar

OPTIONAL GRAMMAR LEAD-IN

Focus on statement 2 in Ex. 2b. Offenders <u>have to do</u> a course at Traffic School. This is false. Ss find the true sentence in the text: They <u>can do</u> a course at Traffic School or they <u>can get</u> points on their licence. Write *They <u>have to do</u> a course.* and *They <u>can do</u> a course.* on the board. Ask: *What is the difference between these two sentences?* (*have to* means there is obligation, they must do it; *can* means it is possible to do it if they want, but it is also possible not to do it.).

3a ▶ Ss look at the pictures. Elicit where each picture is. (E.g. A on a train; B at an airport; C in a restaurant or shop; D, E, F – on a road.) Ss match the six sentences to the pictures. Check answers in pairs, then as a whole class.

> **Answers:** 1 C   2 E   3 A   4 F   5 D   6 B

b ▶ Ss work in pairs. They match the verbs to the meanings. The first one has been done for them.

> **Answers:** 2 b   3 a   4 c

4 ▶ Ss look at the road signs. Teach *overtake* (to pass another car in front of you). Ss write the rules using *can/can't* and *have to/don't have to* using the words and phrases in the box to help them. The first two have been done for them. Ss check answers in pairs, then as a whole class.

> **Answers:** 3 You can't go faster than 120 km per hour
> 4 You can't overtake   5 You must give way to traffic
> 6 You can park here   7 You have to turn left
> 8 You can get petrol here   9 You can't enter here   10 You can go

▶ Explain that *can/can't* and *have to/don't have to* are often used to describe rules and when something is allowed. We use *have to* when there is an obligation and *don't have to* when there is no obligation to do something. We use *can* to say that something is allowed and *can't* when it is not allowed. Note: Focus on the difference in meaning between *can't* and *don't have to*.

▶ Teach the form of *have to*: *I/You/We/They* <u>have</u> *to* but *He/she/it* <u>has</u> *to* do something. The auxiliary *do/does* is used to make negative and question forms. Direct Ss to the reference section on page 113.

5a ▶ Tell Ss they are going to listen to a computer operated information line. Ss look at the list of options. Play recording 11.2. Ss listen and identify which information is not mentioned. Check answers in pairs, then as a whole class.

> **Answers:** Flights and museums are not mentioned.

b ▶ Ss look at the information box on driving in Britain. Teach *documents* (ID card, driving licence, etc.) and a *valid* licence (up to date). Play the recording again. Ss listen and complete the information box. Ss check answers in pairs, then as a whole class.

> **Answers:** have to   have to   have to   have to
> don't have to   can't

6 ▶ Ss write four sentences about Sami using *can/can't* and *have to/don't have to*.

> **Possible Answers:** 2 He doesn't have to get a British driving licence.   3 He can drive in Britain without a British licence.   4 He can't turn right at red lights.

OPTIONAL EXTENSION

Write *mobile phones/eating/arriving late/drinks/speak English/leave early/exams* on the board. Ss work in pairs and take turns to describe the 'rules' in their English class. Monitor closely, correcting any errors you hear.

Person to person

7 ▶ Ss work in pairs. They discuss the rules and regulations in their country in relation to the headings given. (E.g. How old do you have to be to get a passport? Do you need a credit card to rent a car? etc.)

Pronunciation

8a ▶ Ss read the sentence. *Have* is underlined twice. Play recording 11.3. Ss listen and decide if the pronunciation of *have* changes.

> **Answer:** No. The ending of have is different in each case: /f/ and /v/.

b ▶ Ss look at the pairs of words. Write the phonetic symbols /f/ and /v/ on the board. Play recording 11.4. Ss listen and identify which sound they hear. Ss check answers in pairs, then as a whole class.

> **Answers:** 1 b 2 a 3 a 4 a

c ▶ Ss listen to the sentences in recording 11.5 and practise saying them to each other in pairs.

Speaking

9a ▶ Teach *military service* (a compulsory year in the army). Play recording 11.6. Ss listen and note down what Steve says about the six topics. Ss then write sentences about the USA using *have to/don't have to* and *can/can't*. The first one has been done for them. Ss check answers in pairs, then as a whole class.

> **Answers:** 1 Americans don't have to have identity cards 2 You can drive at 16 3 You can buy a gun at 21 4 You have to be 21 to go into a bar or nightclub 5 You can't smoke in offices, shops or restaurants 6 You have to pay to see a doctor or go to a hospital

b ▶ Ss work in small groups. They discuss the rules in the USA and compare them to rules in their country.

> **OPTIONAL EXTENSION**
>
> Ss write up an information leaflet for tourists similar to the one in Ex. 5b about their country. They can use the headings in Ex. 9a.

11.2 School systems

In this lesson Ss find out about the different types of schools in the UK and read about the educational system in Japan. They listen to a teacher describe her education in New Zealand. Through this context Ss review *wh-* questions and learn how to understand and produce a simple explanation.

> **OPTIONAL WARMER**
>
> Ss work in pairs. They ask each other *Did you like school? Why/Why not?* (I didn't like school. The day was very long and we had to wear a really ugly uniform, etc.)

Reading and vocabulary

1a ▶ Ss look at the photos of various learning situations. Direct Ss to the questions. Elicit answers as a whole class.

> **Answers:** A: around 15/16, secondary school pupils B: around 8/9, primary school children C: around 3/4, pre-school children D: 20/21, higher education students

b ▶ Ss complete the Education column in the table. Ss check answers in pairs, then as a whole class.

> **Answers:** primary secondary university

2a ▶ Scanning. Explain to Ss that before they read the text properly they will read it very quickly to find the answers to the three questions. Teach *compulsory/optional* (you have to do it/you don't have to do it). Tell Ss they have two minutes to find the three pieces of information as quickly as possible. Explain they do not need to understand the text fully at this point. They should ignore the gaps at this stage. Stop the activity after two minutes. Ss call out the answers.

> **Answers:** 1 9 years 2 high school 3 90%

b ▶ Ss read the text more slowly, this time focusing on the gaps in the text. Ss use the red words in the box to complete the text. They can use their dictionaries for this exercise. The first one has been done for them. Ss check answers in pairs, then as a whole class.

> **Answers:** 1 private 2 academic 3 subjects 4 optional 5 specialised

c ▶ Ss read the text again to complete the information for Japan in the table. Ss check answers in pairs, then as a whole class.

> **Answers:** 3–6: kindergarten 6–12: elementary school 12–18: high school 18+: college/university

Listening

OPTIONAL LISTENING LEAD-IN

Ss work in small groups. They discuss what they consider to be the five most important qualities of (1) a good teacher and (2) a good student. Encourage Ss to use *have to/don't have to* which they learnt in the previous lesson. (E.g. I think a good teacher has to be patient. He/she doesn't have to be young, etc.)

3a ▶ Tell the Ss they are going to listen to a teacher talk about her education. Play recording 11.7. Ss listen and find out where the speaker is from and the type of school she teaches in. Ss check answers in pairs, then as a whole class.

Answers: She is from New Zealand and teaches in a primary school.

b ▶ Ss look at the questions. Play the recording again. Ss listen and find the answers. Ss check answers in pairs, then as a whole class.

Answers: 1 12 years 2 She wanted to be a teacher, three years 3 between 2,000 and 20,000 dollars

c ▶ Ss work in pairs. They use the blue words in the box to complete the information for New Zealand in the table. If necessary, play the recording again.

Answers: 4–5: kindergarten 5–10: primary school 10–12: intermediate school 12–16 or 18: secondary school 18+: university, polytechnic, college of education

OPTIONAL EXTENSION

Ss work in pairs. Student A writes two questions about the Japanese educational system and Student B writes two questions about the New Zealand educational system. (Student B can look at the tapescript on page 159) Ss close their books and ask each other the questions.

Grammar

4a ▶ Elicit one or two *wh-* questions from the previous exercise. Write the question words which Ss used on the board. Elicit the other question words Ss know and write them on the board. Ss look at the eight question words and match them to the correct sentence ending. Ss check answers in pairs, then as a whole class.

Answers: 1 e 2 h 3 d 4 a 5 g 6 c 7 b 8 f

▶ Direct Ss to the reference section on page 113.

OPTIONAL VARIATION

Write short answers (not full sentences) to the questions in Ex. 4a on the board. These should be in a jumbled order. Ss match the answers to the questions in pairs. (E.g. between 2,000 and 20,000 dollars; a college of education; mathematics and geography; at 6; etc.)

b ▶ Elicit the question words which are not in the list in Ex. 4a (why, who, whose). In pairs, Ss match the words and phrases in the box to the appropriate question word. The first one has been done for them. Check answers in pairs, then as a whole class.

Answers: How long – periods of time Where – places What – things and ideas When – times How many – numbers or quantity Which – a choice between two (or more) things Whose – possession Why – reason How much – prices or cost Who – people

▶ Review the pronunciation of question words, especially the initial /h/ and /w/ sounds (see Lesson 7.3).

Pronunciation

5a ▶ Direct Ss to the four questions. Play recording 11.8. Ss listen and decide whether the voice goes up or down at the end. Ss check answers in pairs, then as a whole class.

Answer: down

b ▶ Ss look at the questions in Ex. 5a again. Play recording 11.9. Ss listen and repeat the questions. Remind them of the different intonation of *Yes/No* questions. (See Lesson 9.3.)

Speaking

6 ▶ Ss prepare ten questions to ask other students about their education. (E.g. When did you start school? Where did you go to secondary school? etc.) Ss work in small groups. They use their questions to discuss their educational backgrounds.

Writing

7a ▶ Ss focus on the table again. In pairs they complete the information for their country.

b ▶ Ss make further notes about the educational system in their country using the prompts provided.

c ▶ Ss use the completed table and their notes to write a short article describing the educational system in their country for an international students' magazine.

OPTIONAL EXTENSION

Ss work in pairs. They compare a modern education system with that of their grandparents' time. Ask: *What were the main differences between then and now?* Write *subjects/pay for school/length of courses/compulsory/discipline/age* on the board to guide their discussion.

11.3 Lifelong learning

Lifelong learning and adult education have become increasingly popular phenomena in recent years. Many people return to learning later in life for various reasons and most colleges and universities have become much more flexible and accessible in their approach. Many universities have followed the Open University's lead and now offer distance learning courses where students can study from home.

OPTIONAL WARMER

Explain *distance learning* (you don't attend college but do all the work at home and contact lecturers and other students by email or phone). Ss work in pairs. They list three reasons why people choose to study this way. (E.g. can't give up job; live far away from the university, etc.) Elicit reasons in feedback and write them on the board.

Reading

1a ▶ Scanning. Explain to Ss that they will read the email twice, the first time very quickly and the second time much more slowly. Direct them to the questions and tell them they have one minute to find the information. Explain that they do not need to understand the text fully at this point. Stop the activity after a minute. Ss call out the answer.

Answers: return to study   at the Open University

b ▶ Ss read the text more slowly and decide whether the four statements are True or False. Teach *distance learning* (see Optional warmer above). Ss check answers in pairs, then as a whole class.

Answers: 1 F 2 F 3 T 4 T

Lifelong learning

2a ▶ Ss look at the words in italics in the text and decide what type of word they are. Ss check answers in pairs, then as a whole class. Ask: *What helped you decide?*

Answers: can't afford – verb (*can't* + base form of the verb)   degree – noun (the indefinite article a comes before the word)   academic – adjective (-*ic* is a suffix for adjectives, it comes between any and qualifications)   distance-learning – adjective (comes between a and course)   tutor – noun (comes after the definite article a and an adjective personal)

b ▶ Ss match the words in italics to the meanings. Check answers.

Answers: 1 degree 2 academic 3 tutor 4 can't afford 5 distance-learning

Grammar

3a ▶ Ss focus on the two sentences in the Active grammar box. Write them on the board. Underline next month and in March. Ss discuss the four questions in pairs. Ss check answers in pairs, then as a whole class.

Answers: 1 Present Continuous 2 Yes 3 Yes 4 the future

b ▶ Ss find other examples of the Present Continuous used to talk about the future in the text. Ss check answers in pairs, then as a whole class.

Answers: I'm returning to studying. I'm taking a degree in Art History. We're having a few days in the country next week. Are you doing anything exciting in the next few weeks?

▶ The Present Continuous is used to talk about actions happening at the time of speaking. Explain that we also use it for definite arrangements in the future. Joanna has made the decision and has already booked her place on the Open University course. The plan is certain.

▶ Direct Ss to the reference section on page 113.

4a ▶ Teach *flatmate* (people you live with, not your family). Direct Ss to the calendar. Ask: *How many flatmates are there? What are their names?* (4: Kimiko, Jesus, Pilar, Radek) Ask: *Are these suggestions or definite arrangements which the four people have made?* (Definite arrangements, times and places are decided on.)

▶ Ss look at the example and write the sentences using the Present Continuous. Ss check answers in pairs, then as a whole class.

Answers: Juan and Pilar are going to the cinema at quarter to nine on Tuesday. Radek is starting his new English class at half past six on Wednesday. Juan is meeting his brother at the Italian restaurant at eight o'clock on Thursday. Everyone is going to a nightclub at half past ten on Friday. Kimiko is taking a flight to Tokyo at ten to twelve on Saturday.

▶ Direct Ss to the How to box.

b ▶ Ss make notes about their plans for the times listed. In pairs, they discuss their plans.

OPTIONAL VARIATION

Ss prepare an empty calendar for next week similar to the one in Ex. 4a. Ss work in pairs. They discuss about their plans and fill in the calendar for their partner with any definite arrangements which have been made for next week. Ss write reminder notes for their partner to give them at the end of class or at the next class. (E.g. Don't forget you're meeting your mum for coffee at 11 on Wednesday morning.)

Listening

OPTIONAL LISTENING LEAD-IN

Ss think of one successful and one unsuccessful learning experience outside of school (e.g. learning to drive, to paint, computer skills, yoga, etc.). In pairs, Ss discuss the two learning experiences and why they think one was successful and one wasn't. (E.g. I learned to drive last year. My teacher was very patient. I needed to learn for my job so I was very interested in it, etc.)

5a ▶ Ss look at the four adverts for different courses. Write *retired/life-saving/career prospects/gain* on the board. Ss guess what these words mean as they read the adverts. (Over 65, not working/how to save a life in an emergency/your job in the future/get). Ss match the adverts to the headings. Ss check answers in pairs, then as a whole class.

Answers: 1 D   2 C   3 B   4 A

b ▶ Tell Ss they are going to listen to four people describe the different courses. Teach *extras* (when you have to pay for extra things, e.g. books, photocopying, etc.). Play recording 11.10. Ss listen and put the adverts in the order the speakers talk about them. Ss check answers in pairs, then as a whole class.

Answers: Haresfield College, Open University, MicroMatters Ltd, University of the Third Age

6 ▶ Play the recording again. Ss listen and complete the table. Ss check answers in pairs, then as a whole class.

Answers: <u>Haresfield College</u>: £100 a year   3 hours a week   History, Languages, Computing. <u>Open University</u>: at home   about £500 a year   12 hours a week   doesn't say. <u>MicroMatters Ltd</u>: the centre   £900 computer skills. <u>University of the Third Age</u>: halls or schools all over the country   £2.50 to join   doesn't say   doesn't say

Vocabulary

7a ▶ Ss look at the words in the box. They categorise the words in any way they wish. Two examples are given. Ss compare categories with a partner.

Possible categories: people who learn   people who teach   places you learn   qualifications   types of learning, etc.

b ▶ Ss write sentences about their education using some of the words in the box.

Speaking

8 ▶ Ss work in small groups. They discuss the four questions in their group. Don't worry about Ss making mistakes during this activity. Note down any obvious errors you hear to deal with later.

Communication: Arrangements and appointments

OPTIONAL WARMER

Teach *appointment* (when you arrange to meet someone like a doctor or teacher). Elicit examples of people you make appointments to see. (Doctor, dentist, hairdresser, etc.) Ss work in pairs. They discuss (1) whether they like/don't like the appointments they make (e.g. I like going to the hairdresser. I relax and read lots of magazines, etc.) and (2) how far in advance they usually make appointments (e.g. the day before, two weeks in advance, just show up, etc.).

1a ▶ Ss discuss the questions as a whole class. Elicit which of the appointments Ss have made and how they made them.

b ▶ Ss read the expressions and decide in pairs whether they mean the person can or can't see you. Check answers in pairs, then as a whole class.

Answers: a 1 and 3   b 2 and 4

2a ▶ Ss read the questions. Play recording 11.11. Ss listen and answer the questions. Ss check answers.

Answers: 1 an appointment with his son's teacher   2 to talk about his examinations   3 Tuesday morning at 9 o'clock

b ▶ Play the recording again. Ss listen and complete Jill's diary. Ss check answers in pairs. Draw the diary on the board for feedback.

Answers:

	morning	afternoon
Tuesday	teaching	swimming
Wednesday	teaching	teaching
Thursday	teaching	free

c ▶ Ss read the tapescript on page 160. Play the recording while they read. Ss use expressions from the tapescript to complete the How to box. Check answers as a whole class.

Answers: <u>Can</u> you come on Thursday?   I'm afraid I <u>can't</u> come then ...   ... because <u>I'm</u> working; I <u>can</u> come on Tuesday   How <u>about</u> earlier in the morning?   OK. <u>Let's</u> meet at nine.

▶ Teach the expression *I'm afraid I can't* to refuse politely. It means *I'm sorry* in this context, not *I'm scared*. Review *How about* + noun and *Let's* + base verb for making suggestions. Ss practise saying the phrases.

3a ▶ Ss work in pairs. Student A is a university lecturer and student B is a student who wants to make an appointment to see the lecturer for an hour. Student A's timetable is on page 128 and student B's timetable is on page 112. They try to find a suitable time to meet.

b ▶ Ss compare appointment times with another pair.

Review and practice

1 ▶

Answers: 1 You can't take photographs. 2 You have to wear a seat-belt. 3 You can find a restaurant here; 4 You don't have to be a hotel guest.

2 ▶

Answers: 1 can't 2 can't 3 doesn't have to 4 can 5 has to 6 can't 7 can't 8 doesn't have to 9 can

3 ▶

Answers: 2 When/c 3 How/g 4 What/a 5 How long/d 6 Who/h 7 Why/b 8 How much/f

4 ▶

Answers: 1 You're arriving 2 am I doing 3 You're not doing 4 I'm watching 5 you're meeting 6 are they showing 7 you're coming

5 ▶

Answers: 1 college (isn't a subject) 2 trainee (isn't a teacher) 3 Training (isn't a qualification) 4 kindergarten (isn't higher education) 5 Petrol (isn't a direction) 6 Driving licence (isn't a rule of the road)

Notes for using the Common European Framework (CEF)

CEF References

11.1 Can do: understand signs and rules

CEF A2 descriptor: can understand everyday signs and notices: in public places, such as streets, restaurants, railway stations; in workplaces, such as directions, instructions, hazard warnings (CEF page 70)

11.2 Can do: understand and produce a simple explanation

CEF A2 descriptor: can communicate in simple and routine tasks requiring a simple and direct exchange of information (CEF page 81)

11.3 Can do: talk about future arrangements

CEF A2 descriptor: can communicate in simple and routine tasks requiring a simple and direct exchange of information on familiar and routine matters to do with work and free time (CEF page 74)

CEF quick brief

There are hundreds of Can do statements in the Common European Framework, which can make it difficult for a learner to assess their level. To simplify matters The CEF contains a 'self-assessment grid' containing brief descriptions of what a learner Can do at each of the six major levels. This grid is in the Total English Portfolio.

Portfolio task

Download the Total English Portfolio free from www.longman.com/totalenglish.

Objective: to reinforce student autonomy in updating the Portfolio.

This task can be done in Ss' own language.

1 ▶ For homework, ask Ss to update the Biography section of their Portfolio. They might like to reassess their language learning aims, history or significant experiences. They might also like to go over the Can do statements again and tick the new objectives at A1 and A2 level that they can now achieve.

2 ▶ Ask Ss to bring their Biography sections in and show them to other Ss.

12 Ambitions

Overview

Lead-in	**Vocabulary:** adventure sports
12.1	**Grammar:** *be going to* for intentions
	Vocabulary: future time expressions
	Can do: talk about intentions
12.2	**Grammar:** infinitive of purpose; revision of *be going to*
	Vocabulary: ambitions
	Can do: write an informal letter
12.3	**Grammar:** verbs + infinitive/-*ing* form (*want, would like, like*, etc.)
	Vocabulary: leisure activities
	Can do: talk about likes, dislikes and ambitions
Com. Focus	Planning study objectives

Summary

Lesson 1: Ss read about various engineering projects which seek to link together different places in the world by tunnel or bridge.

Lesson 2: Ss hear the song *Fame!* and listen to three people who would like to be famous one day talk about their plans for the future. They read a letter written by one of the people to her sister, in which she describes her life now and her immediate plans.

Lesson 3: Ss read part of a website for Charity Challenge, an organisation which helps people raise money for charity. They listen to a telephone call where several questions about the organisation are answered and then read the Summary of Expeditions webpage for Charity Challenge.

Communication: Ss discuss and write study objectives to improve their English.

Film bank: Ten great adventures (3'44")
A travel writer gives her top ten of holiday adventures.

Gill Williams, a TV presenter and travel writer, counts down her personal top ten recommendations for exciting holiday adventures. Her recommendations include bungee jumping, whale watching and sky diving. We see Gill trying each of these activities.

Possible places to use this short film are:

▶ before the Unit Opener to get Ss talking about their own ambitions

▶ after lesson 3 to extend the topic of physical challenges

▶ at the end of the unit to round up the topic and language

For ways to use this short film in class, see Students' Book page 142 and Teacher's Book page 194.

Lead-in

OPTIONAL WARMER

Write *adventure holiday* on the board. Elicit the activities people do on adventure holidays in summer and winter (e.g. canoeing; surfing; horse-riding; rock climbing, etc.; downhill skiing, snowboarding; tobogganing, etc.) Ss work in pairs. They tell each other which type of activity holiday they would like best: (1) a winter or summer adventure holiday, (2) which adventure sport they would choose and (3) which country/area they would go to.

1 ▶ Ss look at the four photos of various adventure sports. They choose one word or phrase from box A and from box B to match each of the pictures. Ss check answers in pairs, then as a whole class.

> **Answers:** A white water rafting, river B sailing, bridge C trekking, canyon D cycling, tunnel

2a ▶ Ss discuss the two questions in pairs. Check answers.

> **Answers:** 1 photo B and D – a tunnel links two places underground a bridge links two places overground 2 Ss give their opinions on how safe the four activities are

b ▶ Ss list other activities which can be done in these places. An example is given.

> **Suggested answers:** river: canoeing, fishing sea: surfing, water-skiing canyon: horse riding, rock climbing tunnel: rally driving, rollerblading, etc.

3a ▶ Tell Ss that some of the photos are from Dario and Mia's holiday last summer. Play recording 12.1. Ss listen and identify which photos are described. Ss check answers in pairs, then as a whole class.

> **Answers:** A, C and D

b ▶ Ss look at the four questions. Play the recording again. Ss listen and answer the questions. Ss check answers in pairs, then as a whole class.

> **Answers:** 1 white water rafting 2 horse-riding 3 in the hills behind San Francisco 4 horse-riding

4 ▶ Ss work in pairs. They ask and answer the questions about the four activities in the photos.

▶ Ss write an advert for an adventure holiday in their country. Put the adverts around the room. Ss circulate reading the adverts. Each student chooses a holiday to go on.

12.1 One world

In this lesson Ss read about various engineering projects which seek to link together different places in the world by tunnel or bridge. Through this context, Ss learn *going to* for intentions and how to talk about future intentions.

> **OPTIONAL WARMER**
>
> Write *tunnels* and *bridges* on the board. Elicit any famous tunnels or bridges Ss know. (E.g. the Mont Blanc tunnel, the Golden Bridge in San Francisco, etc.) Ss discuss how they feel crossing very high bridges and going through very long tunnels (scared; excited, etc.).

Reading and vocabulary

1 ▶ Ss look at the map of the world. They name the continents and ways of travelling between continents.

> **Answers:** 1 Continents: Africa, Antarctica, Asia, Australia, Europe, North America, South America
> 2 Ways of Travelling between them: By sea, by air, by land

2a ▶ Scanning. Explain to Ss that they will read the text twice, the first time very quickly and the second time much more slowly. Direct them to the questions in this exercise and tell them they have one minute to find the answers. Explain they do not need to understand the text fully at this point. Stop the activity after a minute. Ss choose the right option.

> **Answer:** 2

b ▶ Ss read the text more slowly and match the places 1–6 with the places a–f. Ss check answers with a partner and match the pairs to the places on the map. Check answers as a whole class.

> **Answers:** 1 c – E on map   2 a – D on map
> 3 d – B on map   4 f – F on map   5 b – A on map
> 6 e – C on map

3a ▶ Ss look at the words in the box and find them in the text. They answer the questions. Ss check answers in pairs, then as a whole class.

> **Answers:** 1 connect, link, join   2 continent, island, mainland   3 difficult, modern, different

b ▶ Ss complete the questions with the words and write the answers.

> **Answers:** 1 difficult   rivers, mountains and seas
> 2 connect   1994   3 island   a tunnel
> 4 continent   Asia

Grammar

> **OPTIONAL GRAMMAR LEAD-IN**
>
> Ss find the sentence in the text which describes the Sicily – Italian project. (The Italian government is going to build a 5 km long bridge between Sicily and the Italian mainland). Write it on the board. Ss underline the other sentences describing the other projects. (the *going to* construction is used in two of the other three sentences). Underline *is going to build* in the sentence on the board.

4 ▶ Ss look at the two sentences and tick the correct explanation of *going to*. Ss check answers in pairs, then as a whole class.

> **Answer:** 1 intentions

▶ Write *Spain and Morocco + are + going to + build …* on the board. The *going to* future is formed with *to be* (Present Simple) + going to + infinitive of the verb. We use the *going to* future to describe intentions and plans about the future. I am *going to* visit Spain next year on holiday. This is my intention, a definite plan. I have decided to go.

5 ▶ Ss focus on how to form negatives and questions using the *going to* future. They complete the Active grammar box in their books. Direct Ss to the Reference Section on page 123.

> **Answers:** 're   's   isn't   Are   Is

6 ▶ Ss work in pairs. They use the prompts to write sentences using *going to*. Two examples have been done for them. Check answers.

> **Answers:** 1 Britain isn't going to build any more airports.   2 My parents are going to retire next year.
> 3 They are going to open a new bridge in 2020.
> 4 Are the Americans going to build a space station?
> 5 I'm going to start a new course in September.
> 6 We're not going to have a holiday next Summer.

Pronunciation

7a ▶ Direct Ss to the stress pattern for the *going to* sentence. Play recording 12.2. Ss listen and note the sentence stress. Ask: *What do you notice about the pronunciation of to?* Ss compare answers in pairs, then as a whole class. Ss practise saying the sentence.

> **Answer:** to is pronounced /t/

b ▶ Play recording 12.3. Ss listen and repeat the sentences, then mark the sentence stress. Ss check answers in pairs, then as a whole class.

> **Answers:** 1 She's going to lose weight.   2 They're going to sell their car.   3 We're going to learn French.
> 4 I'm going to buy a laptop.

▶ Ask: *Which type of words are stressed?* (Main verbs and nouns, not pronouns, prepositions, suffix endings, auxiliary verbs.)

Vocabulary

8a ▶ Ss look at the future time expressions and put them in order starting from the nearest in time from now. Ss check answers in pairs, then as a whole class.

> **Answers:** 1 today 2 tomorrow 3 the week after next 4 later this year 5 next summer 6 in two year's time 7 three years from now

b ▶ Ss work in pairs. They take it in turns to ask each other about their future intentions using the time expressions from Ex. 8a. An example is given.

Person to person

9a ▶ In pairs, Ss discuss intentions using the prompts in the exercise and some of the verbs in the box. Explain that they will use the questions to ask their partner about their future intentions in relation to the topics in this exercise. (E.g. Are you going to improve your health? Are you going to change your job? Are you going to travel abroad next year? etc.) Ss write sentences about their partner. They take turns to ask each other their questions. Monitor closely, correcting any errors you hear.

b ▶ Ss compare future intentions with other pairs.

Speaking

10 ▶ Nominate each student as A, B, C or D. As Bs and Cs look at page 128. Ds look at page 117. Ss circulate, asking the other Ss in the class about their intentions for next year or so until they find Ss who correspond to the information on their card. (E.g. Are you going to get married in the next two years? Are you going to move house soon?, etc.)

▶ In feedback, ask: *How many Ss are going to visit another country? How many Ss are going to make lots of money?*, etc.

> **OPTIONAL EXTENSION**
>
> Ss work in groups of three or four. They imagine that student elections are going to be held in the school. Each group represents a party and prepares an election manifesto describing their intentions to the voters. Elicit one or two suggestions before Ss start. (E.g. We are going to introduce coffee during the lessons; We are going to provide free books, etc.) The suggestions do not need to be serious ones. Each group prepares four points for their manifesto and then presents the manifestos to the class.

12.2 Fame and fortune

In this lesson Ss listen to the song *Fame!* and listen to three people who would like to be famous one day talk about their plans for the future. They read a letter written by one of the people to her sister, in which she describes her life now and her immediate plans. Through this context, Ss review *be going to* and learn the infinitive of purpose and how to write an informal letter.

> **OPTIONAL WARMER**
>
> Ss work in small groups. They list three good things and three bad things about being very famous (e.g. good: lots of money; bad: no privacy, etc.). Elicit the advantages and disadvantages on the board during feedback. Ask: *Would you like to be famous?*

1 ▶ Elicit different ways people can become famous. Two examples are given. Accept all suggestions and write them on the board.

Listening

2a ▶ Ss look at the two statements. Play recording 12.4. Ss listen and decide which of the statements is true about the singer in the song. Ss check answers in pairs, then as a whole class.

> **Answer:** 2

b ▶ Ss look at the photo of a scene from the film *Fame!* and discuss the questions in pairs.

> **Answers:** 1 It's about young people at a special school for Performing Arts. 2 They are going to be singers, dancers, actors, etc.

3 ▶ Ss look at the lines of the song chorus. Play the recording again. Ss listen and put the lines of the chorus into the correct order. Ss check answers in pairs, then as a whole class.

> **Answers:** 1 Fame! 2 I'm going to live forever 3 I'm going to learn how to fly 4 I feel it coming together 5 People will see me and cry 6 I'm going to make it to heaven 7 Light up the sky like a flame 8 I'm going to live forever 9 Baby, remember my name!

4a ▶ Ss look at the photos A–C. Ss choose from the list to decide how the people in the photos can become famous. Ss check answers in pairs, then as a whole class.

> **Answers:** A become President B star in a film C join a famous club

b ▶ In pairs, Ss look at the vocabulary in the box and match three of the phrases to each photo. Ss can use dictionaries for this activity.

> **Answers:** A: politician, election, politics B: acting, drama, a play C: training session, football team, ball control skills

5a▶ Play recording 12.5. Ss listen and match the speakers to the photos. Ss check answers in pairs, then as a whole class.

> **Answers:** 1 B   2 A   3 C

b▶ Ss look at the questions. Teach *reserve team* (not the first team). Play the recording again. Ss listen and answer the sentences. Ss check answers in pairs, then as a whole class.

> **Answers:** 1 a   2 b   3 b

c▶ Ss read the tapescript on page 160. Play the recording as they read. Ss write sentences about what each speaker is going to do. Ss look at the reasons a–c and match them to the sentences.

> **Answers:** Victoria is going to learn how to sing and dance – b   Helena is going to work for a politician next summer – c   Lewis is going to practise with the reserve team twice a week – a

Grammar

6▶ Ss read the two statements made by Lewis and decide which is the correct explanation of the underlined phrases. Ss check answers in pairs, then as a whole class.

> **Answer:** a

▶ Write *Lewis is working hard because he wants a place in the first team.* Explain that we can replace the *because ... * clause with *to get a place in the first team.* Write *Lewis is working hard to get a place in the first team.*

We use the infinitive to explain the reason we do something or the purpose of something. E.g. Helena is working for a politician to learn about elections. Victoria is going to drama school to become a famous performer.

▶ Direct Ss to the reference section on page 123.

7▶ Ss look at the five statements and decide whether they agree with the reasons given or not. If Ss don't agree, they re-write the sentence with a reason which is true for them. An example is done for them.

> **OPTIONAL EXTENSION**
>
> Elicit reasons why people want to become famous (money, meet other famous people, etc.). Ss make sentences using the infinitive of purpose to explain the reasons. (E.g. They want to be famous to meet other famous people; They want to be famous to make a lot of money, etc.)

Reading and writing

8a▶ Ss read Victoria's letter and choose the correct sentence. Ss check answers in pairs, then as a whole class.

> **Answer:** 1

b▶ Ss read the letter again and answer the three questions in pairs. Elicit answers in feedback.

> **Answers:** 1 Victoria thanks Josie for her 'last letter' and responds to Josie's news.   2 The style is informal (exclamation marks, contractions, informal expressions). There's lots of personal news. Victoria finishes the letter 'love Victoria'.   3 Victoria uses three exclamation marks in the letter. We use these at the end of sentences in informal writing to show that a particular piece of news is exciting or different or especially interesting.

▶ Direct Ss to the writing bank on page 145 for information on exclamation marks.

9▶ Ss focus on the underlined expressions in the letter and use them to complete the How to box. Ss check answers in pairs, then as a whole class.

> **Answers:** Thank you very much for ...   It was great to hear about ...   I was sorry to hear that ...   Everything is going well here. Write soon and give my love to ...

10▶ Tell Ss they are going to write an informal letter to a friend or someone in their family. In the letter they will describe their life now and what their future plans are. Ss make notes about these before starting to write.

▶ Focus on the three paragraphs in Victoria's letter and elicit headings for each one. Write the following organisation on the board for Ss to use.

Dear _____
Respond to news
Give your news
Ending
Love

_____

▶ Ss check their letters for mistakes and then swap letters with a partner. They read their partner's letter and check the spelling and grammar. In pairs, Ss correct the mistakes in both letters. Monitor closely, helping correct the spelling and grammar mistakes.

> **OPTIONAL EXTENSION**
>
> Write the following on the board *career prospects/interest/something to do/pass an exam/travel/communication with others/need it for my job/other reason.*
>
> Ss work in small groups of three or four. They discuss their reasons for learning English. *Which are the most important/least important reasons for you?*
>
> Don't worry about Ss making mistakes during this activity.

12.3 Charity Challenge

In this lesson Ss read part of a website for Charity Challenge, which helps people raise money for charity. They listen to a telephone call where several questions about the organisation are answered and then read the Summary of Expeditions web page for Charity Challenge. Through this context, Ss learn verbs + infinitive/-*ing* (*want, would like, enjoy*, etc.) and how to talk about likes, dislikes and ambitions.

> **OPTIONAL WARMER**
>
> Teach *charity* (an organisation which gives money or other help to people in need, give examples e.g. Oxfam). Ss work in pairs. They list all the ways they can think of to raise money for charity. (E.g. raffle tickets; charity shops; collection box in the street, etc.) Put the suggestions on the board in feedback.

Reading

1▶ Ss work in pairs. They look at the photo and answer the questions.

> **Answers:** 1 It is Mark Webber, a Formula One driver. He is kayaking   2 to raise money for charity.

2▶ Teach *challenge* (something very difficult to do). Scanning. Explain to Ss that they will read the text twice, the first time very quickly and the second time much more slowly. Tell Ss they have one minute to find the connection between the photo and the text. Explain they do not need to understand the text fully at this point. Stop the activity after a minute. Ss check answer in pairs, then as a whole class.

> **Answer:** Mark Webber is doing the Charity Challenge.

3a▶ Ss focus on new vocabulary in the text. They look at the words and match them to the definitions. The first one has been done for them. Ss check answers in pairs, then as a whole class.

> **Answers:** 2 f   3 a   4 c   5 b   6 d

b▶ Ss read the text more slowly and decide whether the four statements are true or false. Ss check answers in pairs, then as a whole class.

> **Answers:** 1 F   2 F   3 T   4 T

4▶ Teach *fit/fitness* (when your body is in a good condition) and *sponsor* (to give you some money to do the trip). Ss work in pairs. As turn to page 129 and Bs turn to page 130. Ss read the information and ask and answer each other's questions. Ss check answers with another pair, then as a whole class.

> **Answers:** Student A's questions: 1 you pay for yourself   2 you choose the charity yourself   3 find people to sponsor your trip and other ways like a car boot sale. Student B's questions: 1 yes   2 half an hour three or four days a week at the start   3 give advice and help at training weekends.

Listening

5▶ Tell Ss they are going to hear a phone call between David and one of the workers in Charity Challenge. Play recording 12.6. Ss listen and note down the questions which David asks. Play the recording again. Ss listen and note down the answers.

> **Answers:** See tapescript on page 160.

> **OPTIONAL VARIATION**
>
> Ss work in pairs and predict the questions David might ask. Elicit the questions in feedback and write them on the board. Play the recording. As Ss listen they note whether the questions are the same or different.

6▶ Teach *can't stand* (when you really dislike something). Play the recording again. Ss listen and match the sentence halves. The first one has been done for them. Ss check answers in pairs, then as a whole class.

> **Answers:** 2 b   3 g   4 a   5 c   6 f   7 h   8 d

Grammar

7a▶ Ss focus on the sentence endings a–h in Ex. 6. Ask: *What do you notice about the form of these verbs?* (some are -*ing* form of the verb and some are infinitives. Write *He wants ...* on the board. Ask Ss *Which form of the verb goes after want?* (the infinitive). Write *He wants to think about it.* Explain that the -*ing* form goes after some verbs and the infinitive goes after some verbs.

▶ Ss look at the completed sentences in Ex. 6 and use them to complete the Active grammar box. Ss check answers in pairs, then as a whole class.

> **Answers:** Verb + infinitive: Positive meaning: would like, want   Negative meaning: doesn't want, wouldn't like   Verb + -*ing* form: Positive meaning: likes, enjoys, loves   Negative meaning: doesn't like, hates, can't stand

▶ Ss use the different verbs to complete the rules.

> **Answers:** want/would like ... like/enjoy/hate ...

We usually use the -*ing* form after verbs of liking and disliking.

▶ Explain the difference in meaning between *I like ...* and *I'd like ...*; *I like playing tennis* (in general) but *I'd like to play tennis tomorrow* (a specific choice). *I'd like/I wouldn't like* are followed by the infinitive. *I like/don't like* are usually followed by the -*ing* form of the verb.

▶ Direct Ss to the reference section on page 123.

8 ▶ Ss choose the correct form of the verb to complete the sentences in pairs. Check answers.

> **Answers:** 1 dancing, to be 2 learning, to leave
> 3 to travel, flying 4 living, to leave 5 staying, to get

9 ▶ Ss look at the summary of expeditions list from the Charity Challenge website. Ask: *Which is more difficult: a challenging or a tough expedition?* (tough). Review Present Perfect for experience. (See Lesson 10.1.) Ss work in small groups of three or four. They discuss the questions together. (E.g. I've never been to China. Have you? I'd love to do that expedition because I really enjoying trekking and I'd love to go to China, etc.)

> **OPTIONAL EXTENSION**
>
> Ask Ss to imagine they are going on one of the Charity Challenge expeditions. Elicit a few different well-known charities. Ss discuss in pairs which charity they would choose to support and why.

Pronunciation

10a ▶ Ss look at the sentence. They listen to recording 12.7 to determine if the pronunciation of the vowel sound in the underlined word is the same or different. Ss check answers in pairs, then as a whole class.

> **Answer:** No. The vowel sound in like is /aɪ/. The vowel sound in play is /eɪ/.

b ▶ Ss look at the pairs of words. Play recording 12.8. Ss listen and underline the words on the recording. Ss check answers in pairs, then as a whole class.

> **Answers:** 1 b 2 a 3 a 4 b 5 a

▶ Ss practise saying the words in pairs.

c ▶ Play recording 12.9. Ss write down the sentences they hear. Ss check answers in the tapescript on page 160.

> **Answers:** 1 I hate waiting for bus rides in the rain.
> 2 Mike likes riding his bike but he hates playing games.
> 3 We prefer safe day trains to late night flights.

Speaking

11a ▶ Give an example of a personal ambition of your own. (E.g. Take a year off work and travel around the world.) Elicit one or two other ideas of things people have never done but would really like to do one day. (E.g. write a book; go scuba diving on a coral reef, etc.) Ss write down four or five personal ambitions.

b ▶ Ss work in small groups. They compare ambitions and whether they would like to do similar things or not. In whole class feedback, elicit the different ambitions and establish what the most popular ambition is.

Communication: Planning study objectives

> **OPTIONAL WARMER**
>
> Ss discuss their preferences in relation to study habits in small groups. Put these heading on the board to guide the discussion *time of day/where/noise/food/ drink/who with*.

1 ▶ Ss look at the photos. In pairs, they use the pictures to make a list of ways of learning English. Ss add to the list with ideas of their own.

> **Answers:** Read English newspaper watch a film in English listen to English/American music use a monolingual dictionary read graded readers listen to tapes/CDs of English look at websites in English

2a ▶ Ss think about the different techniques used to learn English. They complete Part 1 of the questionnaire individually.

b ▶ Ss compare answers in pairs.

3a ▶ Ss focus on their own strengths and weaknesses as language learners. They complete Part 2 of the questionnaire individually.

b ▶ Ss work in groups of five or six. They compare answers to Part 2 of the questionnaire and find other Ss who want to improve at similar things.

4a ▶ Working in the same groups, Ss think of things they can do to improve their English. Elicit examples on the board in feedback.

Lifelong learning

▶ Explain the importance of having clear goals and objectives when learning a language and of establishing clear strategies to help achieve those goals.

b ▶ Ss look at part 2 of the questionnaire and focus on the areas in which they want to improve. Elicit the main areas on the board first. Ss write up clear objectives and strategies for achieving them for their group. (If you have large sheets of paper or card, Ss can design posters for this.)

▶ Put the objectives up around the room. Ss circulate looking at the various strategies and ideas for ways to improve in specific areas. They re-group and discuss the strategies, adding to their original list if they choose.

> **OPTIONAL ACTIVITY**
>
> Ss work in pairs. They think back over their English course for this term/year and list the main things that they are able to do now that they couldn't do at the beginning of the course. Ss look at the Can do section of the contents page of their coursebook.

Review and practice

1 ▶

> **Answers:** 1 They're going to build an old people's home in the suburbs. 2 They're going to open a local history museum in the town centre. 3 Our town is going to close the swimming pool in Rectory Rd. 4 Our town is going to introduce a 35 kph speed limit in the central area. 5 Our town is going to start a new 24-hour telephone information line.

2 ▶

> **Answers:** 1 Toyota isn't going to build new factories in Europe. 2 Is the situation going to get better or worse? 3 Are all the students going to pass the examination? 4 My parents aren't going to sell their house. 5 Is your father going to retire next year? 6 Your team isn't going to win the next swimming competition.

3 ▶

> **Answers:** 1 I am going 2 The children are 3 going to go back 4 to meet 5 isn't going to

4 ▶

> **Answers:** 1 to see the Acropolis 2 to use the Internet 3 to meet new people 4 to commute to work 5 to send text messages

5 ▶

> **Answers:** 1 studying/to go 2 flying/to travel 3 eating/to work 4 smoking/to marry 5 feeling/to live

6 ▶

> **Answers:** 1 rafting 2 driving 3 horse-riding 4 mountain biking 5 kayaking 6 cycling 7 mountain climbing 8 surfing Activity X = trekking

Notes for using the Common European Framework (CEF)

CEF References

12.1 Can do: talk about intentions

CEF A2 descriptor: can perform and respond to basic language functions, such as information exchanges and requests and express opinions and attitudes in a simple way (CEF page 122)

12.2 Can do: write an informal letter

CEF A2 descriptor: can write about everyday aspects of his/her environment, e.g. people, places, a job or study experience in linked sentences (CEF page 62)

12.3 Can do: talk about likes, dislikes and ambitions

CEF A2 descriptor: can explain what he/she likes or dislikes about something (CEF page 59)

CEF quick brief

One of the implications of the Common European Framework and the Can do statements is that Ss are assessed in terms of how well they can achieve a communication objective. The aim is not to perform the task with perfect accuracy but to perform well enough at that particular reference level. The Can do statements set appropriate objectives for each reference level.

Portfolio task

Download the Total English Portfolio free from www.longman.com/totalenglish.

Objective: to reinforce student autonomy in updating the Portfolio.

This task can be done in Ss' own language.

1 ▶ For homework, ask Ss to update the Dossier section of their Portfolio. They might like to add another piece of work to their folder or choose another task to work on with the aim of adding it to their Biography.

2 ▶ Ask Ss to bring their Biography sections in and show them to other Ss.

Photocopiable Worksheets

Family tree

Part 1

Listen to your teacher and write the names and ages of the people below into the family tree.

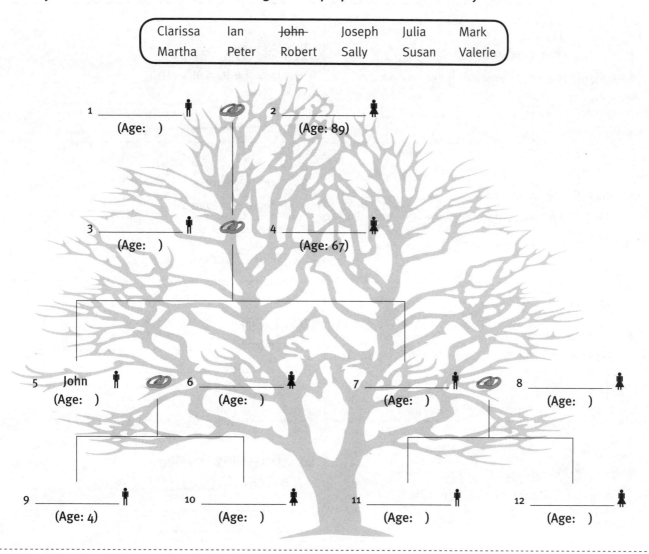

| Clarissa | Ian | ~~John~~ | Joseph | Julia | Mark |
| Martha | Peter | Robert | Sally | Susan | Valerie |

1 _____ (Age:)

2 _____ (Age: 89)

3 _____ (Age:)

4 _____ (Age: 67)

5 John (Age:)

6 _____ (Age:)

7 _____ (Age:)

8 _____ (Age:)

9 _____ (Age: 4)

10 _____ (Age:)

11 _____ (Age:)

12 _____ (Age:)

Part 2

Now use the information in your family tree to complete these sentences.

1 Robert is John's _____ and Clarissa's _____ .

2 Peter is Robert's _____ .

3 Clarissa is Ian's _____ , and John is Ian's _____ .

4 Martha is John's _____ , and Ian is his _____ .

5 Sally and Joseph are Ian and Martha's _____ .

6 Sally is Joseph's _____ .

7 Mark is Valerie's _____ .

8 Susan is Clarissa's _____ .

9 Mark is Sally and Joseph's _____ , and Susan is their _____ .

10 Peter is (a) 82 years old (b) 88 years old (c) 92 years old (d) 96 years old.

11 _____ is six years old.

12 _____ and _____ are the same age.

Photocopiable © Pearson Education Limited 2005

Sentence building

Complete the following sentences.

1 Eduardo (♂)/São Paolo

Eduardo is from São Paolo. São Paolo is in Brazil.

He is _____.

2 Mike (♂)/Melbourne

Mike is from Melbourne. Melbourne is in Australia.

He _____ _____.

3 Susan (♀)/Manchester

Susan is from Manchester. Manchester is in Britain.

_____ _____ _____.

4 Jordi (♂)/Barcelona.

Jordi is from Barcelona. Barcelona is in Spain.

_____ _____ _____.

5 My brother and I/Munich

My brother and I are from Munich. Munich is in

_____. _____ _____ _____.

6 Natalia and Dimitri/St Petersburg

Natalia and Dimitri are from St Petersburg.

St Petersburg is _____ _____.

_____ _____ _____.

7 Maria (♀)/Milan

Maria is from Milan. Milan _____ _____

_____. _____ _____.

8 Peter (♂)/Warsaw

Peter is from Warsaw. _____ _____

_____ _____. _____ _____

_____.

9 I/Helsinki

I am from _____. _____ _____

_____. _____ _____.

_____.

10 Mei Chuen (♀)/Guangzhou

Mei Chuen is _____ _____. _____

_____ _____. _____

_____ _____.

11 Hitoshi (♂)/Kyoto

Hitoshi _____ _____ _____.

_____ _____ _____.

_____ _____ _____.

12 My best friend and I/Thessaloniki

_____ _____ _____

_____ _____ _____.

_____ _____ _____.

_____ _____ _____.

© Pearson Education Limited 2005 Photocopiable

Complete the crossword.

1 from/parents/but/and/their/Emma/New York/
London/are/Mike/are/from

Mike and Emma _____ _____ _____ ,

_____ _____ _____ _____

_____ New York.

2 Cambridge/phone/is/812825/John/and/his/from/
number/is

John _____ _____ _____ _____

_____ _____ _____ _____ 812825.

3 beautiful/is/Maria/very/she/married/Is

Maria _____ _____ _____ . _____

_____ married?

4 Greek/speaks/Alan/Greece/from/he/Is

Alan _____ _____. _____ _____

_____ Greece?

5 husband/and/an/teacher/I'm/my/is/English/
engineer/an

I'm _____ _____ _____ , _____

_____ _____ _____ _____

engineer.

6 phone/me/is/your/mobile/this/Excuse

Excuse _____ , _____ _____

_____ _____ phone.

7 are/parents/I/are/French/My/but/our/Germany/
sister/and/from

My _____ _____ _____ _____

_____ _____ _____ _____

_____ _____ Germany.

8 school/aren't/work/and/Dave/Hilary/teachers/a/
but/they/in

Dave _____ _____ _____ _____ ,

_____ _____ _____ _____

_____ school.

9 Australian/is/her/Clare/husband/married/and/is

Clare _____ _____ _____ _____

_____ _____ Australian.

10 Spanish/brother/I/in/My/but/home/our/aren't/
Spain/and/is

My _____ _____ _____ _____

_____ , _____ _____ _____

_____ _____ Spain.

Complete the crossword with the pronouns.

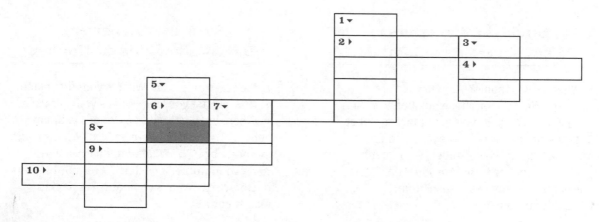

Photocopiable © Pearson Education Limited 2005

Get it right!

Student 1	✂ Student 2

Finish ☺
12   Is this Mark pen?
11   What your job?
10   Are your brother a doctor?
9   What's you nationality?
8   What's your mother job?
7   Is you German?
6   What's your address of email?
5   Where you are from?
4   What's surname?
3   How you are old?
2   How is your first name?
1   Are you a single?
Start ☝

Finish ☺
12   Is this she camera?
11   Where Atsushi from?
10   Are your two sister teachers?
9   Is this you mobile phone?
8   Are you student?
7   Is John and Carrie married?
6   What your father his job?
5   What's do your job?
4   Are you a Japanese?
3   What's your a phone number?
2   How old you are?
1   Where your home?
Start ☝

Student 2's answers.
Do not show this to him/her.

1   Where is your home?   2   How old are you?   3   What's your phone number?   4   Are you Japanese?   5   What's your job?   6   What does your father do?   7   Are John and Carrie married?   8   Are you a student?   9   Is this your mobile phone?   10   Are your two sisters teachers?   11   Where's Atsushi from?   12   Is this her camera?

Student 1's answers.
Do not show this to him/her.

1   Are you single?   2   What is your first name?   3   How old are you?   4   What's your surname?   5   Where are you from?   6   What's your email address   7   Are you German?   8   What's your mother's job?   9   What's your nationality?   10   Is your brother a doctor? / Are your brothers doctors?   11   What's your job?   12   Is this Mark's pen?

© Pearson Education Limited 2005   Photocopiable

My name is Harry Jones.

Part 1

Student 1

My name is Harry Jones, and I am from Australia, so I am Australian. I'm 19 years old. I'm not married. My home is in Britain and I'm a university student. My address is 30 Martins Lane, Cambarnet, CT13 3BV, my home phone number is 01723 875243 and my mobile number is 01729 053426. I also have an email address. It's harry.jo@yahmail.com. My parents are in Australia; my father (Ted) is a bank manager, my mother (Mary) is a doctor.

✂ -

Students 2 and 3

> ### Welcome to the Republic of Bratania.
>
> Please complete all this information before you arrive,
> and keep this form in your passport.
>
> First name: _____   Surname: _____
>
> Place of origin: _____   Nationality: _____
>
> Age: _____   Marital status: _____
>
> Occupation: _____   Address: _____
>
> Phone number: Home: _____   Mobile: _____ Email: _____
>
> Family: Father's name: _____   Job/Occupation: _____
>
>   Mother's name: _____   Job/Occupation: _____

✂ -

Part 2

> ### Welcome to the Republic of Bratania.
>
> Please complete all this information before you arrive,
> and keep this form in your passport.
>
>
>
> First name: Henry   Surname: Janes
>
> Place of origin: Austria   Nationality: Austrian
>
> Age: 18   Marital status: Married
>
> Occupation: School student   Address: 13 Martins Street, Cambarnet, CT30 3VB
>
> Phone number: Home: 01723 875432   Mobile: 01729 035426   Email: henry.jo@yahmail.au
>
> Family: Father's name: Fred Jones   Job/Occupation: Doctor
>
>   Mother's name: Mary Jones   Job/Occupation: Bank manager

Photocopiable   © Pearson Education Limited 2005

Find the hidden words.

Use the clues to complete the puzzle.

Colours

1						V		
2		H						
3				C				
4					E			
5		P						
6		O						
7			E					

Adjectives

8		A						
9				N				
10			D					
11		I						
12			E					
13	H							
14			U					
15				F				
16	U							

1 Expensive jewellery (e.g., a bracelet or a watch) is usually gold or _____ .

2 Snow is _____ .

3 Coal, or the sky at night, is _____ .

4 The flags of Britain, the USA, Malaysia and Cuba are red, white and _____ .

5 Roses are usually red, white, yellow or _____ .

6 Early in the morning or in the evening, the sun is _____ .

7 Grass is _____ .

8 He's a very _____ student: he doesn't come to his lessons.

9 I don't like classical musical: I like _____ music.

10 My grandfather is very _____ ; he's 96 or 97, I think.

11 Old mobile phones were very _____ , but new mobile phones are very small.

12 I don't like this pizza; it's not very _____ .

13 Yuk! This hamburger is _____ .

14 She's very _____ . I think she's only three or four.

15 Credit cards are very _____ when you go shopping.

16 This pen doesn't work. It's _____ .

Use the hidden words above to complete this sentence:

I think that _____ food is _____ .

© Pearson Education Limited 2005 Photocopiable

Can you remember?

Photocopiable   © Pearson Education Limited 2005

Three in a row

Complete the sentences. Try to get three in a row.

clean	feed	go	have	help	invent	like	live	make
organise	play	sleep	start	talk	walk	wash	watch	work

Game 1

1 Antonio's Italian, but he _____ in Switzerland.

2 Janice _____ for ten hours every night.

3 Carl _____ his car at the weekend.

4 Claribel _____ excursions for a travel company.

5 At seven o'clock, he _____ the news on the television.

6 Our English lesson _____ at half past nine.

7 Emma _____ to her friends on the phone every evening.

8 My mother really _____ coffee, and drinks it all day.

9 Brian doesn't have a bicycle, so he _____ everywhere.

Game 2

1 Charles _____ to school by bus.

2 Carol always _____ me with my English homework.

3 My father _____ new computers for a big computer company.

4 Every year, Jim _____ a big party on his birthday.

5 She _____ her bedroom every day.

6 Alan _____ from 8 o'clock in the morning until 7 o'clock in the evening.

7 Jackie _____ tennis every afternoon.

8 Mel only _____ his dogs once a day.

9 Jim _____ sandwiches for lunch every day.

© Pearson Education Limited 2005 Photocopiable

Plurals crossword

Arrange the letters in bold and complete the crossword.

Across →

1 This is a picture of my two _____ , Olivia and Claudia. **scinee**

6 These are my _____ ; I have one for work, and one for social events. **seiaird**

8 I have two _____ , an English–French one, and a French–German one. **aitinoseidcr**

12 This club is for _____ only. **nmeow**

13 I'm sorry, but _____ are not welcome in here. **enm**

14 He eats _____ for lunch. **ehasdicwns**

15 I made dinner, so you can wash and dry the _____. **ssidhe**

17 This club has really good _____ every weekend. **iseprta**

18 Do Harry and Gregory bring their _____ to the office party? **eivsw**

19 Every year, I have two or three _____. **dyoliahs**

Down ↓

2 I'm married to Henrietta, and we have two _____, Tara and Michael. **nrehlcdi**

3 Two _____ go from here to Oxford, the number 2 and the number 7. **subse**

4 My bedroom is very big, with lots of _____ on the wall. **eicpurts**

5 London and Birmingham are two big _____ in Britain. **tseiic**

7 Football supporters often wear _____ with the colours of their favourite teams on. **rasevsc**

9 Don't forget to write the names and _____ on these envelopes before you send them. **essarsded**

10 Two _____ live in the flat next to mine, the Smiths and the Roberts. **ilafesim**

11 I've got two _____ , a cheap plastic one, and an expensive Rolex. **setchaw**

16 The Hilton and the Sheraton are two good _____ in my town. **stoehl**

17 A lot of _____ work in this office. **epploe**

Photocopiable   © Pearson Education Limited 2005

Question and answer

Part 1
Complete the questions using a word from the box.

| are | do | have | how | what | when | where | who |

1 _____'s your name?

2 _____'s your nationality?

3 _____ languages do you speak?

4 _____'s your phone number?

5 _____'s your email address?

6 _____ do you live?

7 _____ do you live with?

8 _____ do you do?

9 _____ old are you?

10 _____ you have brothers or sisters?

11 _____ do your parents do?

12 _____ do you get to school?

13 _____ time do you get up?

14 _____ time do you have lunch?

15 _____ do you go to bed?

16 _____ you married?

17 _____ you have a girlfriend/boyfriend?

18 _____ you go to nightclubs?

19 _____ you like Japanese food?

20 _____ you watch a lot of television?

21 _____ you like English lessons?

22 _____ do you go on holiday?

23 _____ do you do on holiday?

24 _____ do you go on holiday with?

25 _____ do you take on holiday with you?

Part 2
Turn this paper over so you cannot see it. Try to remember the questions. Ask another student the questions, and write their answers.

© Pearson Education Limited 2005 Photocopiable

Write the right number.

Student 1

Read these numbers to your partner.

a		15

b		130

c	☎	01186 587523

d	🕐	2.30

e		19

f		600

g		121

h	🕐	5.08

i		60

j	🕐	5.55

k		50,000,000

l		130

m		16,000

n	☎	01866 877432

o	🕐	3.20

Write the numbers you hear in the table below.

(a)	(b)	(c)
(d)	(e)	(f)
(g)	(h)	(i)
(j)	(k)	(l)
(m)	(n)	(o)

Student 2

Read these numbers to your partner.

a	☎	01855 875523

b		6,000

c	☎	01886 578234

d		113

e		15,000,000

f	🕐	12.15

g	🕐	2.20

h		50

i		140

j		17

k	🕐	8.05

l		70

m	🕐	4.54

n	🕐	8.45

o		5,000,000,000

Write the numbers you hear in this table.

(a)	(b)	(c)
(d)	(e)	(f)
(g)	(h)	(i)
(j)	(k)	(l)
(m)	(n)	(o)

Photocopiable © Pearson Education Limited 2005

Negative matching

Part A

... we don't like our English lessons.	... I don't want lunch.	... she doesn't do her homework at home.	... I don't have any free time.
... we don't eat there.	... we don't watch them.	... she doesn't eat it.	... he doesn't talk a lot.
... I don't listen to him.	... he doesn't read newspapers.	... he doesn't meet his friends during the week.	... she doesn't cook food.
... he doesn't get up early.	... she doesn't work then.	... they don't live with their parents.	... we don't walk.
... I don't sleep very well.	... he doesn't write a diary every day.	... I don't take the bus to school.	... they don't go to bed until one o'clock.

Part B

1 Our teacher is horrible, so ...

2 I'm not hungry, so ...

3 Susan's house is very noisy, so ...

4 I'm always very busy, so ...

5 That restaurant is very expensive, so ...

6 Television programmes in the evening are very bad, so ...

7 Annie hates fish, so ...

8 Bob is a very quiet person, so ...

9 Edward always says stupid things, so ...

10 The news is always so bad, so ...

11 Jeff is always very busy, so ...

12 Helen isn't very good in the kitchen, so ...

13 Richard goes to bed late, so ...

14 Teresa likes to relax at the weekend, so ...

15 Rob and Alex have their own apartment, so ...

16 There's a good bus service to the town, so ...

17 My neighbours make a lot of noise at night, so ...

18 Ian is always very busy at work, so ...

19 The bus service is very slow, so ...

20 Sara and Martin like to go to nightclubs, so ...

© Pearson Education Limited 2005 Photocopiable

Know your partner.

Guess what your partner can and can't do.

ride a bicycle: yes/no	ride a skateboard: yes/no	windsurf: yes/no	sail a boat: yes/no
play the piano: yes/no	drive a car: yes/no	cook a meal for four: yes/no	dance: yes/no
sing: yes/no	make something with wood or metal: yes/no	play tennis: yes/no	swim: yes/no
play chess: yes/no	run 10 kilometres: yes/no	speak three languages: yes/no	touch his/her toes: yes/no
paint or draw: yes/no	write with his/her left hand: yes/no	use a fax machine: yes/no	skate: yes/no
send a text message: yes/no	use a computer: yes/no	repair a car: yes/no	climb a mountain: yes/no

Phone dictations

Students 1 and 2

Students 3 and 4

Student 1: Hello?

Student 2: Hello, can I speak to Sam please?

Student 1: I'm sorry. He isn't here right now. He's in a meeting.

Student 2: Oh, right. Do you know when the meeting ends?

Student 1: I'm sorry, I don't. Can I take a message?

Student 2: Yes, please ask him to call Chris.

Student 1: OK. What's your number?

Student 2: My home number is 01886 724311. My mobile is 0208 448723

Student 1: OK, bye.

Student 2: Thank you. Bye.

Students 3 and 4

Student 3: Hello? Chris here.

Student 4: Hello Chris, it's Sam.

Student 3: Hello Sam. Thanks for calling. How are you?

Student 4: Fine, thanks. And you?

Student 3: Very well, thanks. Can you come out tonight?

Student 4: Yes, I can. What do you want to do?

Student 3: Why don't we meet for dinner at the restaurant on Apple Street?

Student 4: Good idea. Let's meet outside the restaurant at eight o'clock.

Students 1 and 2 to complete:

Student 3: _____ ? _____ _____ .

Student 4: _____ _____ , _____ _____ .

Student 3: _____ _____ . _____ _____ . _____ _____ _____ ?

Student 4: _____ _____ . _____ _____ ?

Student 3: _____ _____ , _____ . _____ _____ _____ _____ _____ ?

Student 4: _____ , _____ _____ . _____ _____ _____ _____ _____ _____ _____ ?

Student 3: _____ _____ _____ _____ _____ _____ _____ _____ _____ _____ _____ ?

Student 4: _____ . _____ _____ _____ _____ _____ _____ _____ _____ .

Students 3 and 4 to complete:

Student 1: _____ ?

Student 2: _____ , _____ _____ _____ _____ _____ _____ ?

Student 1: _____ _____ . _____ _____ _____ _____ _____ _____ . _____ _____ _____ _____ .

Student 2: _____ , _____ . _____ _____ _____ _____ _____ _____ _____ _____ ?

Student 1: _____ _____ , _____ _____ . _____ _____ _____ _____ _____ _____ ?

Student 2: _____ , _____ _____ _____ _____ _____ _____ .

Student 1: _____ . _____ _____ _____ ?

Student 2: _____ _____ _____ _____ . _____ _____ _____ _____ .

Student 1: _____ , _____ .

Student 2: _____ _____ . _____ .

© Pearson Education Limited 2005 Photocopiable

The ideal job for you!

Ask and answer the questions with a partner.

1 Abilities

Can you ...

• drive a car?

• use a computer?

• speak three languages or more?

• play sports?

• repair things (for example, cars, computers)?

• draw or paint?

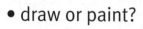

• make things in wood or metal?

• cook?

2 Likes/dislikes

Do you like ...

• working in a large, busy place?

• working at home or in a quiet place?

• physical work (using your body)?

• mental work (using your mind?)

• working indoors?

• working outdoors?

• working on your own?

• working as part of a team?

• working with children?

• working with animals?

3 Personality

Are you ...

• cheerful?

• helpful?

• friendly?

• sensible and practical?

• patient?

Photocopiable   © Pearson Education Limited 2005

Food galore

© Pearson Education Limited 2005 Photocopiable

My question, your answer

Student 1

1	Do you have a car? ❐	**9**	Do you have any credit cards? ❐
2	Do you have any eggs? ❐	**10**	How much water do you drink every day? ❐
3	Do you have any milk? ❐	**11**	Do you have any time to help me? ❐
4	Do you have a mobile phone? ❐	**12**	Do you have any pets? ❐
5	Do you have a DVD player? ❐	**13**	How many holidays do you take every year? ❐
6	How much money do you have? ❐	**14**	Do you have any butter so we can make a cake? ❐
7	How many people are in your class? ❐	**15**	Do you have any brothers? ❐
8	How many children do you have? ❐	**16**	How much pasta do you have? ❐

✂ --

Student 2

a	Yes, I have a Visa and an Amex card.	**i**	No I don't, but I have a video recorder.
b	No, I don't, but I have two sisters.	**j**	Yes, we have an old BMW.
c	Two. We have one in April and one in August or September.	**k**	Not much. I have about £10 in my wallet.
d	Not many. Eight, including the teacher.	**l**	We have two, a boy and a girl.
e	I've got a packet of spaghetti and a packet of ravioli.	**m**	Yes, there are six in the fridge.
f	Usually about two or three litres.	**n**	Yes, I have a new Nokia.
g	No, I don't have any, I'm afraid. I'm very busy at the moment.	**o**	Yes, we have a dog, a cat and a rabbit.
h	Yes, I have, but I don't have any eggs or sugar.	**p**	Yes there are two bottles in the fridge.

Photocopiable © Pearson Education Limited 2005

Object pronouns

Use these words in the sentences below. Cross out each word after you use it.

her	him	it	it	it	that	that	that	that	them	them
them	these	these	those	those	this	this	this	this	us	you

1 I don't understand _____ book.

I don't understand _____ either.

2 _____ woman wants to talk to you.

I don't have the time to talk to _____ .

3 I don't like _____ apples.

I don't like _____ either.

4 I love _____ flowers.

I love _____ too.

5 I know _____ man over there.

Oh, everybody knows _____ .

6 _____ men look a bit frightening.

Right. And I don't like the way they're looking at both of _____ .

7 _____ policemen want to speak to you.

Well, I don't want to speak to _____ !

8 _____ pizza is disgusting.

Really? I quite like _____ .

9 _____ homework is so easy.

I disagree. I find _____ quite difficult.

10 Is _____ hat too big?

Yes, it's much too big for _____ .

© Pearson Education Limited 2005 Photocopiable

First to finish

Start ☞	**1** I usually eat sandwich for lunch.	**2** It's their money; give it to they.	**3** It weighs one kilo and a half.	**4** I'd like a glass of orange juices please.	**5** She isn't looking at you, she's looking at I.
	10 He had five hamburger for lunch and now he's feeling ill.	**9** Can I pay by the credit card?	**8** I don't buy pasta because I don't like them.	**7** I'd like a biscuit and a apple, please?	**6** How much is this computer cost?
	11 How much of water do you drink every day?	**12** Our teacher always gives we lots of homework.	**13** How many milk would you like in your coffee?	**14** It costs £10, but it's £8 if you pay by a cash.	**15** We don't have some eggs, so we can't make an omelette.
	20 We eat a lot of rices every day.	**19** It weighs one hundred fifty and five grammes.	**18** What you would like for lunch today?	**17** Could you buy a beef when you go to the supermarket?	**16** Could I have 2 litre of milk, please?
21 I want a hamburger and any fries please.	**22** I don't want to talk to she at the moment.	**23** How much children do you have?	**24** We don't have car, so we use the bus.	**25** How much moneys do you have in your wallet?	**Finish**

Referee's answers

1 I usually eat **a** sandwich for lunch (*or* I usually eat **sandwiches** for lunch).   2 It's their money; give it to **them**.   3 It weighs **one and a half kilos**.   4 I'd like a glass of orange **juice**, please.   5 She isn't looking at you, she's looking at **me**.   6 How much **does** this computer cost?   7 I'd like a biscuit and **an** apple, please?   8 I don't buy pasta because I don't like **it**.   9 Can I pay by credit card?   10 He had five **hamburgers** for lunch and now he's feeling ill.   11 How much water do you drink every day?   12 Our teacher always gives **us** lots of homework.   13 How **much** milk would you like in your coffee?   14 It costs £10, but it's £8 if you pay by cash.   15 We don't have **any** eggs, so we can't make an omelette.   16 Could I have 2 **litres** of milk, please?   17 Could you buy **some** beef when you go to the supermarket?   18 What **would you** like for lunch today?   19 It weighs one hundred **and fifty-five** grammes.   20 We eat a lot of **rice** every day.
21 I want a hamburger and **some** fries, please (*or* I want a hamburger and fries please).   22 I don't want to talk to **her** at the moment.   23 How **many** children do you have?
24 We don't have **a** car, so we use the bus.
25 How much **money** do you have in your wallet?

Photocopiable   © Pearson Education Limited 2005

Get your orders in!

© Pearson Education Limited 2005   Photocopiable

Complete the maps.

Map symbols

mountain

desert

forest

town or city

village

river

lake

beach

Student 1

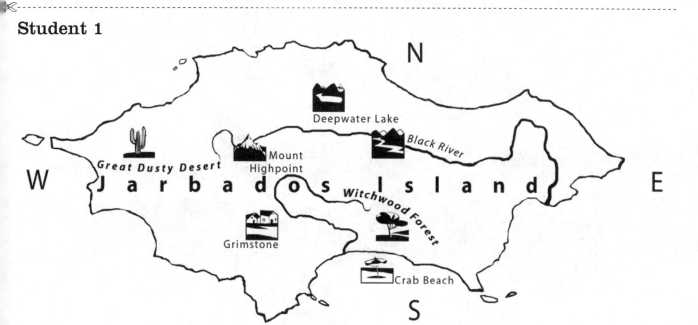

Student 2

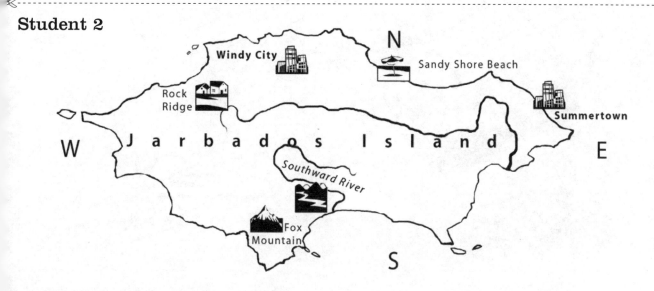

Find the differences.

Students 1 and 2

© Pearson Education Limited 2005 Photocopiable

Find the differences.

Students 3 and 4

Photocopiable © Pearson Education Limited 2005

Name the families.

Student 1

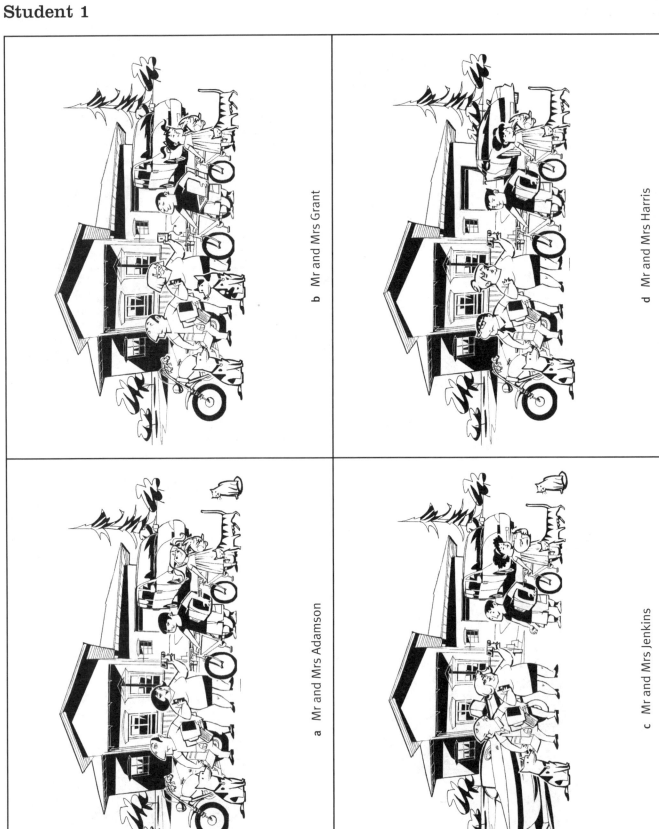

b Mr and Mrs Grant

d Mr and Mrs Harris

a Mr and Mrs Adamson

c Mr and Mrs Jenkins

© Pearson Education Limited 2005 Photocopiable

Name the families.

Student 2

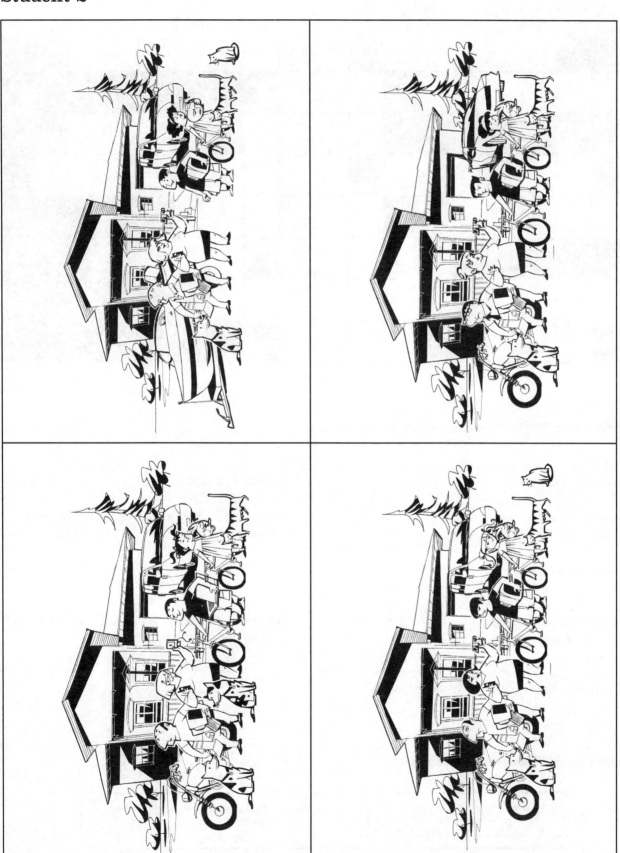

Mr and Mrs Adamson   Mr and Mrs Grant   Mr and Mrs Jenkins   Mr and Mrs Harris

Photocopiable © Pearson Education Limited 2005

Find the hidden modifier.

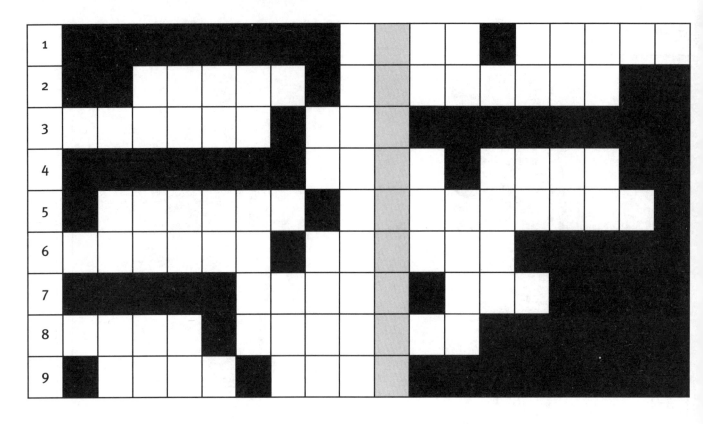

Find the hidden modifier and then complete the crossword.

1. I can't hear what you're saying.
   It's **rvey yinso** in here.

2. I really enjoy playing football.
   It's **utqei tixencgi** to watch, as well.

3. Can we open a window?
   It's **alelry oth** in here.

4. It's December, but the temperature's about 10°C.
   It isn't **evyr dolc** for winter.

5. There are lots of mountains and forests where I live.
   It's a **yaerll teaifbulu** area.

6. Everybody knows the Eiffel Tower in Paris.
   It's a **eylrla osamfu** building.

7. There isn't much rain in my country in the summer.
   It's **tuqei ryd** from about May to September.

8. A lot of people visit my home town.
   It's **yrev rplaopu** with tourists.

9. There are a lot of people in the supermarket today.
   It's always **yerv ybsu** on a Saturday.

Use the hidden modifier to complete this sentence.

The River Nile begins in Uganda and goes all the way to the Mediterranean Sea. It's a/an
_____ long river.

© Pearson Education Limited 2005 Photocopiable

I want, I want ...

What kind of house would you like? (Choose 1 only.)

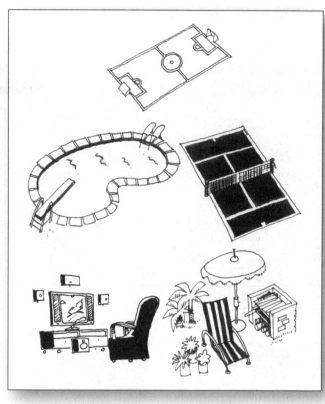

What luxury feature would you most like your house to have? (Choose 1 only.)

Where would you like to live? (Choose 1 only.)

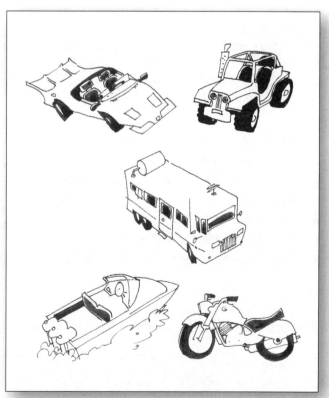

What would your ideal vehicle be? (Choose 1 only.)

Photocopiable © Pearson Education Limited 2005

Where's the bank?

Use the sentences 1–13 to identify the places A–M on your map. Can you find the bank?

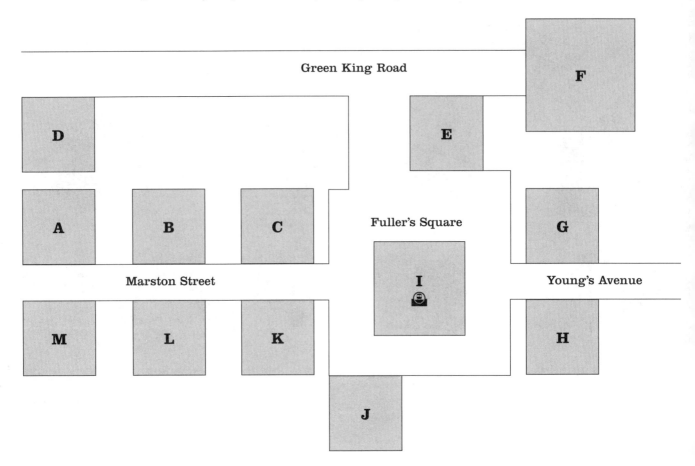

1   The school is behind the cinema.
2   The underground station is in Fuller's Square.
3   The bar is between Green King Road and Fuller's Square.
4   The cinema is on Young's Avenue.
5   The Internet café is behind the car park.
6   The restaurant is between the library and the supermarket.
7   The post office is opposite the cinema.
8   The Internet café is next to the art gallery.
9   The supermarket is on Marston Street.
10 The museum is on Fuller's Square.
11 The restaurant is opposite the art gallery.
12 The car park is on Green King Road.
13 The library is opposite the Internet café.

A = _____   B = _____   C = _____   D = _____

E = _____   F = _____   G = _____   H = _____

I = _____   J = _____   K = _____   L = _____

M = _*library*_

© Pearson Education Limited 2005   Photocopiable

Complete the sentences.

1   I _____ work at seven o'clock this morning.

2   I'm really angry: the bus _____ late again this morning.

3   It _____ a very good film. Don't go and see it.

4   My father _____ my mother in 1986.

5   We _____ television for six hours last night!

6   The building was a shop, but it _____ to a restaurant last year.

7   I _____ hard all day on Monday.

8   Last week we _____ the Past Simple in our English class.

9   For twenty years, the factory _____ keyboards for computers.

10   She _____ her dinner party very carefully.

11   We _____ very tired after such a long day at work.

12   I _____ the door very quietly because everyone was asleep.

13   For seven years I _____ in an apartment in the city centre.

14   On my last visit to London, I _____ with some old friends.

15   He _____ the box very carefully into the living room.

16   You _____ at school yesterday. Why not?

be	work	watch	be
study	start	live	stay
open	plan	be	produce
be	marry	carry	change

Just 10 questions

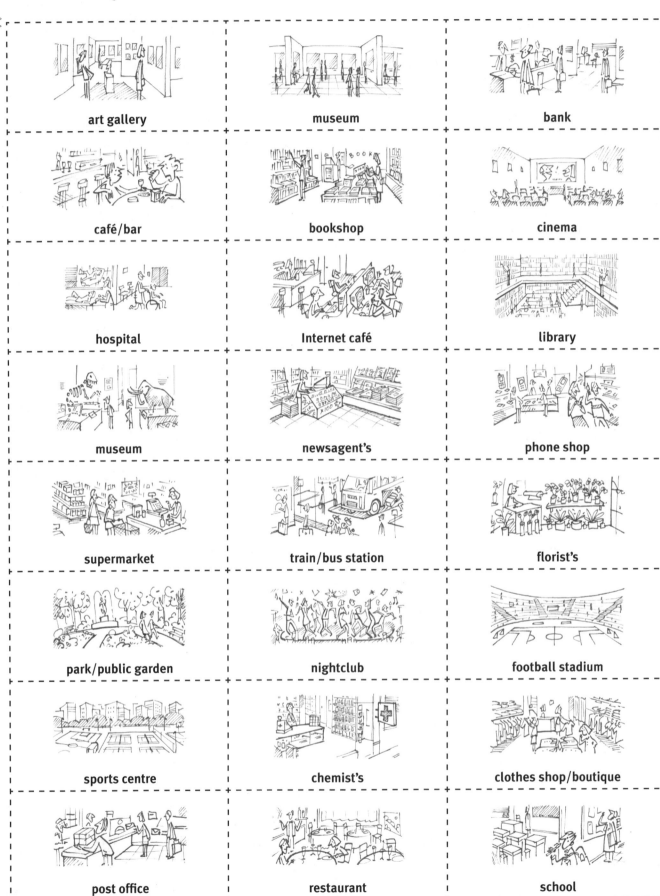

art gallery	museum	bank
café/bar	bookshop	cinema
hospital	Internet café	library
museum	newsagent's	phone shop
supermarket	train/bus station	florist's
park/public garden	nightclub	football stadium
sports centre	chemist's	clothes shop/boutique
post office	restaurant	school

© Pearson Education Limited 2005 Photocopiable

In Ancient Rome ...

Part 1

Part 2

ride	smoke	use	wear	play
eat	drink	cook	watch	listen

Where in the store ...?

Student 1

Third floor	ⓘ		furniture department	computer department	
Second floor					🍽
First floor	women's clothes	👩	women's shoes		
Ground floor				hats	
Basement	🎧				Ⓟ☞

Student 2

Third floor	ⓘ				
Second floor				bookshop	🍽
First floor		👩		stationery	
Ground floor	beauty products				
Basement	🎧	bedlinen	men's clothes		Ⓟ☞

Student 3

Third floor	ⓘ	music department			
Second floor	pharmacy		electronic goods		🍽
First floor		👩			
Ground floor			flowers		
Basement	🎧			men's shoes	Ⓟ☞

Departments

beauty products	bed linen	bookshop	hats
electronic goods	flowers	furniture department	pharmacy
men's clothes	men's shoes	music department	computer department
stationery	women's clothes	women's shoes	

© Pearson Education Limited 2005 Photocopiable

Around the world

Student 1

Listen to your partner and complete these sentences.

1 _____ is St Joseph's Day in _____ .

2 _____ is Scandinavian Union Day in Norway, Sweden and _____ .

3 _____ is Human Rights Day, a very important event in _____ .

4 _____ is National Day in _____ .

5 _____ is Burns' night, when people in _____ remember a famous poet called Robert Burns.

6 _____ is St Patrick's Day, an important day in _____ .

7 _____ is The Queen's birthday in _____ .

8 _____ is Children's Day in _____ .

9 _____ is National Day in _____ .

✂ Student 2

Listen to your partner and complete these sentences.

1 _____ is Independence Day in _____ .

2 _____ is Bastille Day, a national holiday in _____ .

3 _____ is Midori-no-hi ('Green Day'), when people in _____ celebrate spring.

4 On _____ and _____, people in _____ celebrate the Wine Festival.

5 _____ is Victory Day in _____, when people remember the end of the Second World War.

6 _____ is St Nicholas' Day in _____ .

7 _____ is Children's Day in _____ .

8 _____ is Independence Day in _____ .

9 _____ is Bay of Pigs Day in _____ .

Read these sentences to your partner. Do not show him/her your sentences.

1 4 July is Independence Day in the USA.

2 14 July is Bastille Day, a national holiday in France.

3 29 April is Midori-no-hi ('Green Day'), when people in Japan celebrate Spring.

4 On 26 and 27 September, people in Switzerland celebrate the Wine Festival.

5 9 May is Victory Day in Russia, when people remember the end of the Second World War.

6 5 December is St Nicholas' Day in Holland.

7 30 April is Children's Day in Mexico.

8 9 July is Independence Day in Argentina.

9 19 April is Bay of Pigs Day in Cuba.

Read these sentences to your partner. Do not show him/her your sentences:

1 19 March is St Joseph's Day in Spain.

2 7 June is Scandinavian Union Day in Norway, Sweden and Denmark.

3 21 March is Human Rights Day, a very important event in South Africa.

4 1 October is National Day in China.

5 25 January is Burns' Night, when people in Scotland remember a famous poet called Robert Burns.

6 17 March is St Patrick's Day, an important day in Ireland.

7 21 April is the Queen's Birthday in Great Britain.

8 12 October is Children's Day in Brazil.

9 1 March is National Day in South Korea.

Photocopiable © Pearson Education Limited 2005

That's the one!

Put the words in the correct order and match the sentences to sentences 1-12 above.

First sentences

1 My computer is old and doesn't work properly. ❏

2 Is she your sister? ❏

3 I don't like this house very much. ❏

4 That burger was delicious. ❏

5 These shoes are old and full of holes. ❏

6 *(In a shop)* These trousers are too small for me. ❏

7 Would you like one of these biscuits? ❏

8 Who are Mr and Mrs Jones? ❏

9 Which shop do you buy your shoes from? ❏

10 Is he your brother? ❏

11 Who's Anna? ❏

12 Who's John? ❏

Second sentences

a you/don't/Why/some/ones/buy/new/?_____

b one/another/like/you/Would/?_____

c size/blue/be/ones/might/The/the/for/you/right/._____

d and/,/the/No/short/the/glasses/with/brother/one/is/beard/./my_____

e at/want/thank/you/,/one/No/don't/moment/the/I._____

f baby/the/the/The/dog/and/with/./ones_____

g the/with/the/one/He's/long/hair/tall/._____

h one/with/short/the/the/skin/fair/She's/._____

i the/think/,/but/I/the/is/No/with/pool/one/swimming/nice/._____

j with/eyes/No/,/the/the/blue/my/pretty/is/./sister/one_____

k McDonald's/town/next/to/one/The/in/square/the/._____

l don't/new/buy/Why/a/you/?/one_____

© Pearson Education Limited 2005 Photocopiable

Pronouns and adjectives crossword

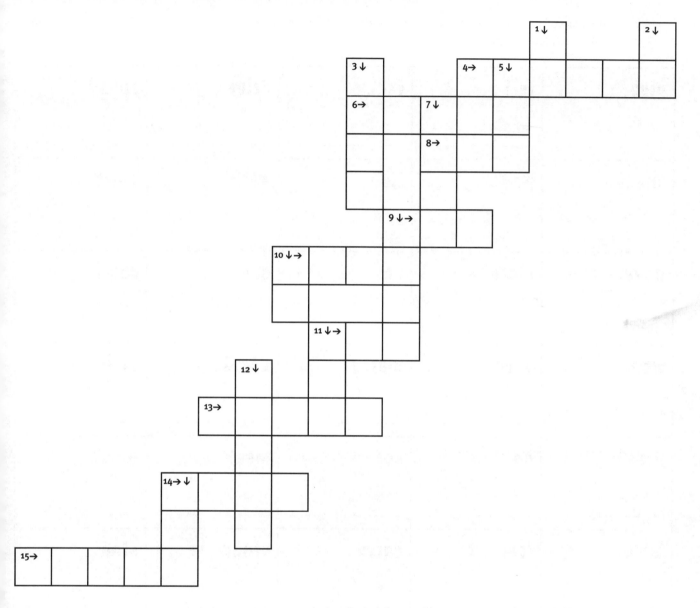

Student A

Across →

4 This car belongs to Jim and Grace; it's **they**.

6 Did Ken go to the party? I didn't see **he**.

8 The hotel we stayed in had **it** own pool and casino.

9 Are these **she** shoes?

10 Last night I visited some friends of **I**.

11 Whose umbrella is this? Is it **he**?

13 Is she a friend of **you**?

14 Please return the ball; it's **we**.

15 They can't come out because **they** son is ill.

Student B

Down ↓

1 She showed **I** her stamp collection.

2 Our teachers always gives **we** lots of homework.

3 Mark and Heidi are my best friends. I see **they** every day.

5 These are **he** keys.

7 This phone belongs to me. It's **I**.

9 Give the money to Jane; it's **she**.

10 Where is **I** mobile phone?

11 I don't like **she** very much.

12 This isn't my money, it's **you**.

14 We really enjoyed **we** last holiday.

Photocopiable   © Pearson Education Limited 2005

Past tense connections

Try to get four squares in a row, horizontally (← →), vertically (↑ ↓) or diagonally (↗ ↖ ↙ ↘). Try to stop the other team getting four squares in a row.

give	tell	feel	drive	spend
change	write	live	work	start
understand	close	be	buy	come
want	open	marry	decide	visit
die	go	see	meet	put
have	look	carry	study	stop
plan	eat	make	own	speak
produce	take	worry	leave	move
finish	jog	keep	pick	think

© Pearson Education Limited 2005 Photocopiable

The usual suspects

Students 1 and 2

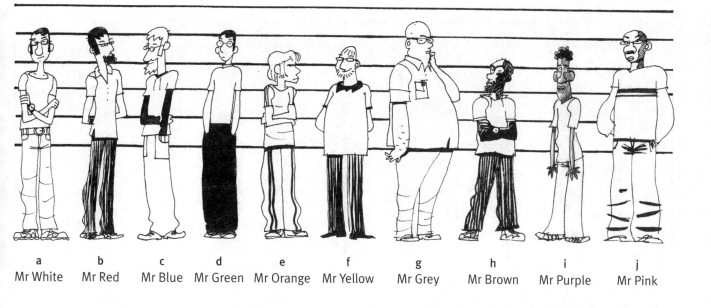

a	b	c	d	e	f	g	h	i	j
Mr White	Mr Red	Mr Blue	Mr Green	Mr Orange	Mr Yellow	Mr Grey	Mr Brown	Mr Purple	Mr Pink

Students 3 and 4

Mr White	Mr Red	Mr Blue	Mr Green	Mr Orange
Mr Yellow	Mr Grey	Mr Brown	Mr Purple	Mr Pink

Photocopiable © Pearson Education Limited 2005

Match them up.

Student 1
Do not show this to your partner.

1	2	3	4
5	6	7	8
9	10	11	12

✂ -

Student 2
Do not show this to your partner.

A	B	C	D
E	F	G	H
I	J	K	L

© Pearson Education Limited 2005   Photocopiable

I always ...

Write *two* **things that you** *always, usually, often, sometimes, hardly ever* **and** *never* <u>are</u> **and** <u>do</u>.

For example:

• I am always on time for my English lessons.

• I always see my friends at the weekend.

• I am never bored.

• I never smoke.

Your name: _____

1 I am always _____ .

I always _____ .

2 I am usually _____ .

I usually _____ .

3 I am often _____ .

I often _____ .

4 I am sometimes _____ .

I sometimes _____ .

5 I am hardly ever _____ .

I hardly ever _____ .

6 I am never _____ .

I never _____ .

Photocopiable © Pearson Education Limited 2005

Twenty verbs

Part 1

Find 20 verbs in the box.

➡	D	R	I	V	E	C	R	Y	W	A	L	K	C	U	T	L	↴
↩	T	A	W	K	N	I	R	D	Y	A	L	P	H	G	U	A	↵
↳	C	H	W	A	S	H	C	Y	C	L	E	J	O	G	R	E	➡
↩	L	A	T	B	M	I	L	C	T	A	E	G	I	D	D	A	↵
↓	K	C	O	O	K	S	H	O	U	T	S	K	I	L	I	S	➡
														N	E	T	↵

Part 2

Use the verbs to complete these sentences. Make the first part *negative*, and the second part *positive*. You need to change the form of the verbs in the box, and add some other words.

1 She _____ because she's happy, she _____ because she's happy.

2 I _____ television, I _____ the newspaper.

3 They _____ biscuits, they _____ coffee.

4 He _____ quietly, he _____ loudly.

5 We _____ in the Swiss mountains, we _____ mountains in the Himalayas.

6 I _____ the piano, I _____ to the radio.

7 They _____ slowly to the shops, they _____ quickly in the park.

8 He _____ our dinner, he _____ the dirty cups and plates.

9 We _____ in our new car, we _____ on our old bicycles.

10 I _____ the garden, I _____ the grass.

© Pearson Education Limited 2005 Photocopiable

Find the secret adverb.

Use the clues to complete the crossword.

1   Good night. I hope you sleep _____ .

2   He plays his music _____ at night, and keeps everyone awake.

3   He drives _____ and always has accidents.

4   We sat _____ on the cold, hard seats and waited for the train to arrive.

5   She sings _____ , but thinks she has a beautiful singing voice.

6   Don't eat so _____ ! Slow down!

7   She always speaks very _____ , and nobody can hear what she says.

8   She looked at him _____ , and then started to cry.

Write your answers here.

1					

2						

(crossword grid for rows 1–8)

Use the letters in the shaded boxes to make an adverb to complete this sentence.

The bus stopped _____ , and we all fell off our seats.

Photocopiable © Pearson Education Limited 2005

Where are they?

✂ -

© Pearson Education Limited 2005 Photocopiable

No numbers or clues crossword

Arrange the letters to make words and complete the puzzle.

yetrpo	liltehrr	apyl
oncrtoa	evnlo	paeor
lusiamc	modecy	nctioa milf
atuleeirtr	eaminc	talble
ascclsila sumci	krco isucm	neceisc otiincf *(film)*

Photocopiable © Pearson Education Limited 2005

Comparative bingo

It's busier today than yesterday.	She's funnier than him.	It was more exciting than this one.
He was faster than me.	My results were worse than yours.	She's shorter than me.
Mine is more modern than yours.	Yours was more expensive than mine.	It's more detailed and more interesting.

✂ -

My results were worse than yours.	She's funnier than him.	She's shorter than me.
He's more serious than me.	She's taller than me.	He was faster than me.
It's more detailed and more interesting.	It was more exciting than this one.	Mine is more modern than yours.

✂ -

I'm a year older than you.	Yours was better than mine.	Mine was cheaper than yours.
He was faster than me.	Yours was more expensive than mine.	It's busier today than yesterday.
Mine is more modern than yours.	It's more comfortable.	My results were worse than yours.

✂ -

Mine is more modern than yours.	Yours was better than mine.	He was faster than me.
She's funnier than him.	I'm a year older than you.	She's taller than me.
It's more detailed and more interesting.	Yours is more popular than mine.	Yours was more expensive than mine.

✂ -

He's fatter than me.	Yours was more expensive than mine.	I'm a year older than you.
Yours was better than mine.	It's busier today than yesterday.	She's taller than me.
My results were worse than yours.	She's funnier than him.	It was more exciting than this one.

✂ -

It's more comfortable	Yours was better than mine.	She's funnier than him.
She's shorter than me.	Mine was cheaper than yours.	He's fatter than me.
It's more detailed and more interesting.	Yours is more popular than mine.	My results were worse than yours.

© Pearson Education Limited 2005 Photocopiable

Superlative word search

Find 18 verbs.

A	H	O	T	B	C	D	E	F	Y	N	N	U	F	I	U
J	T	S	A	F	K	L	M	N	O	P	Q	R	S	T	N
U	V	U	D	W	X	Y	F	D	A	B	C	T	D	R	U
E	F	O	G	R	O	M	A	N	T	I	C	N	H	I	S
E	A	R	L	Y	I	J	M	K	L	P	A	E	H	C	U
M	N	E	O	D	Q	R	O	B	U	S	Y	L	S	H	A
T	U	G	O	O	D	V	U	W	X	Y	Z	O	A	B	L
C	I	N	T	E	R	E	S	T	I	N	G	I	D	E	F
B	E	A	U	T	I	F	U	L	G	H	I	V	J	K	L
M	N	D	O	P	E	L	B	A	T	R	O	F	M	O	C

Put the verbs in the sentences in the superlative form.

1 This film is really good. In fact, it's probably
(g) _____ film of the last ten years.

2 Almost 50 million people use Heathrow Airport in
London every year. It's (b) _____ airport in the
world.

3 He's a really bad teacher. I think he's (b) _____
teacher in the school!

4 He always has good stories to tell us. He's
(i) _____ person I know.

5 Everybody knows him. He's (f) _____ actor
in the world.

6 In this film, over 200 people are killed. It's
(v) _____ film for years.

7 This computer cost me £200. It was (c) _____
computer in the shop.

8 For my last birthday, my boyfriend took me to Venice.
He's (r) _____ person I know.

9 I slept really well last night. This bed is probably (c)
_____ bed I have ever slept on.

10 Bill Gates, the owner of Microsoft, makes many
millions of dollars every year. He's probably
(r) _____ man in the world.

11 Concorde was a passenger aircraft which could fly
from London to New York in 3 hours. It was
(f) _____ airliner in the world.

12 My grandmother's 98 years old. She's (o) _____
person I know.

13 He always makes me laugh. He's (f) _____ man
I know.

14 In the eastern Sahara Desert, temperatures can go
over 50°C. It's (h) _____ place in the world.

Photocopiable © Pearson Education Limited 2005

Spontaneous decision dominoes

meet	drive	eat	get	go	help
open	phone	put	see	send	tell

START (→)

A I feel really ill

B I'll ____ the doctor.

A Goodbye. Take care.

B See you. I'll ____ you when I get home.

A I'm quite hungry.

B OK, I'll ____ you a sandwich.

A I'm really thirsty.

B I'll ____ you a glass of water.

A It's really hot in here.

B I'll ____ a window.

A Have a good holiday.

B Thanks. I'll ____ you a postcard.

A It's really cold in here.

B I'll ____ the heating on.

A I've made you a cake.

B It looks delicious. I'll ____ it later.

A I forgot to ask Alison to our party.

B It's all right, I'll ____ her now. What's her number?

A This homework is very difficult.

B Don't worry, I'll ____ you with it.

A Do you have any plans for the weekend?

B Not really, but I think I'll ____ to that new art gallery.

A My train leaves in ten minutes

B My car's outside. I'll ____ you home.

A These boxes are heavy. I can't move them.

B Don't worry. I'll ____ you with them.

A There's someone at the door.

B Stay there. I'll ____ who it is.

A (On the phone) It's Bernadette here. Is Maria there?

B I'm sorry, she isn't. I'll ____ her you called.

A Let's go to the cinema tonight.

B Good idea. I'll ____ you there at half past six.

A Is John at home today?

B I don't know. I'll ____ him.

FINISH (☺)

© Pearson Education Limited 2005 Photocopiable

A weekend away

Where to stay

Things to do in the afternoon

An early dinner

Things to do in the evening

Things to do at night

Photocopiable   © Pearson Education Limited 2005

Travel quiz

1 Arrange the letters in bold to make words, and match them with the pictures.

an **tcaytiiv** holiday ——

a **eshtesigngi** holiday ——

a **tawre osrstp** holiday ——

a **nitrew topssr** holiday ——

a **haebc** holiday ——

a **rcluulat** holiday ——

Score ☐

2 True or false? The cheapest way to fly is in *business class*.

_____ Score ☐

3 A flight from London to Paris is called a *short-haul* flight. What is a flight from London to San Francisco called?

_____ Score ☐

4 You are on a flight from Singapore to Frankfurt. Your flight stops in Dubai, but you do *not* change aeroplanes here. What do we call this sort of flight?

(a) a non-stop flight (b) a direct flight

(c) an immediate flight (d) a straight flight

_____ Score ☐

5 Complete the gaps in this paragraph about railway travel. *One* word is used *twice*.

Two weeks ago I took a (a) _____ from London to Edinburgh. It went from King's Cross (b) _____. I bought a (c) _____ ticket because I wanted to come back to London a week later. My (d) _____ went from (e) _____ 14 at half past two. It was very busy because there were lots of (f) _____. The (g) _____ took 4 hours. When I returned to London a week later, I took the (h) _____ from King's Cross to my house three kilometres away.

Score ☐

6 Look at this price list for a hotel. The words in bold are wrong. Correct them:

HOTEL ROOM TARIFF	
Simple (1 bed for 1 person)	£45
Dribble (1 large bed for 2 people)	£75
Trim (2 beds for 2 people)	£80
Sweet (1 large bed, living room and bathroom for 2 people)	£120

Score ☐

7 The hotel you want to stay at has these facilities. What do you think they are?

a _____ b _____ c _____

d _____ e _____ f _____

g _____ h _____

Score ☐

TOTAL POINTS SCORED: ☐

© Pearson Education Limited 2005 Photocopiable

Have you ever ...?

A Have you ever been to Italy?	**B** Yes, I have. I went to Tuscany last year with my family and we had a wonderful time.	**C** We visited all the historical sites, and ate lots of delicious pizza and ice cream.
A Have you ever been to a classical concert?	**B** Yes, I have. Two years ago I went to see the New York Symphony Orchestra at Carnegie Hall in New York.	**C** I thought it was a bit boring because I prefer rock music.
A Have you ever been to a rock concert	**B** Yes, I have. Last month I went to see my favourite band, The Hives, in London.	**C** They were really good, and they played all the songs from their latest album.
A Have you ever been to the theatre?	**B** Yes, I have. About three years ago I saw Shakespeare's *Romeo and Juliet* with my sister.	**C** I enjoyed it a lot, and thought the actors were really good.
A Have you ever been to a circus?	**B** Yes, I have. Last year I went to see the Moscow State Circus in Bristol.	**C** I didn't enjoy it because I don't like people making animals entertain an audience.
A Have you ever been to an art gallery?	**B** Yes, I have. I went to the Louvre in Paris with my school two months ago.	**C** It was wonderful and I really liked the impressionist paintings.
A Have you ever been to the USA?	**B** Yes, I have. Three years ago my girlfriend and I went to Los Angeles.	**C** I didn't like it because it was very noisy, there was lots of traffic and everybody spoke English very quickly.
A Have you ever been to a beach?	**B** Yes, I have. Last year I went to Copacabana in Brazil.	**C** I went swimming in the sea, played lots of volleyball and got a beautiful suntan.
A Have you ever been on an aeroplane?	**B** Yes, I have. On my last holiday I flew to Crete with my friends.	**C** The flight was late, there was a terrible storm and all the passengers were sick.
A Have you ever been on a motorbike?	**B** Yes, I have. My brother bought a Harley Davidson last year.	**C** He took me for a ride through the rush hour traffic in Manchester and I loved it!

Photocopiable © Pearson Education Limited 2005

The whole truth

Part 1

Write eight things that you *have* or *have never* done in your life. Some of them must be true, and some of them must be false.

Use the verbs below and any others that you think are useful. Make sure you use the correct form of the verb.

> be   do   eat   have   meet   play   see   take   visit

1 _____

2 _____

3 _____

4 _____

5 _____

6 _____

7 _____

8 _____

Part 2

TRUE	**FALSE**

© Pearson Education Limited 2005   Photocopiable

Communicative crossword

Part 1

camp	commute	drink	drive	eat	fly	go	hike
park	phone	play	stay	swim	take	wait	

Students 1 and 2

Student 3

Clues →

3 _____ your car in Oxford is very expensive.

4 _____ lots of water every day is good for your health.

6 _____ for people who are late makes me angry.

7 _____ by train from my home to the city is slow and boring.

11 _____ is the best way of seeing the countryside.

12 _____ football is better than watching it on television.

13 _____ your friends in the evening is cheaper than doing it in the day.

14 _____ first class on an airline is comfortable but very expensive.

Clues ↓

1 _____ my brother's sports car was the most exciting thing I have ever done.

2 _____ fast food every day is very bad for your health.

5 _____ is a very good way of keeping fit and healthy.

7 _____ is cheap, but not very comfortable.

8 _____ the bus is faster than walking.

9 _____ on holiday with your friends is lots of fun.

10 _____ at home every evening is really boring.

Photocopiable © Pearson Education Limited 2005

The perfect holiday

1 What is your favourite kind of holiday (Choose 1 only.)

2 What kind of hotel room do you want? (Choose 1 only.)

 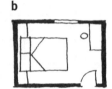  

3 What facilities do you want in your room? (Choose 5 only.)

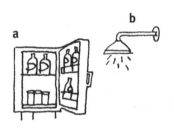   

4 What facilities do you want in your hotel? (Choose 4 only.)

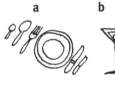  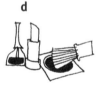  

5 How do you want to get there? (Choose 1 only.)

6 When do you want to go? (Choose 1 only.)

Between 01/01 and 31/03	Between 01/04 and 30/06	Between 01/07 and 30/09	Between 01/10 and 31/12

7 How much money do you have for your holiday? (Choose 1 only.)

Under £500	£500–£600	£601–£800	£801–£1,000	£1,001–£1,200	Over £1,200

© Pearson Education Limited 2005   Photocopiable

Find the hidden expression.

Use the clues to complete the puzzle.

1   Jamie's only four years old, so he goes to _____ .

2   She enjoys learning about living things. _____ is her favourite subject.

3   You have to come to all your lessons. They're _____ .

4   His English classes are twice a week in the evening. It's a _____ course.

5   French and German are my favourite subjects. I love learning _____ .

6   You don't have to come to afternoon classes. They're _____ .

7   At the end of the English course, everybody gets a _____ .

8   She's at university, studying for a _____ in Business.

9   Your English classes are from 9 o'clock to 3 o'clock Monday to Friday. It's a _____ course.

10   Mr Langsdale teaches at Manchester University. He's a _____ in History.

11   Mrs Bevan shows people how to teach. She's a teacher _____ .

12   Between the ages of 5 and 11, British children go to _____ school.

13   Between the ages of 11 and 16, British children go to _____ school.

14   On this course, we are learning how to use computers. It's a _____ course.

15   Sam is learning how to teach. He's a _____ teacher.

16   _____ is my favourite subject at school. I love learning about people and places.

Use the expression in the shaded squares to complete this sentence:

There are no colleges near my home, so I did a _____ _____ course using my computer and the Internet.

Photocopiable   © Pearson Education Limited 2005

Company rules

1 Work begins at 8.30 everyday, so you …	… don't have to …	… eat in the company restaurant.
2 The coffee machine is free, so you …	… don't have to …	… wear a suit.
3 Everybody has one hour for lunch, so you …	… can't …	… get one before you use it.
4 Everybody has a personal code for the photocopier, so you …	… have to …	… use it without her permission.
5 It's very important to ask your boss for permission to go home early, so you …	… can't …	… make personal calls inside the building.
6 There are lots of restaurants and sandwich bars near the office, so you …	… have to …	… make a noise outside his door.
7 The company restaurant is open all day, so you …	… don't have to …	… go outside for a cigarette.
8 Mrs Clark is the only person who can use the fax machine, so you …	… have to …	… pay for hot drinks.
9 It's very important to be quiet when you go near Mr Mansell's office, so you … QUIET	… can't …	… be back in the office by 2 o'clock.
10 Everybody wears informal clothes here, so you …	… can …	… get something to eat without leaving the building.
11 This company has a no smoking policy, so you …	… can …	… be here on time every morning.
12 Please turn off your mobile phone, because you …	… can't …	… leave early without asking her.

© Pearson Education Limited 2005   Photocopiable

Question and answer links

Student 1

Do not show your paper to your partner.

1 **Your first question** → Which do you prefer, Chinese food or Indian food?

2 **Answer** → At the station.
Your next question → How long does the flight take?

3 **Answer** → Her boyfriend has just left her.
Your next question → What do you do on Saturday night?

4 **Answer** → I'm watching television.
Your next question → How much rice have we got?

5 **Answer** → They're Judy and Don, my neighbours.
Your next question → How are you?

6 **Answer** → She's just heard a very funny story.
Your next question → How many eggs have we got?

7 **Answer** → We have an apartment near the station.
Your next question → When's our English exam?

8 **Answer** → It's £120.

9 **Answer** → I'm Roger, your new English teacher.
Your next question → Whose keys are these?

10 **Answer** → Oh, that's Andy, my best friend.
Your next question → How long does the exam last?

11 **Answer** → My parents, but sometimes my friends.
Your final question → Where do you go for your holiday?

12 **Answer** → Somebody has just taken all his money.
Your next question → What do you do?

13 **Answer** → Last Thursday morning.
Your next question → What's Eddie doing?

14 **Answer** → It's not mine. I think it's Tony's.
Your next question → Which subjects do you like the most at school?

Student 2

Do not show your paper to your partner.

a **Answer** → I'm a student at a language school.
Your next question → Who's that man over there?

b **Answer** → There are six in the fridge.
Your next question → When did you take your English exam?

c **Answer** → His homework. Don't interrupt him.
Your next question → Where do you live?

d **Answer** → They're not mine. Maybe they're John's.
Your next question → Why is he so angry?

e **Your first answer** → I like them both.
Your question → Who are they over there?

f **Answer** → We usually go to Spain.
Your final question → How much is this mobile phone?

g **Answer** → The first paper is 2 hours and the second paper is 1 1/2 hours.
Your next question → What are you doing?

h **Answer** → I usually go to the cinema.
Your next question → Whose pen is this?

i **Answer** → Next Thursday morning.
Your next question → Why is she crying?

j **Answer** → There's a small packet in the kitchen cupboard.
Your next question → Who do you go on holiday with?

k **Answer** → I'm very well, thank you.
Your next question → Where are you?

l **Answer** → Chemistry, History and Mathematics.
Your next question → Who are you?

m **Answer** → About 15 hours, with a stop in Singapore.
Your next question → Why is she laughing?

Photocopiable © Pearson Education Limited 2005

A busy Saturday

Part 1

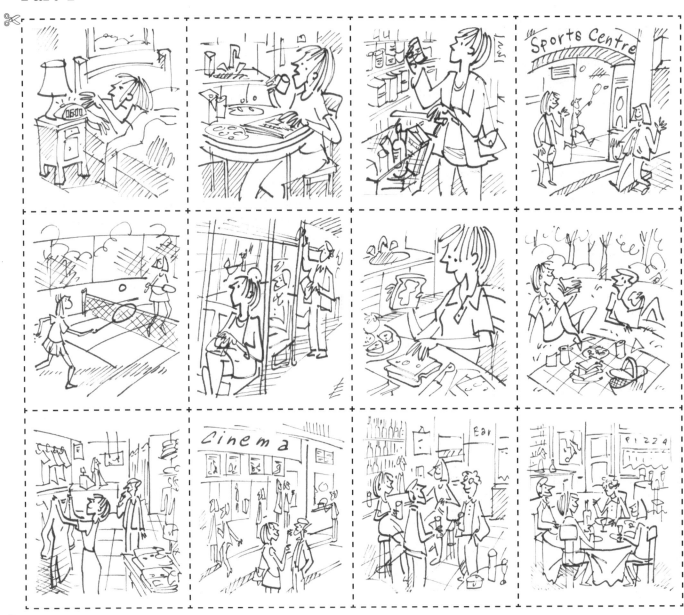

Part 2

Complete this text.

Samantha is a very busy person. This Saturday is a good example. She has a lot to do, so _ _ _'_ _ _ _ _ _ _ _ _ _ early, at _ _ _ o'clock. _ _ _ _' _ _ _ _ _ _ breakfast and then _ _ _' _ _ _ _ _ to the _ _ _ _ _ _ _ _ _ _ _. She likes getting there early, because it's much quieter than it is later in the day. At nine o'clock _ _ _' _ _ _ _ _ _ _ her friend Jo at the _ _ _ _ _ _ centre, and _ _ _ _'_ _ _ _ _ _ _ _ _ _ _ _ _ _. They always do this on Saturday. After that, _ _ _' _ _ _ _ _ _ the _ _ _ home and _ _ _ _ _ _ some _ _ _ _ _ _ _ _ _ _ and a salad, because at twelve o'clock _ _ _' _ _ _ _ _ _ a picnic lunch with her _ _ _ _ _ _ _ _ _ Rob in the park. Then _ _ _ _'_ _ _ _ _ _ some shopping in town because she wants a new _ _ _ _ _ and Rob needs a new jacket. After that _ _ _ _'_ _ _ _ _ _ _ a new film at the _ _ _ _ _ _. In the evening _ _ _ _'_ _ _ _ _ _ _ _ a _ _ _ _ _ in a local bar with Samantha's brother Mick and his wife, and then _ _ _ _'_ _ all _ _ _ _ _ _ at a new Italian _ _ _ _ _ _ _ _ _ _ near her house.

© Pearson Education Limited 2005 — Photocopiable

Making excuses

Student 1

You want to ask Student 2 out, but he/she doesn't want to go with you! Ask him/her to do the following things. Listen to his/her excuses and write the days of the week under the pictures.

Monday: cinema	Tuesday: restaurant	Wednesday: shopping
Thursday: nightclub	Friday: a drink	Saturday: a walk
Sunday: volleyball		

Student 2

Student 1 wants to ask you out, but you don't want to go out with him/her. Look at the pictures below, and use them to help you make an excuse. Be polite!

Monday Tuesday Wednesday Thursday

Friday Saturday Sunday

Photocopiable © Pearson Education Limited 2005

Order the activities.

Arrange the letters in bold and match the sentences to the pictures.

a The week after next I'm going to go **noaumnti gnlicbim**.
_____

b Next month I'm going to go **aykiknga**.
_____

c Next week I'm going to go **eihwt eartw narfgit**.
_____

d Tomorrow I'm going to go **gikins**.
_____

e In two years' time I'm going to go **nciclgy**.
_____

f Later this year I'm going to go **esorh-igirnd**.
_____

g Two days from now I'm going to go **gilsain**.
_____

h This afternoon, I'm going to go **nregktki**.
_____

i Two months from now I'm going to go **onauntim giibnk**.
_____

j Tonight I'm going to go **ngvridi**.
_____

© Pearson Education Limited 2005 Photocopiable

Plans and intentions

1 Have you told your girlfriend you don't want to go out with her again?

2 Have you got any plans for your holiday?

a university/study/They/at/them/.

_____

10 Adam and Liz haven't got enough money to come out tonight.

b I/train/Europe/around/by/travel/.

_____

3 What are Sarah's plans when she finishes her exams?

c wear/you/What/?

_____

d early/have/night/tonight/I/an/.

_____

e Liverpool/visit/They/friends/their/ in/.

_____

4 Peter and Colin have always been interested in languages.

9 Richard's having a party tonight and he's invited me.

f evening/stay/and/home/at/They/ watch/this/television/.

_____

g her/I/tonight/tell/No/,/.

_____

8 It's Erica's birthday next week, and I want to buy her a present.

h university/go/she/to/.

_____

i tonight/I/we/know/,/it/see/.

_____

5 There's a good film on at the cinema in town.

j her/?/get/you/What

_____

7 What are Bill and Claire doing this weekend?

6 You look really tired.

Photocopiable © Pearson Education Limited 2005

This weekend

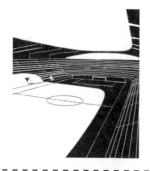

© Pearson Education Limited 2005 Photocopiable

I would like ...

Your name: _____

Use these expressions in your sentences:

| I would like to | I would love to | I wouldn't like to | I would hate to | I like |
| I love | I enjoy | I don't like | I hate | I can't stand |

1 A place or country you would like to visit.
(Example: *I would love to go to India because I enjoy eating spicy food.*)

I _____

because I _____ .

2 A job you would like to have.
(Example: *I would like to be a doctor because I like taking care of people.*)

I _____

because I _____ .

3 An activity you would like to do.
(Example: *I would love to climb a mountain because I enjoy doing dangerous things.*)

I _____

because I _____ .

4 A place or country you *wouldn't* like to visit, a job you *wouldn't* like to have or an activity you *wouldn't* like to do.
(Example: *I would hate to go to an art gallery because I don't like looking at paintings.*)

I _____

because I _____ .

Photocopiable © Pearson Education Limited 2005

Outside the classroom

Buy an English-English dictionary and use it to help you find out what new words and expressions mean.

Buy a book of grammar-practice activities and try to do one or two every day.

Buy a book of vocabulary-practice activities and try to do one every day.

Listen to English songs and write down the words you hear. Try to sing the songs.

Listen to interesting radio programmes on English-language radio stations.

Watch English-language videos or television programmes, and write down words that you hear.

Start an 'English Club' with other students in your school, and meet every week to speak English, watch English films, etc.

Write down new words and expressions in a notebook, carry it with you, and look at it when you have some free time (for example, on the bus).

Try to use new words and grammar you learn in your spoken and written English.

Get an English-speaking penfriend. There are lots of websites where you can find one.

Write to people in an Internet chat-room.

Find interesting English-language websites on the Internet, and read them.

Use a tape-recorder to record yourself speaking or reading. Then listen to yourself speaking.

Find out if there are English-speaking clubs or groups near your home.

Buy or borrow English newspapers and magazines. Find stories or articles that are interested in, and read them (with a dictionary to help you).

Buy or borrow graded readers, and try to read a few pages every day.

(In an English-speaking country): Join a local club (for example a sports club, or one where people have the same hobbies) and speak to the people there.

(In an English-speaking country): Go shopping and practise your English on the shop assistants.

(In an English-speaking country): Look at posters, advertisements, notices, etc., in shops, public buildings and in the street, and try to understand what they mean.

(In an English-speaking country): Go to museums, art galleries, historical buildings and other places of interest.

© Pearson Education Limited 2005 Photocopiable

UNIT 1 Vocabulary
Family tree

• Use this activity after Lesson 1.2 Ex. 6b on page 9.

Procedure

Ss work in pairs. Give each pair a copy of Part 1 (the family tree).

Tell Ss that they are going to hear a description of a family. They are going to hear the names of the different people in the box, and their ages.

Explain that they will hear the description three times. The first time, they just listen. The second time, they try to complete the family tree with the missing information. The third time, they add any information that they still don't have.

Read the script below, three times, at normal speed. The second and third time you read it, pause briefly between each sentence.

I'd like to tell you a bit about my family. My name is John, I'm 35 years old and I'm married to, Clarissa. She's 33. Our two children are Sally and Joseph. Sally is 6 and Joseph is 4. My brother is Robert and he's 38. His wife is Valerie, and she's 33. Their two children are Ian – he's 13 – and Martha – she's 12. My parents are called Mark and Susan. My father is 68 and my mother is 67. My grandparents are very old now. My grandfather, Peter, is 92. My grandmother, Julia, is 89. It's her birthday today.

Give Ss one or two minutes to discuss their answers, then give them Part 2. Tell them that they should use the information they wrote in their family tree to complete the sentences.

Go through their answers with them. You might find it helpful to draw the completed family on the board *before* you discuss the answers to Part 2.

Answers

Part 1: (numbers in brackets show the ages)   1 Peter (92)
2 Julia (89)   3 Mark (68)   4 Susan (67)   5 John (35)
6 Clarissa (33)   7 Robert (38)   8 Valerie (33)
9 Joseph (4)   10 Sally (6)   11 Ian (13)   12 Martha (12)

Part 2: 1 brother/brother-in-law   2 grandfather
3 aunt *or* auntie/uncle   4 niece/nephew   5 cousins
6 sister   7 father-in-law   8 mother-in-law
9 grandfather/grandmother   10 (c) 92 years old
11 Sally   12 Clarissa/Valerie

UNIT 1 Grammar 1
Sentence building

• Use this activity after Lesson 1.1 Ex. 7b on page 7.

Procedure

Ss work in small groups of three or four. Give each group a set of cards, and tell them to look at number 1 only. Ask them if Eduardo is a *man* or a *woman* (he is a man, as shown by the ♂ symbol). Ask them what word is missing (answer = *Brazilian*). They write this in the space on the card.

Tell them to turn card 1 over so they cannot see it, and do the same with number 2. Then turn number 2 over and do number 3.

Working in their groups, they then do the same for the other cards, using the name of the person, the male/female symbol (where relevant) and the city to help them complete the sentences. Each sentence becomes more difficult as words are removed and more blanks added.

The winning group is the group who has completed the most sentences, with the correct countries and nationalities, after ten minutes.

Answers

1 Brazilian   2 is Australian   3 She is British   4 He is Spanish.   5 Germany. We are German.   6 in Russia. They are Russian.   7 is in Italy. She is Italian.
8 Warsaw is in Poland. He is Polish.   9 Helsinki. Helsinki is in Finland. I am Finnish.   10 from Guangzhou. Guangzhou is in China. She is Chinese.   11 is from Kyoto. Kyoto is in Japan. He is Japanese.   12 My best friend and I are from Thessaloniki. Thessaloniki is in Greece. We are Greek.

UNIT 1 Grammar 2
Complete the crossword.

• Use this activity after Lesson 1.2 Ex. 7 on page 9.

Procedure

Ss work in pairs. Give each pair a copy of the activity.

Explain that in sentences 1–10, the words are mixed up. They must put the words into the correct order. In some cases, more than one order of words is possible.

In pairs, Ss rearrange their sentences, and complete their crossword with the pronoun in each sentence. The first pair in the class to finish is the winner.

Answers

1 Mike and Emma live in London, but their parents live in New York.   2 John is from Cambridge, and his phone number is 812825.   3 Maria is very beautiful. Is she married?   4 Alan speaks Greek. Is he from Greece?
5 I'm an English teacher, and my husband is an engineer.
6 Excuse me, is this your mobile phone?   7 My sister and I are French, but our parents are from Germany.
8 Dave and Hilary aren't teachers, but they work in

a school. **9** Clare is married, and <u>her</u> husband is Australian. **10** My brother and I aren't Spanish, but <u>our</u> home is in Spain.

UNIT 1 Grammar 3
Get it right!

• Use this activity after Lesson 1.3 Ex. 6 on page 11.

Procedure

Ss work in pairs. Give each pair a Student 1 and Student 2 paper. Tell them to cover up the answers at the bottom of their paper so their partner cannot see them.

Tell them that each question on their paper contains a mistake. They put their counter in the start box at the bottom then take it in turns to move their counters up the grid. They try to correct each sentence. Their partner has their answers, and tells them if they are correct (but does not give them the correct answer if they *are* wrong). If they are correct, they stay where they are until their next turn. If they are wrong, they move their counter back to the previous box, then try to correct the sentence again on their next turn. (They only need to find the corrections, they do not need to rewrite the sentences.)

The winning student is the first student to reach the finish box (i.e., the first student to correct all their sentences).

Answers

The Ss have their partner's answers at the bottom of their paper.

UNIT 1 Communication
My name is Harry Jones.

• Use this activity after Communication 1 Ex. 5b on page 12.

Procedure

Before you do this activity, you might like to pre-teach the expressions *Could you repeat that?* and *Could you spell that?*

Part 1

Divide the class into groups of three.

Give one student in each group a copy of the Part 1 Student 1 paper (the description of Harry Jones). He/she should not show this to the others in his/her group.

Give the other Ss in the group a copy of the Part 1 Students 2 and 3 paper.

Explain that the Ss with the Part 1 Students 2 and 3 paper need to complete the form with the correct information.

They do this by asking Student 1 questions (e.g., *What's your name?* etc.). They should make sure that spellings, numbers, etc. are correct, if necessary, by asking confirmation questions, e.g., *Could you repeat that?*

When they have done this, Student 1 should return his/her paper to you. In their groups, they look at the completed table and try to remember as much information as possible. Allow them about a minute for this.

Part 2

The groups return their completed tables to you. Give them a copy of the Part 2 paper.

Explain that the paper contains a lot of mistakes. Working in their groups, Ss try to correct as many of the mistakes as possible.

Answers

This is the correct information.

First name:	Harry
Surname:	Jones
Place of origin:	Australia
Nationality:	Australian
Age:	19
Marital status:	Single
Occupation:	University student
Address:	30 Martins Lane, Cambarnet, CT13 3BV
Phone number:	Home: 01723 875243 Mobile: 01729 053426
Email:	harry.jo@yahmail.com
Family:	Father: Ted Jones. Bank manager Mother: Mary Jones. Doctor.

UNIT 2 Vocabulary
Find the hidden words.

• Use this activity after Lesson 2.3 Ex. 6b on page 21.

Procedure

Before you begin the activity, you might need to pre-teach or concept-check some of the words in the sentences. Alternatively, Ss can use dictionaries to help them during the activity.

Divide the class into pairs or small groups and give each group a copy of the activity. Explain that sentences 1–7 can be completed with a colour, and sentences 8–16 can be completed with another adjective from the unit. They write the answers in the appropriate spaces in the grids. In some cases, more than one answer may be possible for the sentence, but only one can fit in the space in the grid.

If they do this correctly, they will reveal two hidden words in the shaded vertical strip. These words can be used to complete the sentence at the bottom of the activity.

Answers

1 silver   2 white   3 black   4 blue   5 pink   6 orange
7 green   8 bad   9 modern   10 old   11 big   12 nice
13 horrible   14 young   15 useful   16 useless

The sentence says: I think that <u>Italian</u> food is <u>delicious</u>.

UNIT 2 Grammar 1
Can you remember?

• Use this activity after Lesson 2.1 Ex. 4 on page 17.

Procedure

Ss work in small groups of three or four. Give each group a set of cards. Ask them to look at the pictures, and tell one another what the woman is doing in each (they can use the Present Simple for this, e.g., *She goes to bed*).

Tell them to turn the cards over so that they cannot see the pictures. Explain that you are going to read them a short text, and they must try to remember as much information as possible (they can make notes).

Read the text below. Read it three times. The first time, read it through once with pauses after each sentence. You will need to read it out a second and third time, too.

> I get up at 6 o'clock, and at quarter past six I have breakfast. At half past six I have a shower, and then I leave home at 7 o'clock. I walk to the bus stop, and at ten past seven I take the bus to work. I get to my office at quarter to eight and I start work at eight o'clock. At ten o'clock, I have a break, and I start work again at half past ten. At quarter past twelve I have lunch. After lunch, at quarter past one, I meet my boss, and then at half past two I finish work and leave the office. I get home at quarter past three, and at 4 o'clock I play tennis with my friends. At quarter past six I watch the news on television, and at quarter to seven I eat dinner. After dinner, at about half past eight, I meet my friends for a drink. I go to bed at about 11 o'clock.

Tell Ss to turn their cards over. Using the information they heard, they try to write the correct times for each activity on the picture cards. They must also put the times in the correct order.

Answers

The pictures are in the correct order on the activity page.

UNIT 2 Grammar 2
Three in a row

• Use this activity after Lesson 2.2 Ex. 5 on page 19.

Procedure

Most Ss are familiar with the game of noughts and crosses (tic-tac-toe), but before you do the activity you could illustrate/play a quick game on the board.

Ss work in pairs. Give each pair a copy of the activity.

Tell them that they are going to play two games of noughts and crosses with each other. They need to get three squares in a row, horizontally, vertically or diagonally. To do this, they choose a square, look at the sentence, and decide which verb in the box at the top can be used to complete the sentence. They write the verb in the box, making sure that their spelling is correct. Some verbs can be used more than once.

Ss play the games. When they have played both games, they check their answers with you. If their answers are correct, and they were the first in their pair to get three squares in a row, they are the winner.

Answers

Game 1:   1 lives/works   2 sleeps   3 washes/cleans
4 organises   5 watches   6 starts   7 talks   8 likes
9 walks

Game 2:   1 goes   2 helps   3 invents   4 has
5 cleans (*not* washes)   6 works   7 plays   8 feeds
9 makes

UNIT 2 Grammar 3
Plurals crossword

• Use this activity after Lesson 2.3 Ex. 8c on page 21.

Procedure

Ss work in pairs. Give each pair a copy of the activity.

Ask Ss to look at sentence 1 across. Tell them that the letters in **bold** can be rearranged to make a word. What do they think this word is? (Give them a clue: it is a member of the family). When they identify the word *niece*, ask them what they must do to the word to make it fit in the sentence (i.e., they must make it plural – *nieces*). They write this word on the crossword grid.

Working in pairs, Ss then try to complete the rest of the crossword, making words out of the jumbled letters, and then making these words plural.

Answers

Across: 1 nieces   6 diaries   8 dictionaries   12 women
13 men   14 sandwiches   15 dishes   17 parties
18 wives   19 holidays

Down: 2 children 3 buses 4 pictures 5 cities
7 scarves 9 addresses 10 families 11 watches
16 hotels 17 people

UNIT 2 | Communication
Question and answer

• Use this activity after Communication 2 Ex. 4b on page 22.

Procedure

Ss work in pairs. Give each pair a copy of the activity. Ask them to work together to complete questions 1–25 with an appropriate question word from the box.

Feedback their answers, then give them one minute to look at the questions and try to remember as many of them as possible.

Tell them to turn their paper over so that they cannot see it. Ask student pairs to interview each other, asking and answering as many questions as they can remember from the activity. They write their answers on a separate sheet of paper.

Allow them about 10–15 minutes for this, then ask them to tell the rest of the class about their partner, using the third person singular (*His name is ...*, *He lives in ...*, *he comes to school by ...*, etc.). If the class is quite large, spread this over a few lessons.

Answers to Part 1

1 what 2 what 3 what 4 what 5 what 6 where
7 who 8 what/how 9 how 10 do 11 what
12 how/when 13 what 14 what 15 when 16 are
17 do 18 do 19 do 20 do 21 do 22 where
23 what 24 who 25 what

UNIT 3 | Vocabulary
Write the right number.

• Use this activity after Lesson 3.3 Ex. 9b on page 31.

Procedure

Ss work in pairs. Give each pair a Student 1 and Student 2 paper. They should not show these to each other.

Tell them to *read* the numbers to their partner, who writes down the numbers that they hear. Sometimes these numbers are telephone numbers and sometimes they are times (shown by the symbols). Monitor the pairs to make sure they are not showing their papers to each other.

When they have read, listened to and written down all the numbers, they compare the numbers they have written with the numbers that were read to them. If they are all correct, and they are the first pair to finish, then they are the winner.

UNIT 3 | Grammar 1
Negative matching

• Use this activity after Lesson 3.1 Ex. 4b on page 26.

Procedure

Before you do this activity, you might need to pre-teach the meaning of *so*.

Ss work in small groups of four. Give each group a copy of the cards. They spread these on the desk in front of them so that they can see all of the cards.

Ask them to read all of the cards, and check the meanings of any words they don't know (either by asking one another, by asking you, or by looking in a dictionary).

Tell them to turn all the cards over so that they are face down. Give them a copy of the B sentences 1–20.

Explain that sentences 1–20 are the *first* part of a sentence, and the cards are the *second* part. Students take it in turns to choose a sentence from 1–20, and try to remember where the second part of the sentence is. They turn over the card that they think is the correct second part. If they are correct, they write their name next to the first part of the sentence. The card is then replaced face down.

Play the game for about ten minutes then review their answers. The winner is the student who made the most correct matches in that time.

Answers

The cards and the sentences are in the same order on the activity.

UNIT 3 | Grammar 2
Know your partner.

• Use this activity after Lesson 3.2 Ex. 6 page 29.

Procedure

Ss work in pairs. Give each student a copy of the activity.

Tell them to look at the pictures and accompanying text. The pictures illustrate the verbs and other words in the text, but you could go through these with Ss, checking how the words are pronounced, and making sure they understand what the words mean.

Ask them to think about their partner. Which of the skills and abilities on their paper do they think their partner has? For each picture, they circle yes or no.

When they have chosen all their answers, they go through each picture, saying either *You can ...* or *You can't ...* For each one, their partner answers. *That's true, I can/I can't ...* or *That's false, I can/I can't ...*

UNIT 3 | Grammar 3
Phone dictations

• Use this activity after Lesson 3.3 Ex. 3b on 30.

Procedure

Ss work in groups of four. Divide each group into pairs. Give each pair a 'Students 1 and 2', or 'Students 3 and 4' paper. They should not show these to the other pair.

Ss 1 and 2 read their phone conversation in the box to Ss 3 and 4. Ss 3 and 4 listen. Ss 3 and 4 then read their conversation to Ss 1 and 2, who listen.

Ss unfold their papers for the second time they read the conversations. Ss 1 and 2 then read their conversation two more times. This time, Ss 3 and 4 write down what they hear on the gapped text under their conversation. They then read their conversation two more times, while Ss 1 and 2 write down what they hear.

The first group in the class to complete both conversation 'dictations' successfully is the winner.

UNIT 3 | Communication
The ideal job for you!

• Use this activity after Communication 3 Ex. 3b on page 32.

Procedure

Ss work in pairs. Give each student a copy of the activity. Tell them to read through the questions and use a dictionary or ask you for the meanings of any words that they don't understand (alternatively, you could pre-teach and/or concept-check some of the more difficult or unusual vocabulary).

Tell Ss to ask each other the questions on the paper, ticking (✓) any that are true for their partner. Allow them about 5–10 minutes for this.

Ask Ss to find a new partner. With the new partner, they look at the qualities, skills, etc., that they ticked, and try to choose a job for their original partner.

When they have done this, they return to their original partner and tell them what they decided. Their partner can then say whether or not they would like the job that has been chosen for them.

UNIT 4 | Vocabulary
Food galore

• Use this activity after Unit 4 Lesson 2 Ex. 1b on page 38.

Procedure

Ss work in small groups of five or six. Ask each group to choose a referee. Ss should be able to sit in a group around a desk.

Give each group a set of cards, which they should place face-down on their desk. Give the referee a copy of the complete activity.

The aim of this activity is for Ss to take it in turns to look at the cards, say what they can see, and remember what they have seen. One student begins by taking a card, looking at the picture and saying what is there (e.g., *500 grammes of coffee*). The referee writes the number 1 next to the picture of the coffee on his/her sheet. The card is then placed face-down on the desk next to the original pile of cards. A second student repeats what the first student said, then takes the next card from the top of the pile, and says what is there (e.g., *2 pineapples*). The referee writes the number 2 next to the pineapples on his/her sheet. This is repeated around the group, each student remembering the articles that came before and then adding another one. A typical game might go something like this: Student 1: *500 grammes of coffee;* Student 2: *500 grammes of coffee and 2 pineapples;* Student 3: *500 grammes of coffee, 2 pineapples and one kilogramme of bread,* etc. While they are doing this, the referee checks his/her list to make sure that the foods/quantities mentioned are correct and said in the correct order. If a student makes a mistake, he/she drops out of the game. The winning student is the last student remaining.

The game can be repeated, with another student taking the referee's role (so that the referee gets a chance to play the game).

UNIT 4 | Grammar 1
My question, your answer

• Use this activity after Lesson 4.1 Ex. 4b on page 37.

Procedure

Ss work in pairs. Give the students in each pair a Student 1 or Student 2 paper. They must not show these to each other.

Explain that Student 1 has questions, and Student 2 has the answers to the questions. They must try to match the questions and answers without looking at each other's papers.

Student 1 begins by reading question 1 (*Do you have a car?*). Student 2 looks for the answer on his/her paper. When he/she finds it, he/she reads out the answer, they decide together if it is the correct answer, and Student 1 writes the letter of the answer (in this case, *j*) in the box.

The first pair to correctly match all the questions and answers is the winner.

Although students have not learnt *do you have* … (an American English alternative to *have you got* …) it is used to avoid exposing students to *have you got* … before it is introduced in the Students' Book (Unit 5).

Answers

1 j   2 m   3 p   4 n   5 i   6 k   7 d   8 l   9 a   10 f
11 g   12 o   13 c   14 h   15 b   16 e

UNIT 4 | Grammar 2
Object pronouns

• Use this activity after Lesson 4.3 Ex. 6 on page 41.

Procedure

Ss work in pairs. Give each pair a copy of the activity.

Explain that each pair of sentences can be completed with the words in the box at the top of the activity (you could explain that the first sentence in each pair can be completed with *this*, *that*, *these* or *those*, or you could let your students work this out for themselves).

Working in pairs, they complete the sentences. Each time they use a word from the box, they cross it out. When the words are crossed out, they cannot be used again in another sentence.

Allow them about ten minutes for this, then stop the activity. The winning pair is the pair who have correctly completed most of the sentences.

Answers

1 I don't understand **this** book. I don't understand **it** either.
2 **That** woman wants to talk to you. I don't have the time to talk to **her**.   3 I don't like **these** apples. I don't like **them** either.   4 I love **those** flowers. I love **them** too.
5 I know **that** man over there. Oh, everybody knows **him**.   6 **Those** men look a bit frightening. Right. And I don't like the way they're looking at both of **us**.   7 **These** policemen want to speak to you. Well, I don't want to speak to **them**!   8 **This** pizza is disgusting. Really? I quite like **it**.   9 **This** homework is so easy. I disagree. I find **it** quite difficult.   10 Is **this** hat too big? Yes, it's much too big for **you**.

UNIT 4 | Grammar 3
First to finish

• Use this activity after Lesson 4.3 Ex. 5 on page 41.

Procedure

Ss work in groups of four. Give each group a copy of the playing board and a dice. Give one student in each group a copy of the referee's answers. He/she should not show this to the others in the group.

Tell Ss that each sentence in the grid contains one mistake. The aim of the activity is for Ss to place their counters in the Start box, take it in turns to roll their dice, move along the board and correct the mistake in each sentence on the board. The referee tells them if their answers are right or wrong, but does not give them the correct answer if they are wrong.

If a student does *not* make a proper correction, he/she moves back along the board by the same number that he/she moved forward, and then waits for his/her next turn.

If a student lands on a sentence that has already been corrected, he/she rolls his/her dice again.

The winning student is the first student to reach the Finish point.

Answers

The answers are on the referee's sheet.

UNIT 4 | Communication
Get your orders in!

• Use this activity after Communication 3 Ex. 7 on page 41.

Procedure

Ss work in groups of four. Give each student in each group a copy of the pictures.

Explain that three of the Ss are customers in a restaurant, and one student is a waiter. The customers must each choose five items of food and drink from their paper. They tick the food/drink they want, but do not show their choice to their waiter.

They then order their food and drink from the waiter, without showing him/her their paper. The waiter writes the name of the Ss next to the items they order. He/she then reads the order back to the customers, who check that they are getting what they want.

The first group in the class to order all the correct food and drink that they want from their waiter successfully is the winner.

UNIT 5 Vocabulary
Complete the maps.

• Use this activity after Lesson 5.3 Ex. 3b on page 50.

Procedure

Ss work in pairs. Give each pair a copy of the map symbols.

Give the Ss in each group a copy of a map showing towns, lakes, rivers, etc. He/she must not show this to his/her partner.

Explain that the Ss must draw in the different geographical features. They do this by listening to their partner, who describes what is on their map. They should also write the names of the different features next to each feature, making sure that their spelling is good. They can ask questions if necessary (e.g., *Where is the beach? How do you spell …?, What is the name of …?, Is there a …?*, etc.). Tell them that the different features do not have to be in *exactly* the same place, but they should make sure that they are in the north, south, etc.

Allow them about 10–15 minutes for this then ask them to compare their maps.

UNIT 5 Grammar 1
Find the differences.

• Use this activity after Lesson 5.1 Ex. 6 on page 47.

Procedure

Ss work in groups of four. Divide each group into pairs. The student pairs should try to sit so that they are facing each other.

Give each pair a copy of the Students 1 and 2 or Student 3 and 4 paper. They should *not* show these to each other.

Explain that their pictures are very similar, but that there are a lot of small differences between them (29 in total). By asking the other pair questions (e.g., *Is there a …* or *Are there any …*), they try to find 10 differences. When they find them, they put a circle around them.

Allow them about ten minutes to find the differences. Then stop and check their answers. Monitor the class to ensure that they are asking the correct kind of questions.

UNIT 5 Grammar 2
Name the families.

• Use this activity after Lesson 5.2 Ex. 7b on page 49.

Procedure

Ss work in pairs. Give each student a Student 1 or Student 2 set of pictures. They must not show these to each other.

Explain that Student 1 and Student 2 have the same pictures, but they are in a different order. Student 1 has the names of the families on the pictures, Student 2 has the names of the families in a box at the bottom of his/her pictures. The aim of the activity is for Student 2 to identify the names of the different families in the pictures.

Student 1 begins by reading one of the family names to Student 2 (e.g., *Mr and Mrs Adamson*). Student 2 then looks at his/her pictures and asks Student 1 questions using has/have got, + any other questions that would help them (e.g., *Has Mr Adamson got a motorbike? How many children have they got? Has the boy got a skateboard?* etc.). Student 1 can only reply *Yes, they have/he has* or *No, they haven't /He/she hasn't*. As soon as Student 2 identifies which picture matches Student 1's picture, he/she writes the family name under the picture.

When they have completed all the pictures, they compare their picture sets to check their answers.

UNIT 5 Grammar 3
Find the hidden modifier.

• Use this activity after Lesson 5.3 Ex. 5 on page 50.

Procedure

Ss work in pairs. Give each pair a copy of the activity.

Explain that the jumbled letters in **bold** in each sentence pair 1–9 can be rearranged to make words. Ss identify these words, and write them in the grid above the sentences.

If these words are written correctly, *another* modifier will appear in the shaded vertical strip which can be used to complete the sentence in the box at the bottom of the page.

Answers

1 very noisy   2 quite exciting   3 really hot   4 very cold   5 really beautiful   6 really famous   7 quite dry   8 very popular   9 very busy

The hidden modifier is *extremely*.

UNIT 5 Communication
I want, I want …

• Use this activity after Communication 5 Ex. 3 on page 54.

Procedure

Ss work in groups of four. Tell each student in the groups to choose a letter, A, B, C or D. Give each group a copy of the activity. Tell them to write their names (but not their chosen letters) at the top of the paper.

In their groups, Ss look at the different sets of pictures, and decide which house/object they would most like, or which area they would most like to live in, from each set. They can only choose one object from each. They tell the others in the group why they like/would like it.

For each set of pictures, students write their letter (A, B, C or D) next to their chosen picture.

Allow them about 10–15 minutes for this, then collect their papers. Redistribute the papers to other groups in the class.

Working in their groups, students then decide who chose the objects on the paper (they match the letters next to the pictures with the names at the top of the paper, e.g., A = Laura, B = Odile, C = Wei Xing, etc.). They then check with the original group to see if they are correct.

UNIT 6 Vocabulary
Where's the bank?

• Use this activity after Lesson 6.2 Ex. 3b on page 58.

Procedure

This activity introduces the preposition *opposite*. Pre-teach this with an example in the classroom (e.g., *Juan is sitting opposite Abdullah. Who is opposite Kyoko?*, etc.)

Ss work in pairs. Give each pair a copy of the activity. Tell them to read through sentences 1–12.

Explain that, using the information in the sentences they have to work out what the buildings and other places A–M on their map are. In some cases, they have to look at more than one sentence to work out where a building is.

One building (the bank) is not mentioned in any of the sentences. The first pair to identify which building is the bank is the winner.

Answers

A = Internet café   B = Art gallery   C = Bank
D = Car park   E = Bar   F = School   G = Cinema
H = Post office   I = Underground station   J = Museum
K = Supermarket   L = Restaurant   M = Library

UNIT 6 Grammar 1
Complete the sentences.

• Use this activity after Lesson 6.1 Ex. 6 on page 57.

Procedure

Ss work in pairs. Give each pair a copy of the sentences and a set of cards. They should place the cards face down in a pile on their desk.

Explain that each sentence can be completed with a Past Simple form of the verbs on the cards. Ss take it in turns to take a card from the top of the pile, look at the

verb, decide which sentence it goes in, and write it (in its correct Past Simple form) in the appropriate sentence.

When they have finished, they check their answers with you. The student in each pair who completed the most sentences (with the right verb in its correct form and with the correct spelling) is the winner.

Answers

1 started   2 was   3 wasn't   4 married   5 watched
6 changed   7 worked   8 studied   9 produced
10 planned   11 were   12 opened   13 lived   14 stayed
15 carried   16 weren't

UNIT 6 Grammar 2
Just 10 questions

• Use this activity after Lesson 6.2 Ex. 7 on page 59.

Procedure

Ss work in groups of four. Each group should divide itself into pairs. If possible, the student pairs should sit facing each other.

Give each group a set of cards and ask them to look at the different pictures. They should tell one another what people do/buy in these places (e.g., *in a florist's, people buy flowers, or they can send flowers to friends*). Allow them about five minutes for this.

Tell Ss to mix the cards well, and place them face down on the desk between them. Each group of four should split into two pairs at this point.

One pair then takes a card from the top of the pile. They must not show this to the second pair.

The second pair has to find out what is on the card by asking the first pair questions with *Did you ... *+ a verb (e.g., *Did you catch a train? Did you buy a book? Did you have a meal?*, etc.). The first pair answers with *Yes, we did* or *No, we didn't*. If the first pair says *Yes, we did*, the second pair say what they think is on the card. If they are correct, they 'win' the card.

The second pair can only ask a maximum of ten questions per card. If they don't find out what is on the first pair's card after ten questions, the card is placed face up on the desk.

It is then the second pair's turn to take a card, and the first pair's turn to ask the questions.

Steps 4–7 above are repeated for about 10–15 minutes. The winning team is the pair in each group who 'won' the most cards.

UNIT 6 Grammar 3
In Ancient Rome ...

• Use this activity after Lesson 6.3 Ex. 4 on page 61.

Procedure

Ss work in pairs or groups of three. Give each group a copy of Part 1. Explain that this is a picture of an ancient Roman family from almost 2,000 years ago.

Ask them to work together and circle or cross all the things that people didn't have or use 2,000 years ago.

Tell them to turn the picture over or put it somewhere they can't see it. Give them Part 2 (the verbs). Working from memory, and using the verbs in the box, they write sentences beginning *In Ancient Rome, people didn't ...*

Allow them about ten minutes for this and then check their answers. The pair/group that writes the most sentences, using the correct verbs, is the winner.

UNIT 6 Communication

Where in the store ...?

- Use this activity after Communication 6 Ex.2c on page 62.

Procedure

Ss work in groups of three. Give each group a list of departments. Give them a few moments to look at these and to check that they all know what these different departments sell.

Give each student in each group a Student 1, 2 or 3 floor plan. They can't show these to one another. Ask them what they think the symbols on their plan mean (ⓘ = information counter 🍽 = restaurant ☎ = public telephone Ⓟ = car park 🚻 = toilets).

Tell Ss that they all have the floor plan of the same department store, but with the names of departments missing. They must work together to ask and tell one another where the different departments are. The departments they need to find are on their list of departments (e.g., *Where can I find the bookshop? It's on the second floor next to the restaurant. Where can I find bedlinen? It's in the basement next to the public telephones*). While they are doing this, they cannot look at the other floor plans. When they know where a department is, they write the name on their plan.

When they have finished, they compare their floor plans. They should all be the same.

UNIT 7 Vocabulary

Around the world

- Use this activity after Lesson 7.2 Ex. 8c on page 69.

Procedure

Ss work in pairs. Give each student a Student 1 or Student 2 paper. They cannot show these to each other.

Explain that they must fill in the missing information in their sentences by listening to their partner. He/she reads out the sentences at the bottom of his/her sheet, while his/her partner listens and completes the sentences.

Monitor the pairs while they are doing this, making sure that they are saying the ordinal numbers correctly (e.g., *the twenty-first of February*, not *twenty-one February*).

The first pair in the class to finish is the winner.

UNIT 7 Grammar 1

That's the one!

- Use this activity after Lesson 7.1 Ex. 5b on page 67.

Procedure

Ss work in pairs. Give each pair a copy of the activity.

Explain that sentences 1–12 in the first box are each followed by one of the sentences a–l in the second box. However, the words have been mixed up.

Working in their pairs, Ss arrange the words in a–l to make sentences and then match the sentences with those in the first box. The first pair to do this correctly is the winner.

Answers

1 l (Why don't you buy a new one?) 2 J (No, the pretty one with the blue eyes is my sister) 3 i (No, but I think the one with the swimming pool is nice) 4 b (Would you like another one?) 5 a (Why don't you buy some new ones?) 6 c (The blue ones might be the right size for you) 7 e (No thank you, I don't want one at the moment) 8 f (The ones with the baby and the dog/The ones with the dog and the baby) 9 k (The one next to McDonald's in the town square/The one in the town square next to McDonald's) 10 d (No, the short one with the beard and glasses is/No the short one with the glasses and beard is my brother) 11 h (She's the short one with the fair skin) 12 g (He's the tall one with the long hair)

UNIT 7 Grammar 2

Pronouns and adjectives crossword

- Use this activity after lesson 7.2 Ex. 4 on page 69.

Procedure

Ss work in pairs. Give each pair a copy of the activity; Student A gets the Across clues and Student B gets the Down clues.

Explain that the words in **bold** in the sentences are wrong: they are *subject pronouns*, but they should be *object pronouns*, *possessive pronouns* or *possessive adjectives*. You could refer them back to Units 1 and 4 of their Students' Book to remind them what possessive adjectives and object pronouns are.

One student reads out their sentence clue while their partner tries to correct the wrong word. The second student, who is correcting the mistake in the sentence, writes their answers in the crossword grid. To make it a bit more difficult, there are no 'filled' squares in the crossword grid. The arrows (➔ ↓) show them when a word goes across or down.

The first pair to correctly complete their crossword is the winner.

Answers

Across: 4 theirs 6 him 8 its 9 her 10 mine 11 his 13 yours 14 ours 15 their

Down: 1 me 2 us 3 them 5 his 7 mine 9 hers 10 my 11 her 12 yours 14 our

Unit 7 Grammar 3
Past tense connections

• Use this activity after Lesson 7.3 Ex. 9 on page 71.

Procedure

Ss work in groups of two pairs. Give each pair a copy of the activity.

The pairs take it in turns to choose a verb on the grid, and write its past tense form underneath. The aim of the activity is to collect rows of four squares, either horizontally, vertically or diagonally, while at the same time trying to prevent the other pair from doing the same (rather like noughts and crosses – see the Grammar activity 'Three in a row' for Lesson 2.2).

When one pair gets a row of four squares, they ask you to check their answers. If their words are correct (including the spelling), they win 1 point. If any of their answers are wrong, the point is awarded to the other pair.

The winning pair is the pair in each group who wins the most rows of four squares after about 15 minutes of play.

Answers

gave	told	felt	drove	spent
changed	wrote	lived	worked	started
understood	closed	was/were	bought	came
wanted	opened	married	decided	visited
died	went	saw	met	put
had	looked	carried	studied	stopped
planned	ate	made	owned	spoke
produced	took	worried	left	moved
finished	jogged	kept	picked	thought

Unit 7 Communication
The usual suspects

• Use this activity after Communication 7 Ex. 4 on page 72.

Procedure

Ss work in groups of four. Divide each group into pairs. If possible, the two pairs should sit opposite each other. Give each pair a copy of the Students 1 and 2 or the Students 3 and 4 sheet. They cannot show these to the other pair.

Explain that the Ss have a picture of the same men, but in a different order. Ss 1 and 2 have the names of the men below each man. Ss 3 and 4 have the names in a box at the bottom of their picture.

The aim of the activity is for Ss 3 and 4 to match the names to each man by asking Ss 1 and 2 questions (e.g., *What does Mr Pink look like? Is he tall? Has he got a beard?*, etc.). Ss 1 and 2 can also give descriptions of the men without waiting to be asked (e.g., *Mr White is tall and slim, he has glasses. He's quite young.* etc.).

The first group to match all ten names to the men is the winner.

Unit 8 Vocabulary
Match them up.

• Use this activity after Lesson 8.1 Ex. 4 on page 76.

Procedure

Ss work in pairs. Ideally they should sit facing each other. Give both Ss in each pair a Student 1 and Student 2 paper. They should not show these to each other.

Explain that the pictures they have are of the same people, but Student 1 has the left half and Student 2 has the right half. The aim of the activity is for the students to match the two halves together by describing the people's clothes to each other.

Student 1 begins by describing what he/she can see in the first picture on his/her paper. Student 2 looks for the identically dressed second half of the person, and writes number 1 next to that picture. Student 2 then describes the first picture on his/her paper to Student 1, who looks for the identically dressed person on his/her paper and writes the letter A next to it. This is repeated until they have matched all their pictures.

Answers

1 E   2 K   3 D   4 H   5 F   6 A   7 L   8 C   9 J 10 G   11 B   12 I

UNIT 8 Grammar 1
I always ...

• Use this activity after Lesson 8.1 Ex. 6 or 7 on page 77.

Procedure

Give each student a copy of the activity, and tell them to write their name at the top. Then tell them to choose eight of the twelve sentences and write true sentences about themselves based on the adverbs of frequency on their paper. The first sentence of each pair uses the verb *be,* so remind them if necessary that this is followed by an adjective. When they are writing their sentences, it is important that nobody else can see what they are writing.

Do step 1 above as a pairwork activity, with Ss asking each other about the things they are or do, and writing down their partner's answers.

Collect in the papers and read them out to the class. Ss guess who is being described and write the names down as in step 3. When all the Ss have been described, they check their answers with you.

Build in a correction stage where teachers monitor and help students identify and correct any mistakes while they are doing the activity.

UNIT 8 Grammar 2
Twenty verbs

• Use this activity after Lesson 8.2 Ex. 4b on page 79.

Procedure

Ss work in pairs. Give each pair a copy of the activity.

Explain that in the box at the top, there are 20 verbs to identify. These read from left to right, and from right to left (indicated by the arrows).

When Ss find the verbs, they use them to complete the sentences using the Present Continuous. The first part of the sentence is negative, and the second part is positive (e.g., *She* isn't *crying because she's happy, she's laughing because she's happy.*) The teacher should demonstrate the first sentence before the class starts the activity.

Answers

1 She isn't crying because she's happy, she's laughing because she's happy.

2 I'm not watching television, I'm reading the newspaper.

3 They aren't eating biscuits, they're drinking coffee.

4 He isn't talking quietly, he's shouting loudly.

5 We aren't skiing in the Swiss mountains, we're climbing mountains in the Himalayas.

6 I'm not playing the piano, I'm listening to the radio.

7 They aren't walking slowly to the shops, they're jogging quickly in the park.

8 He isn't cooking our dinner, he's washing the dirty cups and plates.

9 We aren't driving in our new car, we're cycling on our old bicycles.

10 I'm not digging the garden, I'm cutting the grass.

UNIT 8 Grammar 3
Find the secret adverb.

• Use this activity after Lesson 8.2 Ex. 7 on page 79.

Procedure

Ss work in pairs. Give each pair a copy of the activity.

Explain that each sentence can be completed with an adverb of manner from Unit 8 Lesson 2 (but they cannot look at their books while they are doing this). Working together, they decide what these adverbs are, then write them in the table.

They then take the letters in the shaded box and rearrange them to make a new adverb that isn't in their book. This adverb can be used to complete the sentence at the bottom of the page.

The first pair to identify this new adverb is the winner.

Answers

1 well   2 loudly   3 carelessly   4 uncomfortably
5 badly   6 fast   7 quietly   8 sadly

The letters in the shaded boxes can be rearranged to make *suddenly.*

UNIT 8 Communication
Where are they?

• Use this activity after Communication 8 Ex. 4 on page 82.

Procedure

Ss work in groups of four. Give each group a copy of the shop pictures *only*.

Ask two Ss from any of the groups to come to the front of the class and show them the pictures of the objects. They choose *one* of the objects, then do a brief roleplay in which one of them is a customer and one of them is a shop assistant. The customer wants to return the object he/she has chosen and tries to get a refund or exchange, but *without saying what the object is* (e.g., *I bought this last week, but I want to return it and get my money back. It doesn't speak. In fact I think it's dead*). The shop assistant can ask questions to get more information. Each roleplay should last about one minute.

The groups in the class listen, decide where the customer/shop assistant are, and at the end of the dialogue, write the two Ss' names next to the appropriate shop. This is then repeated with other pairs coming to the front of the class, until everyone has had a chance to do a roleplay dialogue. The winning team is the group who correctly identified the most shops.

UNIT 9 Vocabulary
No numbers or clues crossword

• Use this activity after Lesson 9.2 Ex. 2 on page 88.

Procedure

Ss work in pairs. Give each pair a copy of the activity.

Explain that the crossword can be completed by rearranging the letters in the table to form words related to the arts and films. The words in the table are not in the same order as the crossword, and there are no numbers in the crossword, but to help them some letters of each word have already been put into the crossword.

Allow them about 10–15 minutes for this, then ask them to stop, and check their answers. The winning pair is the pair who has completed most of the crossword.

Answers

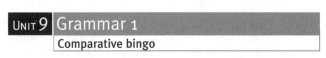

```
C A R T O O N   N
    H         N
    R   S     O
    I   C O M E D Y
    L   I     L
  A L   E           L
  C E   N           I
  T R O C K M U S I C
  I   E             T
  O   F       C I N E M A
  N   I             R
  F M C             A
  I U             T
C L A S S I C A L M U S I C
  M   I   O           R
      C   N       P O E T R Y
      A           P
B A L L E T       E
                  R
            P L A Y
```

UNIT 9 Grammar 1
Comparative bingo

• Use this activity after Lesson 9.1 Ex. 4 on page 87.

Procedure

Before you begin, make sure that Ss are familiar with the game of bingo, with a brief demonstration/diagram on the board.

Divide the class into six teams, and give each team a bingo card. Make sure all the team members can see it (you might need to make more than one copy of each card if you have a big class, or enlarge the photocopies).

Ask Ss to look at the sentences and make sure that they understand the meanings of the adjectives (they have all appeared at some point in the *Total English Elementary* course).

Tell them that you are going to read them some sentences. Each sentence that you read to them has another sentence which comes after it. These 'follow-on' sentences appear on their cards.

Read out the sentences below, choosing them at random, and allow a few moments between each sentence for students to look for the follow-on sentence on their card. You should read each sentence out twice. If they find it, they tick (✓) or put a line through the sentence. Tick your sentences as you read them out so that you don't repeat any (which could cause confusion).

The first student to tick all their sentences calls *Bingo!* and wins the game.

Check their answers. Here are the sentences you need to read out (the Ss' answers are in brackets afterwards – don't read these out!)

• You're 16 and I'm 17. (I'm a year older than you.)
• My computer cost £700 and yours cost £800. (Yours was more expensive than mine.)
• Your mobile phone cost £150, and mine cost £120. (Mine was cheaper than yours.)
• My homework was good, but your homework was *very* good. (Yours was better than mine.)
• You got 40% in the exam, but I only got 20%. (My results were worse than yours.)
• There were 200 people in the bar last night, but there are 300 here this evening. (It's busier today than yesterday.)
• This football match is good, but the match I saw at the weekend was *really* good. (It was more exciting than this one.)
• I weigh 95 kilogrammes, but my father weighs over 100 kilogrammes. (He's fatter than me.)
• Michael came first in the race, and I came second. (He was faster than me.)
• Tom always makes me laugh, but Susie makes me laugh a lot. (She's funnier than him.)
• I'm 1 metre 75 cm tall, but Alison's 1 metre 82 cm tall. (She's taller than me.)
• I'm 1 metre 68 cm tall, but Marnie's 1 metre 55 cm tall. (She's shorter than me.)

• The *Sun* newspaper doesn't give us a lot of information, but the *Daily Telegraph* newspaper gives us a lot of information. (It's more detailed and more interesting.)

• That bed feels very hard, but this bed feels very soft. (It's more comfortable.)

• I work quite hard at school, but Henry works *very* hard at school. (He's more serious than me.)

• Last year, 20,000 people visited my town, but 30,000 visited yours. (Yours is more popular than mine.)

• I bought my camera last year, but you bought your camera in 1998. (Mine is more modern than yours.)

UNIT 9 | Grammar 2
Superlative word search

• Use this activity after Lesson 9.2 Ex. 7 on page 89.

Procedure

Ss work in pairs. Give each pair a copy of the activity.

Explain that there are 18 adjectives hidden in the grid. Ss must find these adjectives, then use 14 of them to complete the sentences. They must change the adjectives to their superlative forms.

The words in the grid can be read horizontally from left to right (→), and from right to left (←), and also vertically top to bottom (↓) and bottom to top (↑).

The winning pair is the pair who find the most adjectives and put them correctly into the sentences after 10–15 minutes.

Answers

1 the best   2 the busiest   3 the worst   4 the most interesting   5 the most famous   6 the most violent   7 the cheapest   8 the most romantic   9 the most comfortable   10 the richest   11 the fastest   12 the oldest   13 the funniest   14 the hottest

UNIT 9 | Grammar 3
Spontaneous decision dominoes

• Use this activity after Lesson 9.3 Ex. 9 on page 91.

Procedure

Ss work in groups of three or four. Give each group a set of cards and a list of verbs.

Explain that their cards contain pairs of sentences, A and B. Sentence B 'follows on' from sentence 'A' (give them an example to illustrate this, e.g., A *The music is very loud*. B *I'll turn the radio down*). The aim of the activity is for Ss to join all the cards together, the B sentences following on from the A sentences. To help them, the first and last cards are marked *Start* and *Finish*. However, the verbs

have been removed from the B sentences. Your students will find these in their verb list. They must also put these into the B sentences.

The first group to join all the cards together and complete the B sentences with the right verb is the winner.

Answers

The cards are in the correct order on the activity page. The missing words are:

I'll **phone** the doctor. I'll **phone** you when I get home. OK, I'll **get** you a sandwich. I'll **get** you a glass of water. I'll **open** a window. Thanks. I'll **send** you a postcard. I'll **put** the heating on. It looks delicious. I'll **eat** it later. It's all right, I'll **phone** her now. What's her number? Don't worry, I'll **help** you with it. Not really, but I think I'll **go** to that new art gallery. My car's outside. I'll **drive** you to the station. Don't worry, I'll **help** you with them. Stay there. I'll **see** who it is. Good idea. I'll **meet** you there at half past six. I don't know. I'll **phone** him. I'm sorry, she isn't. I'll **tell** her you called.

UNIT 9 | Communication
A weekend away

• Use this activity after Communication 9 Ex. 3b on page 92.

Procedure

Ss work in groups of four. Give each group a copy of the activity.

Explain to Ss that they have decided to go in their group to a big city for the weekend, and they must decide what to do. They should each choose *one* picture in each set (they cannot choose the same picture as another student in their group), and write their name under that picture.

Working together, they try to persuade the others in their group that their choice is the best. They then decide on one picture in each set.

UNIT 10 | Vocabulary
Travel quiz

• Use this activity after Communication 10 Ex. 3b on page 102.

Procedure

Ss work in pairs. Give each pair a copy of the activity.

Explain that the questions in the activity all require answers that your students have met in this unit. Working in their pairs, Ss complete the activity. Tell them to read the questions carefully before answering the questions.

Allow them about fifteen minutes for this, then tell them to stop. Tell them to change their papers with another pair, and check their answers. For each correct answer, award them 1 point (see the answers below for points that they can score for each question). The winning pair is the pair who got the most points.

Answers

1 activity (c) sightseeing (f) water sports (b) winter sports (e) beach (a) cultural (d) (10 points: 1 point for each word correctly written, and 1 point for matching it with its correct picture)

2 False. The cheapest way to fly is *economy* class (*coach* class in the USA). (1 point – plus a bonus point if they change business to economy)

3 A long-haul flight. (1 point)

4 (b) a direct flight. (1 point)

5 (a) train (b) station (c) return (d) train (e) platform (f) passengers (g) journey (h) underground/metro (8 points)

6 Simple = Single, Dribble = Double, Trim = Twin, Sweet = Suite (4 points)

7 (a) (swimming) pool (b) tennis (court) (c) sauna (d) gym (also sometimes called a *health club* or *fitness centre)* (e) beauty salon (f) shops (g) restaurant (h) golf (course) (8 points)

Ss can get a maximum of 34 points.

UNIT 10 | Grammar 1
Have you ever ...?

• Use this activity after Lesson 10.1 Ex. 7 on page 97.

Procedure

Ss work in groups of three or four. Give each group a copy of the activity.

Explain that on the 'A' cards there are ten questions with *Have you ever been ...?* On the other cards there are 10 answers to the questions. The answers are divided into two sentences (sentence 1 on card B and sentence 2 on card C).

Working in their groups, Ss match the questions and answers to form ten mini-dialogues.

Answers

The questions and answers are in the correct order in the activity.

UNIT 10 | Grammar 2
The whole truth

• Use this activity after Lesson 10.2 Ex. 6 on page 99.

Procedure

Ss work in groups of equal size (minimum two Ss in each group, recommended maximum of five). Give each student a copy of the activity and a True and False card.

Tell Ss to write eight sentences about themselves using the Present Perfect (some of their sentences can be negative with *haven't* or *have never*). Some of their sentences should be *true* and some of them should be *false*.

Each student then reads out his/her sentences to the rest of the class. After each sentence, the other groups decide if that sentence is true or false. They discuss this, then 'vote' using their *True* or *False* card (the group containing the student who is speaking cannot vote). The individual team members do not have to vote the same way (e.g., some Ss in one group can vote *True*, while others in the same group can vote *False*).

For each correct vote, the teams win one point (for example, if one team has three *true* votes and two *false* votes, and the speaking S's sentence was *true*, the team wins three points). The winning team is the team with the most points after all the Ss in the class have read out their sentences.

UNIT 10 | Grammar 3
Communicative crossword

• Use this activity after Lesson 10.3 Ex. 6 on page 101.

Procedure

Ss work in groups of 3. Give each group a copy of the Part 1 verbs. Ss should demonstrate that they understand them by creating a sentence each using one of the verbs.

Tell them to put the verbs somewhere they cannot see them, then give two Ss in each group a copy of the crossword grid, and one student a copy of the clues. He/she must not show these to the other two in his/her group.

Explain that Student 3 reads out the sentences to the others in his/her group. There is a word missing from the beginning of the sentence. These words were on their verbs list. The two Ss with the grid decide what that word is, and write it in its correct *-ing* form in the appropriate space on their grid. They must be careful, as sometimes more than one answer may be possible for some of the sentences (advise them to use a pencil so that they can erase their mistakes, or have a few extra crossword grids on standby).

The first group to complete the crossword is the winner.

Answers

Across: 3 parking   4 drinking   6 waiting
7 commuting   11 hiking   12 playing   13 phoning
14 flying

Down: **1** driving **2** eating **5** swimming **7** camping **8** taking **9** going **10** staying

UNIT 10 | Communication
The perfect holiday

• Use this activity after Communication 10 Ex.4 on page 102.

Procedure

Ss work in pairs. Give each student a copy of the activity. Ask them to look at the different icons, and decide what they all mean. You could spend a few minutes discussing these with your class.

Tell them to work individually and choose pictures from each set. Sometimes they need to choose just one picture, sometimes they need to choose more than one. They must *not* show their choices to their partner. They put a tick below each picture(s).

Tell them to imagine that one of them is a travel agent and one of them is a customer. The customer tells the travel agent about his/her choice of holiday, using the pictures he/she has chosen as prompts (e.g., *I want to go on a winter sports holiday. I want a single room with shower, toilet, mini bar and safe box*, etc.) The travel agent listens, asks questions if necessary, and writes the customer's name below each picture.

When they have finished, they compare their activity sheets. The pictures the customer chose in step 2 and the pictures that the travel agent wrote his/her name under should be the same.

They then change roles: the customer becomes the travel agent, and the travel agent becomes the customer. They repeat steps 3 and 4 above.

UNIT 11 | Vocabulary
Find the hidden expression.

• Use this activity after Lesson 11.3 Ex. 8 on page 111.

Procedure

Ss work in pairs. Give each pair a copy of the activity.

Explain that each sentence can be completed with a word from Unit 11 Lesson 3 (but they cannot look at their books while they are doing this). Working together, they decide what these words are, then write them in the grids.

If they do this correctly, they will reveal a two-word expression in the shaded vertical strips.

The first pair to identify this expression is the winner.

Answers

1 kindergarten **2** Biology **3** compulsory **4** part-time **5** languages **6** optional **7** certificate **8** degree

9 full-time **10** lecturer **11** trainer **12** primary **13** secondary **14** vocational **15** trainee **16** Geography

The expression in the shaded vertical strip is *distance learning*.

UNIT 11 | Grammar 1
Company rules

• Use this activity after Lesson 11.1 Ex. 6 on page 107.

Procedure

Ss work in pairs. Give each pair a copy of the activity.

Explain that twelve sentences have been split into three parts and they must join all three parts together. The sentences are rules and other information for somebody starting a new job in a company.

The first pair to do this correctly is the winner.

Answers

1 Work begins at 8.30 everyday, so you have to be here on time every morning.

2 The coffee machine is free, so you don't have to pay for hot drinks.

3 Everybody has one hour for lunch, so you have to be back in the office by 2 o'clock.

4 Everybody has a personal code for the photocopier, so you have to get one before you use it.

5 It's very important to ask your boss for permission to go home early, so you can't leave early without asking her.

6 There are lots of restaurants and sandwich bars near the office, so you don't have to eat in the company restaurant.

7 The company restaurant is open all day, so you can get something to eat without leaving the building.

8 Mrs Clark is the only person who can use the fax machine, so you can't use it without her permission.

9 It's very important to be quiet when you go near Mr Mansell's office, so you can't make a noise outside his door.

10 Everybody wears informal clothes here, so you don't have to wear a suit.

11 This company has a no smoking policy, so you have to go outside for a cigarette.

12 Please turn off your mobile phone, because you can't make personal calls inside the building.

UNIT 11 | Grammar 2
Question and answer links

• Use this activity after Lesson 11.2 Ex. 5b on page 109.

Teacher's notes

Procedure

Ss work in pairs. Give each pair a Student 1 and Student 2 paper. They must not show these to each other.

Tell Ss that they are going to ask and answer questions on their paper. Student 1 begins by asking the first question on his/her paper (*Which do you prefer, Chinese food or Indian food?*). Student 2 looks for the answer on his/her paper and answers Student 1's question. He/she then asks the question that follows that answer. Student 1 then looks for the answer on his/her paper.

This is repeated until they have asked and answered all the questions. The first pair to match the questions and answers is the winner.

Answers

The questions and answers follow this sequence:

1 → e → 5 → k → 2 → m → 6 → b → 13 → c → 7 → i → 3 → h → 14 → l → 9 → d → 12 → a → 10 → g → 4 → j → 11 → f → 8

UNIT 11 Grammar 3
A busy Saturday

• Use this activity after Lesson 11.3 Ex. 4a or 4b on page 110.

Procedure

Ss work in groups of three or four. Give each group a set of cards. They do not look at them – they should put them face down on their desk.

Tell them you are going to read them a short passage. They listen and try to remember what happens.

Read the text below at normal speed. Read it twice.

I'm a very busy person. This Saturday is a good example. I have a lot to do, so I'm getting up early, at 6 o'clock. I'm having breakfast and then I'm going to the supermarket. I like getting there early, because it's much quieter than it is later in the day. At nine o'clock I'm meeting my friend Jo at the sports centre, and we're playing tennis. We always do this on Saturday. After that, I'm taking the bus home and making some sandwiches and a salad, because at twelve o'clock I'm having a picnic lunch with my boyfriend Rob in the park. Then we're doing some shopping in town because I want a new dress and Rob needs a new jacket. After that we're seeing a new film at the cinema. In the evening we're having a drink in a local bar with my brother Mick and his wife, and then we're all eating at a new Italian restaurant near my house.

Tell Ss to turn their cards over and put the pictures in the correct order.

When all the groups have done this, give them a copy of Part 2. Using their cards as prompts, they fill in the gaps with appropriate words.

UNIT 11 Communication
Making excuses

• Use this activity after Communication 11 Ex.3b on page 112.

Procedure

Ss work in pairs. Give each student in each pair a Student 1 or Student 2 paper. They do not show these to each other.

Explain that Student 1 wants to go out with Student 2, but Student 2 doesn't want to go out with him/her. Student 1 uses the prompts in the grid (e.g., *Would you like to go to the cinema with me on Monday?*) and Student 2 uses his/her pictures to give a reason why he/she can't go, using the Present Continuous (e.g., *I'm sorry, but I'm washing my hair*). Student 1 listens, and writes the days of the week under each appropriate picture.

When they finish, they compare their papers. The days of the week on Student 1's pictures should be the same as the days of the week on Student 2's pictures.

Answers

Here are some possible questions and responses that Ss could use:

Would you like to come to the cinema with me on Monday night? I'm afraid I'm washing my hair.

How about a meal with me on Tuesday? Thanks for asking, but I'm doing my homework.

Let's go shopping on Wednesday evening. I'm afraid not. I'm going swimming.

Why don't we go to a nightclub on Thursday night? Sorry, but I'm watching a video with my friends.

What about a drink on Friday night? I'm afraid that's not possible. I'm cooking dinner for my friends.

Would you like to go for a walk on Saturday? That sounds nice, but my mother's coming to see me.

Let's play tennis on Sunday. I'd love to, but I'm already playing volleyball.

UNIT 12 Vocabulary
Order the activities.

• Use this activity after Lesson 12.3 Ex. 3b on page 120.

Procedure

Ss work in pairs. Give each pair a copy of the activity.

Explain that the letters in **bold** at the end of each sentence can be rearranged to make words. These words are activities illustrated by the pictures at the bottom of the activity.

When Ss have made the words, they then look at the sentences again and, using the time indicators at the beginning (*This afternoon, Tomorrow*, etc.), they put the pictures in order of when they happen. They do this by writing a number in the box next to each activity.

The first pair to do this is the winner.

Answers

The activities are: **1** mountain climbing **2** skiing **3** mountain biking **4** white water rafting **5** cycling **6** trekking **7** horse-riding **8** kayaking **9** sailing **10** driving

The correct order of activities is: trekking   driving   skiing   sailing   white water rafting   mountain climbing   kayaking   mountain biking   horse-riding   cycling

Unit 12 | Grammar 1
Plans and intentions

• Use this activity after Lesson 12.1 Ex. 6 on page 117.

Procedure

Ss work in pairs. Give each pair a copy of the activity. They should all read through the numbered sentences first to ensure that they understand them, before attempting the matching exercise.

Tell students that there are three things they have to do in this activity. They have to:

   a Match sentences 1–10 to sentences a–j.

   b Rearrange the words [a–j] to make sentences.

   c Make those sentences grammatically correct by adding *is* or *are + going to*.

The first pair in the class to do all three of the above is the winner (alternatively, stop them after fifteen minutes and see who got the most correct).

Answers

1 g (No, I'm going to tell her tonight.)

2 b (I'm going to travel around Europe by train/by train around Europe.)

3 h (She's going to go to university.)

4 a (They're going to study them at university.)

5 i (I know, we're going to see it tonight.)

6 d (I'm going to have an early night tonight/Tonight I'm going to have an early night.)

7 e (They're going to visit their friends in Liverpool.)

8 j (What are you going to get her?)

9 c (What are you going to wear?)

10 f (They're going to stay at home and watch television this evening.)

Unit 12 | Grammar 2
This weekend

• Use this activity after Lesson 12.2 Ex. 7 on page 119.

Procedure

Ss work in pairs. Give each pair a set of cards, which they should place face down on their desk.

One student begins by taking a card, looking at the picture and saying *This weekend I'm going to go to the ___ to ___* (e.g., *This weekend, I'm going to go to the library to borrow a book*). The card is then placed face-down on the desk next to the original pile of cards.

The second student then takes the next card from the top of the pile, repeats what the first student said and then says what he/she is going to do (e.g., *This weekend I'm going to go to the library to borrow a book, and I'm going to go to the pet shop to buy a dog*).

This is repeated until one of the Ss either forgets a place or forgets why he/she is going to go there. When this happens, the other student is the winner.

They can then play the game again. Allow them about fifteen minutes in total. Monitor the pairs to make sure they are using the correct grammatical structures and other language.

Unit 12 | Grammar 3
I would like ...

• Use this activity after Lesson 12.3 Ex. 8 on page 121.

Procedure

Give each student a copy of the activity, tell them to write their names at the top, and then write sentences about themselves using the key language in the box and the examples to help them. They cannot show their sentences to their neighbours.

Allow them about ten minutes for this, then collect in their papers. Redistribute them to other Ss in the class. Again, they cannot show the paper to their neighbours.

One student then reads out all the sentences on the paper he/she has been given, beginning *This person ...* (e.g., *This person would love to go to India because he/she enjoys eating spicy food*). They cannot say the name of the student. Make sure Ss begin with *This person …* and use *he* or *she* while speaking.

The other Ss in the class try to decide who is being described. On a separate piece of paper, they write the number 1, and the name of the student who they think is being described.

This is then repeated with the other Ss in the class, until all the papers have been read.

They then check their answers with the Ss who read out the sentences. The person who correctly identified the most Ss is the winner.

Unit 12 | Communication
Outside the classroom

• Use this activity after Communication 12 Ex. 4b on page 122.

Procedure

Distribute the cards around the class. (If you have more than 20 Ss, some of them can share a card. If you have fewer than 20, some Ss can have more than one card).

Tell Ss that their cards contain useful ideas on ways of improving, developing or practising their English outside the class. They should walk around the classroom telling others about the ideas on their card, and listening to the other ideas they are given. They cannot make notes at this point.

Allow them about ten minutes to share their ideas with one another, then tell them to return the cards to you, form groups of four and sit down.

In their groups, Ss then try to remember as many of the ideas as possible, and use them to write a 'useful information' sheet.

Before watching

1 Choose the correct responses, a) or b).

1 Good morning.
   a) *Good morning.*   b) *Is it?*
2 How do you do?
   a) *How do you do?*   b) *I do very well, thank you.*
3 How are you?
   a) *How are you?*   b) *I'm fine, thanks. And you?*
4 I'd like you to meet Mrs Lewis.
   a) *Hello, pleased to meet you.*   b) *Not at all.*
5 My name is Julius Caesar. I represent the Roman Empire.
   a) *Pleased to meet you.*   b) *No thanks, not today.*
6 Good evening. I hope I'm not too early.
   a) *Not at all.*   b) *Thanks a lot.*
7 May I introduce Mr Lawson?
   a) *How do you do?*   b) *Yes, you may.*

While Watching

2 Watch the film. Are these statements true (T) or false (F)?

1 Mrs Wilberforce is very popular.
2 Mr Wakefield and Mr Grigg are old friends.
3 Mr Jenkins isn't very attractive. ...
4 The nurse asks Mr York his name, address, age and occupation.
5 Miss Madderly is very strong.
6 Julius Caesar is happy.
7 Mrs Wilberforce doesn't know her visitors.

After Watching

3 Order the words to make questions.

is / name / what / your   _____?
do / do / how / you   _____?
is / phone number / what / your   _____?
is / occupation / what / your   _____?
address / is / what / your   _____?
are / how / old / you   _____?

4 Write a dialogue for one of the photos on Students' Book page 115. Use the expressions on this page.

Before Watching

1   Use the words below to make questions about the man in the film.

1   Where / work?   *Where does he work?*

2   What / do?   _____

3   like / job?   _____

4   What time / finish work? _____

5   Where / live?   _____

6   What / do / after work? _____

While Watching

2   Watch the first part of the film, and answer the questions in Ex. 1.

3   Watch the rest of the film and describe these things with the adjectives in the box.

1   The man's flat
2   The place in his dream
3   The girl in his dream

> beautiful   colourful   friendly   grey   horrible
> nice   old-fashioned   sunny   young

4a Translate these words to your language. Use a dictionary.
Catch   butterfly   sad   key   wings

b   Use the words above to answer these questions.

1   What do the man and the girl do in the dream?
2   How does the man feel when he breaks the box?
3   What is on the floor next to the key?
4   Are the man and the girl happy at the end of the film? Why?

After Watching

5   Use the prompts in Ex. 1 to ask your partner questions about his/her life.
Where do you work?

© Pearson Education Limited 2005   Photocopiable

Before Watching

1 Match each verb (1–5) with one of the expressions (a–e) in the box.

1 check *your e-mails*
2 do _____
3 run _____
4 send _____
5 talk _____

a) in the park
b) on the phone
c) text messages
d) yoga
e) ~~your e-mails~~

While Watching

2 Watch the video and match each verb (1–10) with one of the expressions (a–j) in the box.

1 have *breakfast at a café*
2 fly _____
3 go _____
4 go out _____
5 listen to _____
6 look in _____
7 play _____
8 read _____
9 ride _____
10 swim _____

a) a bike
b) a book
c) a kite
d) ~~breakfast at a café~~
e) in the pond
f) music
g) roller-blading
h) shop windows
i) tennis
j) with friends

3 Complete this description of Deborah's day using expressions from exercises 1 and 2.

Deborah gets up early, and then she **(1)**_____. It helps her to relax. After that she switches on the computer and **(2)**_____. Then, she **(3)**_____ to her agent about a new acting job.

She practises her lines and then she **(4)**_____ to a friend. It's a good way to keep in touch. After putting on her helmet she **(5)**_____ into the town centre. She **(6)**_____ with tables on the pavement.

Later, she **(7)**_____. It's important for an actor to keep fit. While running, she **(8)**_____ on her personal stereo. She often **(9)**_____ after running, and she sometimes **(10)**_____ or **(11)**_____. In the evening, she often **(12)**_____. It's her favourite sport. But it's her friend's birthday today so this evening she **(13)**_____ to a pub.

After Watching

4 Use the expressions in Ex. 1 and 2 to ask your partner questions.
Do you ever have breakfast at a café? / ***When do you*** check your e-mails?

Photocopiable © Pearson Education Limited 2005

Before Watching

1 Which of these things can you *not* usually see in a restaurant?

> bowl of soup   chef   customers   cutlery (fork, knife, spoon)   glass
> magazines   main course   rubbish bin   tablecloth   waitress

While Watching

2 Complete the sentences with the expressions in the box. Watch the video to check your answers.

Waitress: **(1)** _Ready to order, sir? Madam?_ Man: Jane? Jane: **(2)** _____ Waitress: I'll just go and find out. Man: **(3)** _____ Jane: Twenty five to. Man: **(4)** _____	**First part** **a)** Oh, well. That's not too bad. **b)** ~~Ready to order, sir? Madam?~~ **c)** What time's your train? **d)** Yes, what's the soup of the day, please?
Waitress: **(5)** _____ Jane: Yes, I wanted to know what the soup of the day was. Waitress: **(6)** _____ Jane: Look. Let's just have it, shall we? Whatever it is. We'll be here all day. Man: Waitress! We'll have the soup, anyway… We'll have the two soups, anyway… Waitress: **(7)** _____ Man: **(8)** _____ Waitress: Two soups… One soup… and another soup… Right away, sir.	**Second part** **a)** I beg your pardon, sir. I didn't quite catch that. **b)** Ready to order, sir? Madam? **c)** That's right. I'll just go and check with the chef. **d)** We'll have two soups.
Jane: Look. Let's just have a main course, shall we? Skip the soup. Man: Shall we? Jane: **(9)** _____ Man: **(10)** _____ Waitress: Yes, isn't it? Jane: Chicken. Is that the quickest? Man: It's no wonder this place is empty. Waitress: **(11)** _____ Man: **(12)** _____	**Third part** **a)** I don't believe this. These are empty. **b)** Two soups. **c)** Waitress! I'm sorry. We've changed our minds. **d)** Yes, tell her.

After Watching

3 Match the expressions from the script (1–4) with their meanings (a–d).

1 that's correct   3 I didn't hear that
2 I'm sorry   4 right away

> **a)** I beg your pardon   **c)** immediately
> **b)** I didn't quite catch that   **d)** that's right

4 In groups of three practise reading the whole sketch out loud.

ble

Before Watching

1 Complete the description of this ship with the numbers in the box.

1	2	3	4	88	110	196	650	4 million

The World of ResidenSea is (1) _____ metres long. Over (2) _____ people live on it. There are (3) _____ luxury apartments. The smallest luxury apartments have (4) _____ bedroom. An apartment with (5) _____ bedrooms costs just over (6) $_____. There are also (7) _____ rooms for guests. On The World of ResidenSea there are (8) _____ top-class restaurants, and (9) _____ swimming pools.

While Watching

2 Watch the video to check your answers to Ex. 1.

3 Answer these questions with cities and places from the film. Watch the video to check your answers.

1 You can visit a famous Opera house here. _Sydney_
2 You can play football on the beach here. _____
3 You can cross a golden bridge here. _____
4 You can eat a good meal here. _a top-class restaurant_
5 You can keep fit here. _____
6 You can relax here. _____
7 You can read a book here. _____
8 You can see a play here. _____
9 You can admire some paintings here. _____
10 You can stand here and watch the world go by. _____

After Watching

4 Imagine you are staying on the The World of ResidenSea for one week. Work with a partner to fill in the information.

a realistic itinerary for the ship for seven days. (You can't sail from Rio to Sydney in 1 day)

ITINERARY

DAY ONE: _____
DAY TWO: _____
DAY THREE: _____
DAY FOUR: _____
DAY FIVE: _____
DAY SIX: _____
DAY SEVEN: _____

a perfect day aboard
The World of ResidenSea

IN THE MORNING _____

IN THE AFTERNOON _____

IN THE EVENING _____

Photocopiable   © Pearson Education Limited 2005

Before Watching

1a Say where these people's favourite buildings are.

Suzy's favourite building is the Flatiron Building.	Australia
John's favourite building is the Guggenheim Museum.	Bilbao
Adam's favourite building is the Gherkin.	London
Penny's favourite building is the Eiffel Tower.	New York
Laura's favourite building is Sydney Opera House.	Paris

b Find out what your classmates' favourite buildings are and where they are.

While Watching

2 Watch the film. Use the information below to write about the people and their favourite buildings.

Suzy spent 2 years as a waitress in New York. Her favourite building is the Flatiron building. She thinks it's really unusual.

... is from Sydney	because he wanted to see	amazing shape
... lives and works in London	but she didn't visit ... until her last month	fantastic
... lived in Paris for a year	He walks past the ... every day.	really unusual
... spent 2 years as a waitress in New York	She loves	looks modern
... travelled to Bilbao	Her favourite building is	very beautiful

3 Watch the film again to correct the errors in these descriptions.

1 The Flatiron building is the most recent skyscraper in New York. It's 87 metres wide and 2 metres high.

2 The Guggenheim museum is 500 metres high. It's made of plastic and glass and there is a gallery inside.

3 The Eiffel Tower is 30 metres tall so you can't see it from most of the city. It opened last year.

4 It's the Gherkin, but everybody calls it the Swiss-Re Tower. It will open in 2014. It was in the film *Spiderman*.

5 The Sydney Opera House opened 300 years ago. There's a theatre, a cinema and some restaurants near it. Its roofs come from France, it's glass is Danish, and the architect is Swedish.

After Watching

4 Write six clues about a famous building. Read them to a partner. After every clue your partner has *one* guess to identify your building.

© Pearson Education Limited 2005 Photocopiable

Before Watching

1   Match the names of the people with the descriptions.

   1   He's a shy young boy. His parents are dead and he lives with his sister and her husband, Joe.

   2   She's a strange old woman. She always wears an old wedding dress.

   3   She's a pretty young girl. She lives with Miss Havisham.

   4   He's Joe's uncle. He takes Pip to see Miss Havisham.

   a)   Mr Pumblechook

   b)   Pip

   c)   Miss Havisham

   d)   Estella

While Watching

2   Watch the film. Put these events in the right order.

   1   Estella opens the gate.

   2   Miss Havisham asks Pip to visit her.

   3   Mr Pumblechook takes Pip to Satis House.

   4   Pip and Estella go upstairs.

   5   Pip knocks at the door of Miss Havisham's room.

   6   Pip rings the bell.

   7   Pip meets Miss Havisham.

   8   Pip's sister washes and dresses him.

3   Who says these lines in the film? Watch it again to check your answers.

   1   Ring the bell, boy!   6   Your clock's stopped.

   2   A quarter past three.   7   After you, miss.

   3   So this is Pip, is it?   8   Don't be silly.

   4   Do you wish to see Miss Havisham?   9   Come in... Who is it?

   5   Come along, boy!   10   Come nearer. Let me look at you.

After Watching

4   Match the sentences below with appropriate sentences from exercise 3.

   a)   What's the time?   d)   Yes, I do.

   b)   It's me.   e)   Thank you very much.

   c)   Yes, I know.   f)   Yes, it is.

5   Find the past form of the verbs in Ex. 2 and write the story of the film. Use the words in the box.

   | first   then   after that   finally |

Photocopiable   © Pearson Education Limited 2005

Before Watching

1 Do you have carnivals in your country? What things can you do there?

While Watching

2 Watch the film. Which of these things can you see?

1. a big pink flower
2. a Japanese tourist with a camera
3. a man wearing a bullfighter's costume
4. the parade crossing a bridge
5. a gold mask with red eyes
6. a girl using a hair-drier
7. someone ironing a costume
8. a girl painting a mask
9. two little children dancing together
10. a boy talking on a mobile phone
11. some spectators waving to the camera
12. a man dressed as a devil
13. someone eating a hamburger
14. the judges sitting at a table

3 Match the beginnings (1–6) with the continuations (a–f). Watch the film again to check your answers.

1. The streets of Notting Hill   _d_
2. The Queen of my band   ___
3. Tamiko   ___
4. Costumes   ___
5. The people in Clara's team   ___
6. Tamiko's costume   ___

a) are working quickly.
b) is an excellent performer.
c) is very comfortable to wear.
d) are full of people, music and colour.
e) can take months to design and make.
f) is a very special young lady called Tamiko.

After Watching

4 Imagine you are sitting on a café terrace in Notting Hill, watching the Carnival parade. Complete this postcard to a friend describing what you can see.

Hi _____,

Well here I am at the Notting Hill Carnival. I'm sitting at a café watching the parade go by. It's amazing...

LUFTPOST
PAR AVION VIA AEREA
FIRST CLASS

LDN
230405

30p

© Pearson Education Limited 2005   Photocopiable

Before Watching

1 Look at the information and use the words in the box to compare these places in London.

| old   high   popular   beautiful   interesting |

	St Paul's cathedral	Tower Bridge	The London Eye
built in	1708	1894	1999
height	108m	43m	135m
popular with tourists	very	not very	extremely

While Watching

2 Complete this description of London with the words in the box. Watch the film to check your answers.

London is a (1) _huge_ city. It stretches for over (2)_____ along the (3)_____. With a population of nearly (4)_____, it is the (5)_____ city in Europe. Its (6)_____ visitor attraction is the London Eye. The Thames, which is the second (7)_____ river in Britain, is like a (8)_____ of the city: always changing, but always (9)_____. At (10)_____ the buildings become towers of (11)_____, and it looks like a magical (12)_____.

40km	light
8 million	night
~~huge~~	symbol
largest	world
longest	the same
most popular	River Thames

3 Complete this description of Richard Tate with the correct form of the verbs in brackets. Watch the film again to check your answers.

Richard Tate (1) _was_ (be) born in Scunthorpe, a small quiet town in the East of England.

His father (2)_____ (bring) him to London when he (3)_____ (be) 10 After university, Richard

(4)_____ (come) to London to live. To make money, he (5)_____ (work) as a security guard.

During his lunch breaks, he usually (6)_____ (go) up to the roof, (7)_____ (study) the

buildings and (8)_____ (take) photographs, but he (9)_____ (dream) of painting.

Richard still (10)_____ (work) from photographs today. He (11)_____ (use) oil paints and

(12)_____ (spend) a lot of time on each painting. They can (13)_____ (take) 5 months to finish.

He also (14)_____ (enjoy) drawing portraits, but London is his favourite subject. Its landscape

(15)_____ (change) all the time, and there (16)_____ (be) always new views to paint. Richard

also (17)_____ (love) the River Thames.

After Watching

4 Write sentences comparing the city where you live with London.

Photocopiable © Pearson Education Limited 2005

10 Commuting

FILM BANK

Before Watching

1 Order the words and write them in the spaces 1–4 below.

1 describe / journey / to / work / your

2 do / do / to / travelling / what / while / work / you / you're / ?

3 and / are / bad / good / points / the / what / ?

4 are / ever / for / late / work / you / ?

While Watching

2 Watch the film and complete the notes about the commuters.

1 _____

	Penelope	Jonathan	Liz	Mike	Johnny & Rachel
Journey time	(1)_____	(3)_____	------	(7)_____	(9)_____
Means of transport	walks (2)_____	bike	(5)_____ (6)_____ train	(8)_____ tube	car

2 _____?

Penelope usually gets (1)_____ at the station. She tends to have breakfast on the train. She always uses the time to (2)_____ .	Jonathan tends to read a book. He sometimes (3)_____ a newspaper, but he never (4)_____ one.	Liz reads.	On the train Mike can always (5)_____ . But on the tube he has to (6)_____ .	Johnny & Rachel (7)_____ or they listen to the radio. Rachel (8)_____ and they (9)_____ .

3 _____

	Penelope	Jonathan	Liz	Mike	Johnny & Rachel
Good points	a chance to read novels	short journey	(2)_____	(4)_____	(5)_____
Bad points	(1)_____		(3)_____ a bit noisy		(6)_____

4 _____?

Penelope is usually on time because (1)_____	Jonathan is late twice a week on average because (2)_____	Liz is sometimes late if (3)_____	Mike is never late because (4)_____	Johnny & Rachel are hardly ever late, but if they are, it's because (5)_____

After Watching

3 Ask your partner the four questions from Ex. 1.

 © Pearson Education Limited 2005 Photocopiable

Before Watching

1 In groups, grade the following activities in terms of how *a) dangerous, b) fun, c) difficult* they are.

Hang Gliding   Karting   Rock Climbing   White Water Rafting

While Watching

2 Complete this leaflet with the expressions from the box. Watch the film to check your answers.

Are you ready for (1) *a challenge*?
Have you got (2) _____?
Why not (3) _____?
It's really exciting!

Come to the **National Mountain Centre** in Wales.

Instructor Stuart McAleese – more than (4) _____
" (5) _____ *can go climbing!*"

Marian: a satisfied customer
"*I thought I'd be* (6) _____*, but I wasn't! It was*
(7) _____*!*"

Andy: wants to return
"*I definitely want to come and* (8) _____ *again!*"

a bit scary
a challenge
a spirit of adventure
an indoor climbing wall
anybody
lots of fun
really scared
rules and techniques
take up rock climbing
the final climb
the rock face
the ropes
to tie knots
try climbing
10 years experience

DAY ONE: you learn the (9) _____, and practise on (10) _____.
DAY TWO: it's the real thing! You climb (11) _____!
Your instructor shows you how to attach and remove (12) _____, and teaches you how (13) _____ and to make sure they're secure. And then it's time for (14) _____ to the top. It's exciting and (15) _____, but it's always thrilling to get to the top!

3 Complete the final part of the leaflet with appropriate modal verbs.

Climbing is a serious business. You (1) _____ make mistakes. You (2) _____ do things the right way. You (3) _____ learn where to put your hands and feet, but you (4) _____ use a lot of equipment – helmet, harness, rock boots and ropes. It's thrilling and it's fun.

Come on! You (5) _____ **do it!**

After Watching

4 Design an advertising leaflet for a centre which promotes a sport or activity that you enjoy.

Photocopiable © Pearson Education Limited 2005

Before Watching

1 Complete the list of activities with the words in the box.

1 dog _____
2 _____ a ship
3 whale _____
4 _____ the rapids
5 _____ in the mountains
6 _____ under the sea
7 bungee _____
8 _____ through the air
9 _____ with dolphins
10 _____ an expedition

diving
going on
jumping
parascending
riding
sailing
skiing
sledging
swimming
watching

While Watching

2 Match each of Gill's comments with one of the activities in Ex. 1. Watch the film to check your answers.

1 It's fast, dangerous and a lot of fun. *riding the rapids*
2 It's a fast ride. _____
3 I hope you like heights. _____
4 The more you splash, the more they play. _____
5 It's only for people who love taking risks. _____
6 It was a fantastic experience. _____
7 I hope you don't get seasick. _____
8 This icy wilderness is so beautiful. _____
9 It's popular all over the world. _____
10 You can explore a beautiful undersea world. _____

3a Which of these questions does Gill ask?

1 Are you tired of your usual holidays?
2 Do you want to try something new?
3 Do you prefer relaxing holidays?
4 Are you fond of animals?
5 Do you love the sea?
6 Do you like living life in the fast lane?
7 Can you ski?
8 Can you swim?
9 Do you suffer from vertigo?
10 Do you enjoy taking risks?
11 Do you like cold weather?
12 Which one are you going to choose?

b Gill asks three questions beginning *Why not...?* Watch the film again to find the three questions and to check your answers to Ex. 3a.

After Watching

4 Interview a partner about the type of holidays he/she prefers. Use some of the questions in Ex. 3a. Then, recommend a holiday for him/her.

© Pearson Education Limited 2005 Photocopiable

Teaching Notes

1 Meeting People

Before Watching

1 ▶ Ss work in pairs and agree on the most appropriate answers.

While Watching

▶ Tell Ss that they are going to watch the film to check their answers to Ex. 1.

> **Answers:** 1 a)   2 a)   3 b)   4 a)   5 they say
> b) in the film, but a) is more appropriate   6 a)   7 a)

▶ Elicit which of the exchanges (1–7) is not in the film? (3), which of the exchanges (1–7) is not complete (4 *We don't hear Mr Jenkins' greeting to Mrs Lewis*), and in which of the exchanges (1–7) is the response in the film not appropriate (5 *Obviously, it would be more appropriate (but less funny) if the man at the door invited Caesar inside*).

2 ▶ Ss read the statements and decide if they are true or false and why. Watch the film again to check their answers.

> **Answers:** 1 T Everyone says *"Good morning"* to her.
> 2 F Miss Wheeler introduces them.   3 F The young women want to talk to him.   4 T She says '*Name. Address. Age. Occupation.*'   5 T She hurts the Captain's hand.   6 F He is insulted because the man has closed the door in his face.   7 T The professor introduces them to her.

After Watching

3 ▶ Ss work in pairs to make questions.

> **Answers:** 1 What is your name?   2 How do you do?
> 3 What is your phone number?   4 What is your occupation?   5 What is your address?   6 How old are you?

4 ▶ Ask Ss to choose one of the photos on Students' Book page 115. Encourage them to use the expressions from Ex. 1 and 3.

▶ Ss work with a partner to correct any mistakes, then read their dialogues together.

> **OPTIONAL EXTENSION**
>
> Ask Ss to find more informal alternatives for the following expressions. Suggested answers in brackets.
>
> How do you do? (How are you? / How's it going? / How are you doing?)
>
> May I introduce you to...? (This is... / Do you know....?)
>
> Delighted to meet you. (Nice to meet you)

2 Unreal City

Before Watching

1 ▶ Freeze the film on an image of the man at work (10:05:29:24). Ss work in pairs and agree on the answers to Ex. 1.

> **Answers:** 2 What does he do?   3 Does he like his job?
> 4 What time does he finish work?   5 Where does he live?   6 What does he do after work?

While Watching

2 ▶ Watch the first part of the film up to the beginning of the dream (10:07:33:11) and elicit answers to Ex. 1. Rewind and replay the appropriate scenes if Ss find some of the questions difficult.

> **Suggested answers:** 1 He works in a factory in a big city.   2 He operates a machine.   3 No, it's boring.
> 4 He finishes work at 7 o'clock.   5 He lives in a small flat.   6 He listens to his music box and looks at stamps.

3 ▶ Watch the rest of the film, pausing on the relevant frames, and elicit the descriptions.

> **Answers:** 1 It's old-fashioned, grey, horrible.
> 2 It's beautiful, colourful, sunny.   3 She's friendly, young, nice.

4 ▶ Check that Ss understand all the words in Ex. 4a, and that they understand all the questions in Ex. 4b. Check answers.

> **Suggested answers:** 1 They catch butterflies.   2 He is very sad.   3 Two wings.   4 Yes. They're in love.

After Watching

5 ▶ Ss work in pairs. Elicit the correct form of the questions using *do you*. Encourage Ss to give complete answers and to ask follow-up questions when they interview each other. Remind them that they could also use questions from the warmer activity to interview their partners.

> **OPTIONAL EXTENSION**
>
> Freeze the film near the end when the man and the girl are looking at each other. Ask Ss to imagine what they are saying to each other. For homework, they could write a dialogue between the man and the girl.

3 Deborah's day

Before Watching

1 ▶ In pairs, Ss match the verbs with the expressions. Give Ss a short time limit, and then check answers. You may remind them that all the expressions are on Students' Book page 117 .

> **Answers:** 1 check your e-mails   2 do yoga   3 run in the park   4 send text messages   5 talk on the phone

While Watching

2 ▶ Watch the film without pausing, and check answers.

> **Answers:** 1 have breakfast at a café   2 fly a kite
> 3 go roller-blading   4 go out with friends   5 listen to music   6 look in shop windows   7 play tennis
> 8 read a book   9 ride a bike   10 swim in the pond

3 ▶ Ss work in pairs. Check that they understand that they have to find the correct expressions for the gaps, and to put them in the third person singular form. Write a large letter S on the board to remind them. Check answers.

> **Answers:** 1 does yoga   2 checks her e-mails   3 talks on the phone   4 sends a text message   5 rides her bike   6 has breakfast at a café   7 runs in the park
> 8 listens to music   9 swims in the pond   10 flies a kite   11 goes roller-blading   12 plays tennis
> 13 goes out with her friends

After Watching

4 ▶ Ss work in pairs. Remind them of the two questions *Do you ever...?* and *When do you...?* Elicit possible follow-up questions: *Where do you...? Do you like it? etc*

▶ Alternatively you could turn this into a survey-type activity. Ask Ss to circulate, talking to other Ss until they find the person with the most similar routine to their own.

> **OPTIONAL EXTENSION**
>
> Ask Ss to write a description of their perfect day, using any of the expressions from this unit.

4 Two soups

Before Watching

1 ▶ Ask Ss to study the words in the box and choose the items that are not usually seen in a restaurant.

> **Answers:**   *Magazines* and *rubbish bin*

While Watching

2 ▶ In pairs, Ss complete the *first* part of the dialogue with the missing sentences. Elicit the correct answers and then watch the first part of the film to check.

Repeat the procedure for parts 2 and 3.

> **Answers:**
> First part: 1 b)   2 d)   3 c)   4 a)
> Second part: 5 b)   6 c)   7 a)   8 d)
> Third part: 9 d)   10 c)   11 b)   12 a)

After Watching

3 ▶ Elicit the correct answers, and then help Ss with any other expressions they do not understand from the script.

> **Answers:**   1 d)   2 a)   3 b)   4 c)

4 ▶ Ss work in small groups of three or four. Ask them to decide who is going to play each part. Encourage them to act the part, and to make an effort to sound like the characters in the film.

> **OPTIONAL EXTENSION**
>
> Ask Ss to memorise their parts from the sketch. In the next class, you could have volunteers perform the sketch.
>
> As an alternative for stronger groups, you could ask them to prepare their own restaurant sketch, perhaps staging something that went wrong for them in a restaurant.

6

5 ResidenSea

Before Watching

1 ▶ Ss work in pairs. Give them a short time to try to complete the description. If they have done the activity in the Film Bank, they should be able to do it fairly well, but point out that it doesn't matter if they leave some of the gaps blank as they will be watching the film to check their answers.

While Watching

2 ▶ Watch the film to check the answers to Ex. 1, pausing where necessary.

> **Answers:** 1 196   2 650   3 110   4 1   5 3
> 6 4 million   7 88   8 4   9 2

3 ▶ Give Ss a short time to answer the questions. Help with any difficult vocabulary. Elicit the answers and if necessary, play the relevant parts of the film again.

> **Answers:** 1 Sydney   2 Rio de Janeiro   3 San Francisco   4 a top class restaurant   5 a gym
> 6 a spa   7 a library   8 a theatre   9 an art gallery
> 10 your terrace

After Watching

4 ▶ Ss work in pairs. Ensure they understand both parts of the task. Put up some useful expressions on the board, e.g. *I think we should.... .Why don't we...? What do you think? I don't agree I think it's better if we... . What would you like to do? I would like to...*

Give them a time limit to come to an agreement and to write down their decisions.

Ss swap pairs and compare their itineraries and their perfect days.

Discuss with the whole class how enjoyable such a week might be.

> **OPTIONAL EXTENSION**
>
> Ask Ss to write you a postcard from their holiday on *The World of ResidenSea*.

6 Amazing buildings

Before Watching

1a ▶ Elicit where the five buildings are.

> **Answers:** 1 The Flatiron Building is in New York.
> 2 The Guggenheim Museum is in Bilbao.   3 The Gherkin is in London.   4 The Eiffel Tower is in Paris.
> 5 Sydney Opera House is in Australia.

While Watching

2 ▶ Ask Ss to read the information. Watch the film without pausing, and then give Ss a short time to write the sentences. Elicit complete sentences.

> **Answers:**
> Suzy spent 2 years as a waitress in New York Her favourite building is the Flatiron Building. She thinks it's really unusual.
> John travelled to Bilbao because he wanted to see the Guggenheim Museum. He thinks it's fantastic.
> Penny lived in Paris for a year but she didn't visit the Eiffel Tower until her last month. She thinks it looks modern.
> Adam lives and works in London. He walks past the Gherkin every day. He thinks it's an amazing shape.
> Laura is from Sydney. She loves Sydney Opera House. She thinks it's very beautiful.

3 ▶ Give Ss time to read the sentences, and to correct any errors they can. Watch the film again, pausing after each section to check the answers.

> **Answers:** 1 The Flatiron building is the *first ever* skyscraper in New York. It's 2 metres wide and *87* metres high.   2 The Guggenheim museum is *50 metres* high. It's made of *stone* and *metal* and there are 19 galleries inside.   3 The Eiffel Tower is *300* metres tall so *you can see it from all over* the city. It opened *in 1889*.   4 It's the *Swiss-Re Tower*, but everybody calls it the *Gherkin*. It *opened in 2004*. It was in the film *Love, Actually*.   5 The Sydney Opera House opened *over 30* years ago. There's a theatre, a cinema and some restaurants *inside* it. Its roofs come from *Sweden*, it's glass is *French*, and the architect is *Danish*.

After Watching

4 ▶ Remind Ss of the guessing game in the Optional Warmer. Tell them they are going to do the same thing. Remind them to choose well-known buildings, and not to make the first clues too obvious.

> **OPTIONAL EXTENSION**
>
> Ask Ss to prepare a presentation – a speech of no more than 2 minutes – about a building they appreciate. Put some useful language on the board to help them do this, e.g.
>
> *It was built in... .   It's ... metres high.   It's made of... .*
> *It looks... .   It's used as... .   I think it's ... .*

7 Great Expectations

Before Watching

1 ▶ Ask a different Ss to read out each description, and elicit who it corresponds to. Help with any difficult vocabulary.

> **Answers:** 1 Pip   2 Miss Havisham   3 Estella
> 4 Mr Pumblechook

While Watching

1 ▶ Ask Ss to read the sentences in Ex. 2. Watch the film without pausing. Elicit the right answers, watching again, if necessary.

> **Answers:** 2 8   3   6   1   4   5   7

2 ▶ Give Ss a short time to read the sentences in Ex. 3, and to guess who said each line. Watch the film again to check the answers, pausing after each of these lines so that the students can repeat what is said.

> **Answers:** 1 Mr Pumblechook   2 Pip   3 Estella
> 4 Estella   5 Estella   6 Pip   7 Pip   8 Estella
> 9 Miss Havisham   10 Miss Havisham

After Watching

4 ▶ Ask Ss to read the sentences in Ex. 4, and elicit which sentences from Ex. 3 correspond to them.

> **Answers:** a 2   b 9   c 6   d 4   e 7   f 3

5 ▶ Elicit the past forms of the verbs in Ex. 2, and check that Ss understand the meaning of the words in the box. Encourage them to use some of the direct speech in Ex. 3.

> **OPTIONAL EXTENSION**
>
> Tell Ss they are going to write a description of a famous character from literature or the cinema. Read out this example and ask Ss to guess who it is.
>
> *He's a powerful wizard. He lives in Middle Earth. He's got long white hair and a white beard.*
>
> **Answer:** Gandalf from Lord of the Rings.

8 The Notting Hill Carnival

Before Watching

▶ Ask Ss to look at the questions, and elicit as many sentences about them as possible, e.g. *You can dance. You can play musical instruments. You can ride on a float. You can have your face painted. You can wear colourful costumes.*

While Watching

1 ▶ Go through the list of items with Ss, checking they understand them all. Tell them that you are going to play the film, and that you want them to shout out 'Stop!' when they see an item from the list. Play the film and pause where necessary. At the end of the film, elicit which two items are *not* in the film (3 and 13).

2 ▶ Give Ss a short time to match the beginnings and the continuations. Help with any difficult vocabulary. Ss check answers in pairs. Play the film again, pausing appropriately, to check answers.

> **Answers:** 1 d   2 f   3 b   4 e   5 a   6 c

After Watching

1 ▶ Make sure Ss understand the task in Ex. 4. Encourage them to use the present continuous and language from the film. You may decide to set this for homework.

> **OPTIONAL EXTENSION**
>
> Ask Ss to find a photo (in small classes, two photos) of people wearing special clothes and doing something special – it can be one of their own photos, or from a magazine, or downloaded from Internet. Tell them to write a short description of the person or people in their photo(s). Remind them to use the present continuous.
>
> In the next lesson, ask Ss to give you their photos, but to keep the descriptions hidden for the moment. Display all the photos Ss have brought in along with one or two of your own. Give everyone time to see all the photos. Then, ask Ss in turn to read out their description(s) and elicit from the other Ss which photo it corresponds to.

10

9 Spirit of the city

Before Watching

1 ▶ Ask Ss to name the places in the photos and to study the information. Then, elicit sentences comparing the three places. Encourage them to form appropriate comparative and superlative sentences, e.g. St Paul's is older than Tower Bridge. I think London Bridge is more beautiful than the London Eye. St Paul's isn't as high as the London Eye. I think St Paul's is the most interesting building.

While Watching

1 ▶ Ss work in pairs. Ask them to read the text about London. Give them a short time to fill in as many gaps as they can. Watch the film, without pausing. Elicit the correct answers.

> **Answers:** 1 huge 2 40 km 3 River Thames 4 8 million 5 largest 6 most popular 7 longest 8 symbol 9 the same 10 night 11 light 12 world

2 ▶ In the same pairs, set a time limit and ask Ss to complete the description of Richard Tate with the correct form of the verbs in brackets. Once the time is up, watch the film to check answers, pausing where necessary.

> **Answers:** 1 was 2 brought 3 was 4 came 5 worked 6 went 7 studied 8 took 9 dreamed 10 works 11 uses 12 spends 13 take 14 enjoys 15 is changing 16 are 17 loves

3 ▶ Ask Ss where Richard Tate is from, and then ask them to compare London and Scunthorpe using the adjectives, big, busy and noisy. Replay the appropriate section of the film if necessary.

After Watching

1 ▶ Ss work in small groups. Tell them you want them to write as many comparisons as they can in 3 minutes. When the time is up, have Ss read out their sentences.

Alternatively, you could set this task for homework.

> **OPTIONAL EXTENSION**
>
> Ask Ss to write a full description of the city where they live and / or an artist they know a lot about.

10 Commuting

Before Watching

1 ▶ Ask Ss to look at the first example, and elicit the correct answer. Ss work in pairs. Set a short time limit for Ss to re-order the words in the other 3 sentences. Elicit the correct answers, and make sure Ss write the 4 sentences in the correct places (1–4 in Ex. 2).

> **Answers:** 1 Describe your journey to work. 2 What do you do while you're travelling to work? 3 What are the good and bad points? 4 Are you ever late for work?

While Watching

▶ This is quite a challenging task, so you may wish to make it easier by eliciting the meaning of the key words from the answers before you start.

1 ▶ Give Ss a short time to read the information, and check that they understand what they have to do in each of the four parts. Watch the first part of the film, without pausing and elicit the answers. Replay any scenes if necessary.

> **Answers:** 1 about an hour 2 train 3 about 45 minutes 4 train 5 bus 6 tube 7 an hour and a half 8 train 9 30 to 35 minutes

2 ▶ Repeat the procedure for the other three parts.

> **Answers:** Part 2: 1 a cup of coffee 2 prepare for work 3 reads 4 buys 5 get a seat / read or work 6 stand 7 listen to music 8 sings 9 chat
> Part 3: 1 the trains are too crowded 2 time to read 3 smelly 4 personal time / the chance to read or to catch up with work 5 company / someone to talk to 6 traffic
> Part 4: 1 she has a simple journey to work 2 he oversleeps 3 there are problems with the trains 4 transport in Japan always runs on time 5 the traffic is very bad

After Watching

1 ▶ Ss work in pairs and use the four questions to interview each other. Encourage them to ask suitable follow-up questions.

> **OPTIONAL EXTENSION**
>
> Ask Ss to write about their partner using the information they obtained in the previous exercise.

11 Rock climbing

Before Watching

1 ▶ Write the four activities and the three adjectives on the board. Ss work in small groups. Set a time limit and ask Ss to grade the activities. Revise useful expressions for giving opinions, agreeing and disagreeing first if necessary.

While Watching

1 ▶ Check that Ss understand the meaning of the expressions in the box in Ex. 2. Make sure they know what they have to do. Ss work in pairs. Give them a few minutes to complete as many gaps as they can. Watch the film to check their answers and to fill in the gaps they couldn't do before.

> **Answers:** 1 b 2 c 3 i 4 o 5 e 6 g 7 f 8 n
> 9 h 10 d 11 k 12 l 13 m 14 j 15 a

2 ▶ Elicit some modal verbs, write them on the board ensuring that the following verbs are there, e.g. *can / can't / have to / don't have to*. Ask Ss to complete the text.

> **Answers:** 1 can't 2 have to 3 have to
> 4 don't have to 5 can

After Watching

1 ▶ Ask Ss to design an advertising leaflet for a centre which promotes a sport they are interested in. Encourage them to use the language from this unit, and ideas from the leaflets you showed them in the warmer activity.

> **OPTIONAL EXTENSION**
>
> Ask Ss to come up with more information about the centres in the leaflets they prepared for homework, e.g. opening hours, prices, what students can and can't do, what they have to do and what they don't have to do.
>
> In pairs, Ss prepare a role-play in which one person plays the part of a potential customer and the other represents the activity centre in their own leaflet.
>
> The customer should find out all the information he/she can.
>
> The representative should try to sell a course in their centre.

12 Ten great adventures

Before Watching

1 ▶ Elicit the missing words.

> **Answers:** 1 h 2 f 3 j 4 e 5 g 6 a 7 c
> 8 d 9 i 10 b

While Watching

1 ▶ Give Ss time to read the sentences in Ex. 2. Help with any difficult vocabulary, and then have them guess the activities the sentences refer to. Do not tell them if they are right or wrong at this stage. Play the film, pausing appropriately to check the answers.

> **Answers:** 1 riding the rapids 2 dog sledging
> 3 bungee jumping 4 swimming with dolphins
> 5 parascending 6 whale watching 7 sailing a ship
> 8 an expedition to Antarctica 9 skiing 10 diving

2 ▶ Read the questions in Ex. 3a and ask them to predict which questions Gill asks.

Ask Ss to look at Ex. 3b and check that they understand how questions can be formed with *Why not...?* and an infinitive.

Play the film, pausing appropriately to check the answers to both 3a and 3b.

> **Answers:** 3a: She asks questions 1, 2, 5, 6, 12
> 3b: Why not join the crew of a big old sailing ship?
> Why not learn to dive? Why not join an expedition to Antarctica?

After Watching

4 ▶ Encourage Ss to use the questions in Ex. 3a, and elicit other suitable questions, e.g.
Are you an adventurous person?
Do you like driving fast?
Do you enjoy lying on the beach?
Where do you usually spend your holidays?
Are you happy with your normal holidays?

Encourage them to use the construction *Why not...?* to give their recommendations.

> **OPTIONAL EXTENSION**
>
> Ask Ss to write a postcard from their holiday destination. In the next class, pin up the postcards on the wall and let Ss circulate to read them.

Tests

Test 1 Units 1-3

Grammar

to be (positive)

1 Complete the sentences with the correct form of *to be* (*am, is* or *are*). Use contractions where possible (*'m, 's, 're*).

Ralf and Sabine __are__ from Stuttgart.

1 John _____ from Boston.

2 What _____ this?

3 It' _____ a phone.

4 Where _____ you from?

5 We' _____ from Bratislava.

6 Hello, I' _____ Tomas.

[3 points]

Possessive 's; possessive adjectives

2 Put the words in the correct order to make sentences.

teacher Our is Australian
Our teacher is Australian.

1 Victoria wife is David's

_____

2 wife brother's from is My Riga

_____

3 father's is This sister my

_____

4 is cousin Paco her

_____

5 Laura sister is Harry's

_____

6 Mark Lucy's is son is daughter and Natasha her

_____

[3 points]

a/an; to be (questions and negatives)

3 Make the sentences into questions and then write the answers.

Brad Pitt is a singer.
Is Brad Pitt a singer?
No, he isn't a singer. He's an actor.

1 Paris is in Germany.

_____

_____

2 Ferrari cars are French.

_____

_____

3 Pizza is from Sweden.

_____

_____

4 You're in a Spanish class.

_____

_____

5 Your mother is president of the USA.

_____

_____

6 Your name is Britney.

_____

_____

[3 points]

© Pearson Education Limited 2005   Photocopiable

Present Simple: *I/you/we*

4 Write true answers about yourself for the following questions.

Where do you work?

I don't work. I'm a student./I work in a hospital.

1 What do you do?

_____

2 When do you get up?

_____

3 Where do you have breakfast?

_____

4 When do you have lunch?

_____

5 Do you have dinner at home?

_____

6 What do you do in the evening?

_____

(**3 points**)

Present Simple: *he/she/it*

5 Choose the correct form of the verb in italics.

He *play/plays* tennis very well.

1 My brother *talk/talks* for hours on his mobile phone.

2 I *watch/watches* sports on TV.

3 Hashim and Fatima *go/goes* to work by bus.

4 *Do/Does* Janet have a computer?

5 When does Marco *have/has* lunch?

6 *Do/Does* your sisters like football?

(**3 points**)

Present Simple: negative

6 Re-write the sentences in the negative.

Melanie works in an office.

Melanie doesn't work in an office.

1 Wayne plays hockey.

_____

2 I like classical music.

_____

3 We go shopping on Saturdays.

_____

4 She has an expensive guitar.

_____

5 They go to the gym in the evening.

_____

6 Anton and Sonia read computer magazines.

_____

(**3 points**)

can/can't

7 Put the missing word in the correct place in each sentence.

Nicky can play guitar. the

Nicky can play the guitar

1 Can you a bicycle? ride

_____

2 I can't French. speak

_____

3 your brother drive a car? can

_____

4 She can use computer. a

_____

5 Can you judo? do

_____

6 No, but I do yoga. can

_____

(**3 points**)

Photocopiable © Pearson Education Limited 2005

Making suggestions

8 Complete the gaps in the conversation.

A: What *can* we do tonight?

B: (1)_____ don't we (2)_____ dinner in the Italian restaurant?

A: I don't (3)_____ Italian food. How (4)_____ the cinema?

B: OK. (5)_____ film can we see?

A: Why (6)_____ we see *The Incredibles*?

B: That's a good idea. (7)_____ meet at half (8)_____ seven.

4 points

Total: 25 points

Pronunciation

1 Underline the stressed syllables.

Bra<u>zil</u>ian <u>Ger</u>many Aus<u>tra</u>lia

1 Russia
2 Japanese
3 Polish
4 Italy
5 Japan
6 Chinese
7 American
8 Italian

4 points

2 Write the verbs in the correct column.

finishes helps likes listens loves organises plays talks washes

/s/	/z/	/iz/
works	cleans	watches
_____	_____	_____
_____	_____	_____
_____	_____	_____

3 points

3 Write the words in the correct column.

six read big leave three these this listen meet green dinner sister

/ɪ/	/iː/
think	clean
_____	_____
_____	_____
_____	_____
_____	_____
_____	_____
_____	_____

3 points

Total: 10 points

© Pearson Education Limited 2005 Photocopiable

Vocabulary

1 Which word in each group is different?

France/Italy/Spain/<u>China</u>

(China is different because it's in Asia.)

1 Australian/American/Germany/Brazilian

_____

_____

2 mother/father/sister/daughter

_____

_____

3 father/girlfriend/brother/niece

_____

_____

4 parents/children/cousins/uncle

_____

_____

5 secretary/retired/nurse/police/officer

_____

_____

6 student/lawyer/judge/architect

_____

_____

(**2 points**)

2 Complete the sentences with the correct verb.

1 Does your brother _____ you with your homework?

2 I _____ to my friends by mobile phone.

3 I _____ football in the park every evening.

4 What programmes do you _____ on TV?

5 When do you _____ lunch?

6 In the morning I _____ up at 6.30.

(**3 points**)

3 Put the letters in the correct order to write the names of sports and games.

ODJU   _JUDO_

1 CAEOBRIS _____

2 SGIKIN _____

3 GRUINNN _____

4 NTISEN _____

5 OYAG _____

6 MSWIINGM _____

(**3 points**)

4 Complete the missing days of the week.

MONDAY

T_____

W_____

T_____

FRIDAY

S_____

SUNDAY

(**2 points**)

Total: 10 points

Photocopiable © Pearson Education Limited 2005

Reading

1 Read what Luke says about a typical day in his life.

On a typical day I get up at 7 o'clock. I leave home about half an hour later and then I drive to work. The journey takes about 45 minutes, and to fill the time I listen to the news on the radio. I stop in a bar near the office before I get to work and I always have a large black coffee, but I don't have anything to eat. I don't like to eat in the morning. I always go to the same bar so the waiter knows me well and we talk about football or the weather. I start work about half past eight and in the mornings I look at my e-mail, make phone calls and try to help my team with their problems. I have lunch in a restaurant near the office, and then in the afternoon I meet clients and talk to them about our products. I usually finish at about 6 o'clock, but if I have a lot of work, I don't leave until later- sometimes much later.

What do I do in the evenings? Well, every Monday I play five-a-side football with some friends. On Wednesdays I have a three-hour Italian class. It's very difficult because I'm a beginner in Italian. The other days I always go running. It helps me relax. I don't watch TV; I think the programmes are horrible. Most days I read – I like history books, and biographies of famous people. I go to bed about midnight.

2 Are the following sentences true (T) or false (F)?

Luke works in a hospital. *false*

1 Luke goes to work by car.

2 He has breakfast at home.

3 He has a big breakfast.

4 He doesn't have lunch at home.

5 He talks to many different people in a typical day.

6 He finishes work at the same time every day.

7 Luke doesn't like sports.

8 He speaks Italian very well.

9 He doesn't like television.

10 He reads in the evening.

(**10 points**)

3 Answer the questions about Luke's day.

What time does Luke get up?
He gets up at 7 o'clock.

1 What time does he leave home?

_____

2 What does he drink in the morning?

_____

3 What does he talk about with the waiter?

_____

4 When does he look at his e-mail?

_____

5 Who does he meet in the afternoon?

_____

6 What does he do on Monday evenings?

_____

7 What language does he study?

_____

8 Why does he go running?

_____

9 What books does he read?

_____

10 When does he go to bed?

_____

(**10 points**)

Total: 20 points

© Pearson Education Limited 2005   Photocopiable

Listening

1 Listen and complete the table.

Name	Jane	Andrea	Michael	Marga
Nationality	English			
Town/City			Dublin	
Age	31			
Job				teacher
Free time activities				

Total: 20 points

Writing

1 Choose ONE of the following and write a text of about 150–175 words.

1 Your family.

2 A typical day in your life.

3 The free time activities you like and when you do them.

_____

_____

_____

_____

_____

_____

_____

_____

_____

_____

_____

Total: 20 points

100 points

Test 2 Units 4-6

Grammar

Countable and uncountable nouns

1 Choose the correct word in *italics*.

How *much/many* coffee do you drink?

1 How *much/many* fruit do you eat?
2 How *much/many* bananas do you usually buy?
3 I usually buy 1 kg of *rice/rices*.
4 She doesn't eat *fish/fishes*.
5 I buy 12 *egg/eggs* when I go shopping.
6 How much *bread/breads* do you buy?

(**3 points**)

a/an, some and any

2 Complete the sentences with *a, an, some or any*.

I don't drink *any* wine.

1 Do you have _____ oranges?
2 No, but I have _____ watermelon.
3 When I go to the supermarket I usually buy _____ milk.
4 Is that _____ apple?
5 Can you buy _____ coffee?
6 I don't have _____ bananas.

(**3 points**)

Subject and object pronouns

3 Rewrite these sentences replacing the underlined nouns with pronouns.

John lives with Mary.
He lives with her.

1 The pizza is for the children.
   _____

2 Patricia loves chocolate.
   _____

3 Tomás and I go to school with Luisa.
   _____

4 Your mother loves dogs.
   _____

5 Dogs like your mother.
   _____

6 The eggs are for Charles.
   _____

(**3 points**)

there is/there are

4 Underline the correct sentences.

   a) There is some shops in the village.
   b) There are some shops in the village.
   c) There are any shops in the village.

1 a) There is a cupboard in the kitchen.
   b) There is some cupboards in the   kitchen.
   c) There are a cupboard in the kitchen.

2 a) There isn't any restaurant in the hotel.
   b) There isn't a restaurant in the hotel.
   c) There isn't any restaurants in the hotel.

3 a) Is there a swimming pool here?
   b) Is there any swimming pool here?
   c) There is any swimming pool here?

4 a) There is some mountains in the north.
   b) There are any mountains in the north.
   c) There are some mountains in the north.

5 a) How many rooms are there?
   b) How many rooms there are?
   c) How many rooms is there?

6 a) Is there any cars in the street?
   b) Are there a cars in the street?
   c) Are there any cars in the street?

(**3 points**)

© Pearson Education Limited 2005 Photocopiable

have got

5 Put the words in the correct order to make sentences.

has Niurka brothers got three
Niurka has got three brothers.

1 The television hasn't got flat a

_____

2 parents My new have a got car

_____

3 house got a Has your garden?

_____

4 Malta beaches some got has nice

_____

5 cats many got has How he?

_____

6 They got haven't chairs any

_____

(**3 points**)

Past of *to be*

6 Complete the dialogue with the correct past form of *to be*.

A: You weren't at home last night Where (1)_____ you?
B: I (2)_____ at my sister's house.

A: (3)_____ you in the garden?
B: No, we (4)_____. The weather (5)_____ very cold.

A: (6)_____your husband with you?
B: No, he (7)_____. He (8)_____at work.

(**4 points**)

Past Simple of regular verbs

7 Complete the sentences with the Past Simple form of the verbs in the box.

marry study ~~work~~ visit live start open

Last year Gabby *worked* as a chef in a restaurant.

1 I _____ work at 8 o'clock this morning.
2 When I was younger I _____ in a house in the country.
3 My brother _____ philosophy at university.
4 The President _____ the new parliament building last weekend.
5 When I went to Egypt I _____ the Pyramids.
6 My friend _____ his wife in Las Vegas last summer.

(**3 points**)

Photocopiable © Pearson Education Limited 2005

Past Simple: questions

8 Write questions for these sentences.

I lived in **Helsinki.**

Where did you live?

1 The museum opened **last year.**

_____ ?

2 They watched **the football match** on Saturday.

_____ ?

3 She **didn't** have **any** money with her.

_____ ?

4 He studied French **at school.**

_____ ?

5 He asked **the policeman** for directions.

_____ ?

6 She worked **in a bank.**

_____ ?

(3 points)

Total: 25 points

Pronunciation

1 Put the words in the correct column.

some pasta shop hot happy lunch
hat young

/ɒ/	/ʌ/	/æ/
Dog	*sun*	*cat*
_____	_____	_____
_____	_____	_____
_____	_____	_____

(4 points)

2 Put the verbs in the correct column.

liked   lived wanted
started watched finished painted
changed invented moved opened produced

/d/	/t/	/ɪd/
cleaned	*worked*	*visited*
_____	_____	_____
_____	_____	_____
_____	_____	_____
_____	_____	_____

(6 points)

Total: 10 points

© Pearson Education Limited 2005 Photocopiable

Vocabulary

1 Write three more words in each list.

   1 Meat and fish:

     tuna, _____, _____,

     _____.

   2 Fruit:

     watermelon, _____, _____,

     _____.

   3 Vegetables:

     potatoes, _____, _____,

     _____.

   4 Cold drinks:

     cola, _____, _____,

     _____.

(**2 points**)

2 Write the names of three pieces of furniture or equipment for each room.

Living room:

armchair, sofa, TV.

   1 Kitchen:

     _____,_____,

     _____.

   2 Bathroom:

     _____,_____,

     _____.

   3 Bedroom:

     _____,_____,

     _____.

   4 Dining room:

     _____,_____,

     _____.

(**2 points**)

3 Complete the sentences.

You can buy stamps in *the post office*.

   1 We went to the Italian _____
     and ate gnocchi al pesto.

   2 My uncle works in a _____
     that produces cars.

   3 I saw some beautiful impressionist paintings
     in the _____ .

   4 Sandra is a student and she spends a lot of time
     reading books in the _____
     at the university.

   5 It's more convenient to do my food shopping in the
     _____ than in the small local shops.

   6 I need to go to the _____ to have some
     medical tests.

(**3 points**)

4 Put the letters in the correct order to write the names of forms of transport.

SBU *BUS*

   1 ECIYBCL   _____

   2 AXTI   _____

   3 TOBA   _____

   4 RATIN   _____

   5 TMAR   _____

   6 CRA   _____

(**3 points**)

Total: 10 points

Photocopiable   © Pearson Education Limited 2005

Reading

1 Antonella is being interviewed about the city she lives in. Match the questions (1–9) with the answers (a–i).

1 Can you tell us something about the city where you live? c

2 Where is it exactly?

3 Has it got good transport facilities?

4 Are there many famous buildings?

5 Are there any museums or art galleries?

6 What about shopping?

7 What can you do at night?

8 Are there any interesting places to visit near the city?

9 Is there anything you don't like about living in Florence?

a) Oh, yes, of course. There are a lot. There's a very famous cathedral, a lot of palaces and some beautiful churches.

b) It's located on the river Arno, in the north of Italy.

c) I live in Florence. It's the capital of Tuscany, and I think it's the most beautiful city in Italy and probably in the world. It has a population of about half a million people – so it's quite a big city. And of course it's famous throughout the world for it's art and culture.

d) Well, there is a very big train station in the centre of Florence, and there are two airports, named after two famous people in the history of the city: Amerigo Vespucci and Galileo Galilei. There are a lot of buses, but it's usually a good idea to walk around the city centre.

e) There are many other famous towns and cities near Florence that are well worth visiting, like Lucca, Arrezzo, Siena and Pisa. I would recommend going to Fiesole, it's in the mountains to the north-east of Florence. It's about 8 km away.

f) Yes, we have some of the greatest museums and art galleries in the world. The most famous is the Uffizi gallery. It's got a lot of paintings by Italian renaissance artists. And there is also the Accademia, where you can see the famous statue of David by Michelangelo.

g) Oh yes, that's easy. There are too many tourists!

h) There are a lot of bars, cafés and restaurants.

i) There are a lot of shops for tourists in the historical centre and there are some famous jewellery shops on a bridge over the river. But, like in any city, you can also find supermarkets and department stores.

(**12 points**)

2 Read the interview again. Are the following sentences true (T) or false (F)?

Florence is the capital of Tuscany. *T*

1 Florence is a small city.

2 There is a river in Florence.

3 The name of the train station is Galileo Galilei.

4 Florence has got some beautiful churches.

5 There are a lot of paintings in the Uffizi.

6 Arrezzo is near Florence.

7 Fiesole is next to the sea.

8 There aren't any supermarkets in Florence.

(**8 points**)

Total: 20 points

© Pearson Education Limited 2005 Photocopiable

Listening

1 Listen to four people (George, Sarah, Anton, and Muriel) talking about where they live. Answer the questions.

Who has got children? <u>Sarah</u>

1 Who lives in a city? _____

2 Who lives near the sea? _____

3 Who lives in a big house? _____

4 Who lives with animals? _____

5 Who doesn't live with his or her family? _____

(**10 points**)

2 Listen again and say if the sentences below are true (T) or false (F).

George isn't married. *F*

1 Three people live in George's house.

2 George hasn't got a garden.

3 Sarah lives in a house.

4 Sarah has got two bathrooms.

5 Sarah hasn't got a garden.

6 Anton lives with his sister.

7 Anton doesn't like living near the beach.

8 There isn't a dining room in Muriel's house.

9 There's a lake in Muriel's garden.

10 Muriel goes swimming in the river.

(**10 points**)

Total: 20 points

Writing

1 Choose ONE of the following and write a text of about 150–175 words.

1 A description of your house or apartment.

2 Write about what kind of food you normally eat.

3 A description of the town or city where you live.

_____

_____

_____

_____

_____

_____

_____

_____

_____

_____

_____

_____

_____

_____

_____

_____

_____

_____

_____

_____

_____

_____

_____

_____

Total: 15 points

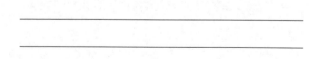

100 points

Photocopiable © Pearson Education Limited 2005

Grammar

Pronoun *one/ones*; possessive pronouns

1 Choose the correct word in italics.

The blue *one/ones* are mine

1 Your house is quite big but *our/ours* is small.
2 These are his trainers and those *one/ones* are hers.
3 Is this umbrella *your/ yours?*
4 No, mine is the black *one/ones.*
5 Which one belongs to *them/theirs?*
6 The red one is *them/theirs.*

(**3 points**)

Past Simple: irregular verbs

2 Complete the sentences with the Past Simple form of the verbs in the box.

> ~~see~~ have spend take
> tell give go

I *saw* a great film on TV yesterday.

1 I _____ my dog to the park this morning.
2 In our old house we _____ a garden.
3 Marta _____ to India on her last holiday.
4 My parents _____ me a beautiful watch for my birthday.
5 Jackie _____ me you passed the exam. Congratulations!
6 He _____ three hours doing his homework.

(**3 points**)

Present Simple; adverbs of frequency

3 Put the words in the correct order to make sentences.

They wine drink never
They never drink wine

1 I wear suit a often

_____

2 He gym to the goes sometimes

_____

3 She work drives to always

_____

4 often It is in Finland cold

_____

5 I at work weekends never

_____

6 They go hardly cinema the ever to

_____

(**3 points**)

Present Continuous

4 Find the errors in each sentence and correct them.

They talking quietly.
They're talking quietly.

1 She are looking for her book.

_____

2 They are sleep in the bedroom.

_____

3 He isn't driving careful.

_____

4 Matthew singing in the bath.

_____

5 I am read an interesting book.

_____

6 Gloria is speak on the phone.

_____

(**3 points**)

© Pearson Education Limited 2005 Photocopiable

Present Simple and Present Continuous

5 Present Simple or Present Continuous? Put the verbs in brackets in the correct tense.

At the moment he is watching TV. (watch)

1 My mother never _____ coffee. (drink)

2 What are they doing?

They _____ their homework. (do)

3 In Canada, people _____ French and English. (speak)

4 Freddy usually _____ a suit when he goes to work. (wear)

5 Katrin _____ a blue shirt today. (wear)

6 What's the weather like at the moment?
It _____ . (rain)

7 I _____ to work every day. (drive)

8 Where's Buddy?
He _____ tennis in the park. (play)

(**5 points**)

Comparison of adjectives

6 Write a comparative sentence for each of the following topics.

Russia / Spain
Russia is bigger than Spain.

1 Italian food / English food

_____

2 basketball / tennis

_____

3 a car / a bicycle

_____

4 Chinese / English

_____

5 New York / your city

_____

6 travelling by plane / travelling by train

_____

(**3 points**)

Comparative and superlative adjectives

7 Choose the correct option for each sentence.

That was the _____ film I've seen this year.
a) better   b) best   c) most good

1 London is the _____ city in the UK.
a) most big   b) biggest   c) bigger

2 What's the _____ hotel in your town?
a) expensivest   b) more expensive
c) most expensive

3 The weather in England is _____ than in Spain.
a) badder   b) worse   c) worst

4 The _____ river in Africa is the Nile.
a) most long   b) longer   c) longest

5 My brother is _____ than me.
a) younger   b) youngest   c) more young

6 A taxi is _____ than a bus.
a) most comfortable   b) more comfortable
c) comfortabler

(**3 points**)

prefer

8 Complete the sentences with an appropriate word.

I prefer *reading* novels to poetry

1 I prefer pizza _____ pasta.

2 _____ you prefer painting or sculpture?

3 I prefer _____ football to watching it.

4 I _____ coffee to tea.

5 He likes classical music more _____ rock music.

6 I prefer _____ to the cinema.

(3 points)

Total: 25 points

Pronunciation

1 Put the words in the correct column.

> brother   bathroom
> three   third
> this   there
> thirteen   those

/θ/	/ð/
thank	*they*
_____	_____
_____	_____
_____	_____
_____	_____

(4 points)

2 Underline the stressed syllables in each word.

Trainers foggy

1 prefer	**5** opera	**9** pullover
2 returned	**6** police	**10** sometimes
3 snowing	**7** carefully	**11** cartoon
4 exciting	**8** newspaper	**12** romantic

(6 points)

Total: 10 points

© Pearson Education Limited 2005   Photocopiable

Vocabulary

Ordinal numbers; months

1 Write the dates as complete sentences.

3/12 *the third of December*
22/7 *the twenty-second of July*

1/8 _____

8/5 _____

12/10 _____

5/2 _____

4/1 _____

25/12 _____

15/6 _____

23/4 _____

(**2 points**)

Phrasal verbs

2 Complete the sentences with the correct word.

I like listening to the radio.

| to back up up together at in |

1 Pick _____ that book and put it on the table!

2 We handed _____ out homework to the teacher.

3 I'll give you _____ the money tomorrow.

4 Look _____ Joanna! What's she doing?

5 Irina gets _____ at 6.30 every morning.

6 I can't put_____ the pieces of this puzzle!

(**3 points**)

Clothes; the weather

3 Complete the words by writing the missing letters.

Clothes:

B _ _ T   J _ _ K _T   S K _ _ _

T _ _ _ S _ _ S   D _ _ S S

Weather:

S _ _ _ Y   S _ _ _ _ N G   H _ _

C _ _ _ D _   F _ _ _ Y

(**2 points**)

4 Put the words in the correct column.

| horror impressionist sculpture abstract musical novels poetry cartoon plays |

Types of film	Painting and art	Literature
_____	_____	_____
_____	_____	_____
_____	_____	_____

(**3 points**)

Total: 10 points

Test 3 Units 7-9

Reading

1 Read the texts about famous writers and painters and answer the questions below.

Ernest Hemingway was born in 1899 in Chicago. His father was a doctor. When he was young he worked as a journalist, but in 1924 he decided to devote himself to writing.

During his life he travelled around the world and he used his experiences as the basis for many of his novels. He was in Italy during the First World War and based A Farewell to Arms on his experience there. During the Civil War he went to Spain and described his experiences in For Whom the Bell Tolls. He was passionately interested in bullfighting, hunting, and fishing.

Hemingway wrote about twenty novels and short stories and received the Nobel Prize for literature in 1954. He died in 1961.

Michelangelo Buonarotti was born on the 6th of March 1475. He lived in Florence and Rome for most of his life. He was a painter, sculptor and architect. His most famous works are probably the paintings in the Sistine chapel, and his statue of David. He never married. He worked continuously all his life until 6 days before his death in 1564.

William Shakespeare was born in Stratford in 1564. His father was an important businessman in the town. In 1582 he married Anne Hathaway, who was eight years older than him, and he had three children. In 1587 he went to London where he worked as a writer and actor. He wrote a lot of plays and poetry. He retired to Stratford in 1612, and died on the 23rd April 1616.

Vincent van Gogh was born in 1853 in a village in Holland. He had a brother, Theo, who was two years younger than him. He was a painter and his most famous paintings are 'Sunflowers' and his paintings of Arles, in the south of France, where he lived in 1888. Today his paintings sell for millions of pounds, but during his life he was not successful, and he was financially dependent on his brother. He had mental health problems all his life, and finally committed suicide in 1890. His brother Theo died one year later.

2 Are the following sentences true (T) or false (F)?

1 Hemingway had the same profession as his father.

2 In 1924 he changed the direction of his life.

3 He didn't have much experience of the situations he described in his books.

4 His life was not very exciting.

5 Michelangelo travelled to many different countries.

6 In the last years of his life he did not work very much.

7 He was more than 80 years old when he died.

8 He didn't have a wife.

9 Shakespeare was younger than his wife.

10 He lived in the same town all his life.

11 He died four years after returning to Stratford.

12 Shakespeare never wrote novels

13 Van Gogh was older than his brother.

14 He lived in Holland all his life.

15 He made a lot of money from his paintings when he was alive.

16 He was not very happy in his life

3 Answer these questions.

1 Who lived the longest?

_____

2 Who travelled the most?

_____

3 Who was the youngest when they died?

_____

4 Who had the most personal problems?

_____

Total: 20 points

© Pearson Education Limited 2005 Photocopiable

Listening

1 Listen to some people describing their friends. Read the sentences below and say if they are true (T) or false (F).

Speaker 1

1 John is quite tall.

2 He's got a lot of hair.

3 He plays rugby now.

Speaker 2

4 Lucy is a university student.

5 She's got dark hair.

Speaker 3

6 David works in a school.

7 He's not very tall.

8 The speaker thinks he's handsome.

Speaker 4

9 Lisa is a translator.

10 She is on holiday in Turkey at the moment.

(**10 points**)

2 Listen again and answer the questions.

1 When does the first speaker see his friend, John?

_____

2 What colour are Lucy's eyes?

_____

3 Write three words the speaker uses to describe Lucy's personality. _____, _____, _____.

4 When is David's birthday?

5 The last speaker says his friend has got _____, _____ eyes.

(**10 points**)

Total: 20 points

Writing

1 Choose ONE of the following and write a text of about 150–175 words.

1 Write a postcard to a friend from a holiday destination. Write about where you are, what you are doing, what you did yesterday, and the weather.

2 Write about a good film you have seen, or a good book you have read this year.

3 Write a description of a friend or a person in your family. Describe their appearance, their personality, and give some information about their life and their likes and dislikes.

_____

_____

_____

_____

_____

_____

_____

_____

_____

_____

_____

_____

_____

_____

_____

_____

_____

_____

_____

_____

_____

_____

Total: 15 points

100 points

Photocopiable © Pearson Education Limited 2005

Test 4 | Units 10–12

Grammar

Present Perfect (*been* with *ever/never*)

1 Choose the correct word in *italics*.

I've ever/<u>never</u> been to Australia.

1 Have you *ever/never* been in a plane?

2 *Has/Have* Silvia been horse-riding?

3 Yes, she *went/has been* last summer.

4 I have never *went/been* to Rome.

5 Have you ever been *in/to* the opera?

6 *I'm/I've* been hiking many times.

(**3 points**)

Present Perfect

2 Complete the sentences with the Present Perfect form of the verbs in the box.

> go see have spend be play arrive

Amanda *has gone* to the post office today.

1 I'm not hungry. I _____ lunch.

2 I _____ seven films at the cinema this month!

3 We _____ three hours in a boring meeting.

4 The Cambridge train _____ at the station.

5 Brian _____ tennis for his university team.

6 Yes, I _____ bungee-jumping once. It was very exciting.

(**3 points**)

can/can't, have to/don't have to

3 Complete the sentences with *can, can't, have to,* or *don't have to.*

You *have to* have a passport to travel to the USA.

1 You _____ drive a car without a driving licence.

2 The exhibition is free. You _____ to pay.

3 You _____ smoke in the hospital.

4 In most restaurants you _____ pay cash or by credit card, as you prefer.

5 You _____ study hard to pass this exam. It's not easy.

6 You _____ come to the cinema with us, if you don't want. There's no obligation.

(**3 points**)

© Pearson Education Limited 2005 Photocopiable

Wh- questions

4 Complete the questions below with an appropriate question word.

How do you go to work? By car.

1 _____ did you move to Oslo?

In 2002.

2 _____languages do you speak? Only two.

3 _____ do you do in the evening?

I usually read or watch TV.

4 _____ does your brother work? He works in a bank in Zaragoza.

5 _____ coffee do you drink?

Two or three cups a day.

6 _____do you spend doing your homework?

Usually about half an hour.

(**3 points**)

Present Continuous for future

5 Write sentences using the prompts.

Jorge/ tennis/ next Saturday

Jorge is playing tennis next Saturday.

1 Peter and Mary/dinner/tomorrow evening

_____

2 I/start/course/next month

_____

3 The president/open/ new museum/ Sunday

_____

4 We/go/Paris/December

_____

5 What/you/do/next weekend?

_____

6 I/cinema/friends/Saturday evening

_____

(**3 points**)

Going to

6 Answer the questions.

When are you going to see your parents?

I'm going to see them this evening.

1 When are you going to have a holiday?

_____

2 Where are you going to go?

_____

3 What are you going to have for breakfast tomorrow?

_____

4 What are you going to do after this class?

_____

5 How are you going to go home today?

_____

6 What are you going to do when you arrive home?

_____

7 What are you going to do next weekend?

_____

8 Are you going to buy anything tomorrow? What?

_____

(**4 points**)

Infinitive of purpose

7 Use your imagination to complete the sentences.

I went to the supermarket
I went to the supermarket *to buy potatoes.*

1 Carrie went to the airport

_____

2 We're going to the stadium

_____

3 I'm studying English

_____

4 Paula went to Egypt

_____

5 Tomorrow I'm going to the hospital

_____

6 Next year my daughter is going to university

_____

(3 points)

Verbs + infinitive/-*ing* form

8 Complete the sentences with a verb in the infinitive or –*ing* form.

Friedrich would like to be a pilot.

1 Peter hates _____ to the cinema.
2 They don't want _____ the football match.
3 I enjoy _____ hockey
4 I would like _____ three or four languages.
5 She doesn't want _____ dinner with me.
6 Katerina can't stand _____ to rock music

(3 points)

Total: 25 points

Pronunciation

1 Put the words in the correct column.

swim   this   these   slim   green   sleep
visit   beach

/iː/	/ɪ/
see	*sing*
_____	_____
_____	_____
_____	_____
_____	_____

(4 points)

2 Underline the stressed syllables in each word.

Biology   college

1 Chemistry   4 Geography
2 History   5 Mathematics
3 polytechnic   6 university

(3 points)

3 Underline the words in the sentences below that contain the sound /aɪ/. (There is one word in each sentence.)

Dave's car is white.

1 You have to wait at the light.
2 I don't like to be late.
3 I often drive to the lake.
4 The blue one is mine.
5 It's faster to fly to Spain.
6 The chocolate cake is nice.

(3 points)

Total: 10 points

© Pearson Education Limited 2005   Photocopiable

Vocabulary

Travel

1 Complete the sentences.

1 It's very expensive to live in the city centre, so I live in the s_____

2 In the morning, during the r_____ hour , there is a lot of traffic on the roads.

3 Would you like a one-way ticket or a r_____ ticket?

4 You have to arrive at the airport one hour before d_____

5 The Majestic is the most l_____ hotel in the city. It has five stars.

6 We went on a s_____ tour of the city.

(3 points)

Education

2 Write three more words in each of the categories.

Subjects:

Biology, Physics, _____,

_____,_____.

Places:

College, primary school,_____,

_____,_____.

People:

Lecturer, teacher, _____,

_____,_____.

(3 points)

Geographical features

3 Put the letters in the correct order to make the names of some geographical features.

LINDSA   ISLAND

1 RGDBEI   _____

2 YNACON   _____

3 NMTAOUIN _____

4 RERVI   _____

5 LSIHL   _____

6 TOSCA   _____

7 UNNLET   _____

8 ASE   _____

(2 points)

Leisure activities

4 Choose the correct answers.

1 You need an animal for this activity:
   a) kayaking
   b) mountain biking
   c) horse-riding

2 An exciting sport you do on a fast river:
   a) white water rafting
   b) sailing
   c) trekking

3 In this activity you walk for a long time in the mountains:
   a) kayaking
   b) mountain biking
   c) trekking

4 You need a bike for this:
   a) trekking
   b) cycling
   c) sailing

(2 points)

Total: 10 points

Photocopiable © Pearson Education Limited 2005

Reading

1 Read the texts about three different hotels in Prague and answer the questions.

Union Hotel, Odstrcilovo nam, 1128 00 Prague 2
The hotel Union was built in 1906 and renovated in 1992. The hotel is situated in Prague's historical centre, five minutes from the Congress Palace and the Vysehrad Castle.
The hotel has 57 modern rooms, equipped with toilet, bath or shower, hair dryer, telephone, satelitte TV, radio and minibar. Money exchange, souvenirs and a safe for valuables are available at reception. Free parking is provided.
The restaurant offers Czech and international cuisine. There is a bar with a view of the Castle and a wide selection of drinks.
English and German is spoken at reception, and we accept payment by all major credit cards.

Price of a double room: 87

Axa Hotel, Na Porici 40, 110 00 Prague 1
The hotel Axa was constructed in 1932. The hotel is ideally situated in the heart of enchanting Prague, just 150 metres from the nearest metro station. The hotel offers 132 rooms equipped with private bathrooms, colour satellite TV and direct-dial telephones. We have a full restaurant service providing Czech specialities as well as international cuisine. We also have excellent recreational and fitness training facilities, including a 25m long indoor heated swimming pool (1.50 per hour). You can enjoy a sauna (3), massage or a visit to the solarium. Parking is available at a price of 260 KC (Czech crowns) Price of a double room: 124

Hotel Mepro, Viktora Huga 23, 150 00 Praha 5
The hotel is very conveniently located near Arbes Square in the historical centre of Prague below Prague castle and on the left bank of the Vltava River, It is a short walk from Charles Bridge or the National Theatre. A tram stop is close to the hotel and the underground station is 3 minutes walk from the hotel.
There are 27 rooms, we speak English and German, and parking is available at the hotel at a price of 150 CZK per night.
A double room costs: 99 including a buffet breakfast.

2 Are the following sentences true (T) or false (F)?

1 The Union is a modern hotel.

2 It is in the suburbs of Prague

3 All rooms have a bathroom

4 You don't have to pay to park your car.

5 The Axa is in the centre of Prague

6 It has got more than 100 rooms

7 You have to eat Czech food in the restaurant

8 You don't have to pay to use the swimming pool.

9 The Mepro is near the river.

10 You can speak French at the reception

11 Parking at the hotel is free

12 You have to pay extra for breakfast

3 Answer the following questions.

1 What services can you find at the reception in the Union?

2 What can you see from the bar in the Union?

3 How can you relax at the Axa?

4 Which forms of public transport can you use if you stay at the Mepro?

5 Which hotel is the biggest?

6 Which hotel has the cheapest rooms?

7 Which hotel is not near the Castle?

8 Which hotel has the best recreational facilities?

Total: 20 points

© Pearson Education Limited 2005 Photocopiable

Listening

1 Listen to Martina talking about her experiences of studying and learning, then answer the questions below.

1 Did Martina like primary school?

_____

2 Did she learn a lot a primary school?

_____

3 Why didn't she like secondary school?

_____

4 What were here favourite subjects at school?

_____

5 Which university did she go to?

_____

6 What did she start to study at university?

_____

7 Who was David?

_____

8 How did he help her?

_____

9 What course did she change to?

_____

10 Was the course she did in new technologies part-time or full-time?

_____

11 What languages has she studied in the past?

_____

12 What language is she studying at the moment?

_____

13 Why is this course unusual?

_____

14 Why doesn't she like it?

_____

Total: 20 points

Writing

1 Choose ONE of the following and write a text of about 150–175 words.

1 Write a description of public transport in your town or region. What kinds of transport are there? Which do you use? What are the advantages and disadvantages of each?

2 Write a letter to a hotel to book a room. Ask for some information about the hotel, for example, it's location, facilities available, etc.

3 Write about your education. Describe where you studied or where you are studying now. What did/do you like or not like? Have your taken any courses apart from your formal education?

_____

_____

_____

_____

_____

_____

_____

_____

_____

_____

_____

_____

_____

_____

_____

Total: 15 points

100 points

Photocopiable © Pearson Education Limited 2005

TEST 1

Grammar

1 1 is/'s; 2 is/'s; 3 's; 4 are; 5 're; 6 'm

2 1 Victoria is David's wife. 2 My brother's wife is from Riga. 3 This is my father's sister. 4 Paco is her cousin. 5 Laura is Harry's sister. 6 Mark is Lucy's son and Natasha is her daughter./Natasha is Lucy's daughter and Mark is her son.

3 1 Is Paris in Germany? No, it isn't in Germany. It's in France. 2 Are Ferrari cars French? No, they aren't French. They're Italian. 3 Is pizza from Sweden? No, it isn't from Sweden. It's from Italy. 4 Are you in a Spanish class? No, I'm not in a Spanish class. I'm in an English class./No, we aren't in a Spanish class. We're in an English class. 5 Is your mother president of the USA? No, she isn't president of the USA. She's ... 6 Is your name Britney? No, it isn't Britney. It's ...

4 Ss' own answers: 1 I'm a (occupation). 2 I get up at (time). 3 I have breakfast in/at (place). 4 I have lunch at (time). 5 Yes, I do./No, I don't. 6 I (verb + activity).

5 1 talks; 2 watch; 3 go; 4 Does; 5 have; 6 Do

6 1 Wayne doesn't play hockey. 2 I don't like classical music. 3 We don't go shopping on Saturdays. 4 She doesn't have an expensive guitar. 5 They don't go to the gym in the evening. 6 Anton and Sonia don't read computer magazines.

7 1 Can you ride a bicycle? 2 I can't speak French. 3 Can your brother drive a car? 4 She can use a computer. 5 Can you do judo? 6 No, but I can do yoga.

8 1 Why; 2 have; 3 like; 4 about; 5 Which/What; 6 don't; 7 Let's; 8 past

Pronunciation

1 1 Russia; 2 Japanese; 3 Polish; 4 Italy; 5 Japan; 6 Chinese; 7 American; 8 Italian

2

/s/	/z/	/ɪz/
likes	plays	washes
talks	listens	finishes
helps	loves	organises

3

/ɪ/	/iː/
six	leave
big	read
this	three
listen	these
dinner	meet
sister	green

Vocabulary

1 1 Germany (the others are nationalities); 2 father (the others are female); 3 girlfriend (not a member of your family); 4 uncle (the others are plural); 5 retired (the others are jobs); 6 student (the others are paid occupations)

2 1 help; 2 talk/speak; 3 play; 4 watch; 5 have; 6 get

3 1 AEROBICS; 2 SKIING; 3 RUNNING; 4 TENNIS; 5 YOGA; 6 SWIMMING;

4 TUESDAY; WEDNESDAY; THURSDAY; SATURDAY

Reading

2 1 true; 2 false; 3 false; 4 true; 5 true; 6 false; 7 false; 8 false; 9 true; 10 true

3 1 He leaves home at half past seven/at 7.30. 2 He drinks a large black coffee. 3 He talks about football or the weather. 4 He looks at his email in the mornings. 5 He meets clients.; 6 he plays (five-a-side) football. 7 He studies Italian. 8 Because it helps him relax. 9 He reads history books and biographies of famous people. 10 He goes to bed about mignight.

Listening
(points per answer in brackets. Total 20 points)

1

Name	Jane	Andrea	Michael	Marga
Nationality	English	Italian (1)	Irish (1)	Spanish (1)
Town/City	Slough (1)	Bari (1)	Dublin	Oviedo (1)
Age	31	19 (1)	48 (1)	35 (1)
Job	architect (1)	student (1)	unemployed engineer	teacher
Free time activities	meet friends, go to restaurant or cinema (2)	football, basketball and swimming (3)	study French (1)	read travel books (1)

Recording
Hi. My name's Jane, and I'm English. I'm an architect. I'm 31 years old and I live in a town in the south of England called Slough. That's S-L-O-U-G-H. I like to meet friends and go to restaurants or to the cinema.

Hello. I'm Andrea. I'm 19 and I'm a student. I'm from Italy, from a town called Bari. That's B-A-R-I. I like sports and I play football, and basketball and I go swimming.

Well, I'm called Michael Brennan and I'm from Dublin. Dublin's in Ireland of course. And, what else? My job? Yeah, well, I'm an engineer but I'm unemployed now. It's difficult to find a job at my age. I'm 48 you see. I have a lot of free time so I study French.

My name's Marga and I come from Oviedo in Spain. That's O-V-I-E-D-O. I'm a school teacher. I'm 35 years old and I have two children. In my free time I read books – travel books.

Writing
Ss own answers.

TEST 2

Grammar

1 1 much; 2 many; 3 rice; 4 fish; 5 eggs; 6 bread

2 1 any; 2 a; 3 some; 4 an; 5 some; 6 any

3 1 It's for them. 2 She loves it. 3 We go to school with her. 4 She loves them. 5 They like her. 6 They are for him.

4 1 a; 2 b; 3 a; 4 c; 5 a; 6 c

5 1 The flat hasn't got a television. 2 My parents have got a new car. 3 Has your house got a garden? 4 Malta has got some nice beaches. 5 How many cats has he got? 6 They haven't got any chairs.

6 1 were; 2 was; 3 Were; 4 weren't; 5 was; 6 Was; 7 wasn't; 8 was

7 1 started; 2 lived; 3 studied; 4 opened; 5 visited; 6 married

8 1 When did the museum open? 2 What did they watch on Saturday? 3 How much money did she have with her? 4 Where did he study French? 5 Who did he ask for directions? 6 Where did she work?

Pronunciation

1

/ɑ/	/ʌ/	/æ/
hot shop	some lunch young	pasta happy hat

2

/d/	/t/	/ɪd/
lived moved changed opened	liked watched finished produced	wanted painted started invented

Vocabulary

1 **Possible answers:** 1 Meat and fish: chicken, beef, trout. 2 Fruit: apples, bananas, pineapple. 3 Vegetables: carrots, tomato, rice. 4 Cold drinks: orange juice, water, milk.

2 Possible answers: 1 Kitchen: fridge, microwave, sink, coffee machine, cooker, dishwasher, washing machine, table. 2 Bathroom: shower, toilet, cupboard, chair, CD/DVD player. 3 Bedroom: bed, chair, cupboard, desk, bookshelves, TV, CD/DVD player. 4 Dining room: chairs, (dining) table, bookshelves, CD/DVD player.

3 1 restaurant; 2 factory; 3 art gallery; 4 library; 5 supermarket; 6 hospital

4 1 BICYCLE; 2 TAXI; 3 BOAT; 4 TRAIN; 5 TRAM; 6 CAR

Reading

1 2 b; 3 d; 4 a; 5 f; 6 i; 7 h; 8 e; 9 g

2 1 false; 2 true; 3 false; 4 true; 5 true; 6 true; 7 false; 8 false

Listening

1 1 Sarah; 2 Anton; 3 Muriel; 4 George; 5 Anton

2 1 true; 2 false; 3 false; 4 false; 5 true; 6 false; 7 false; 8 false; 9 true; 10 false

Recording

NARRATOR: George
GEORGE: I live in a small cottage in the country with my wife and my mother-in-law. The great thing is my kitchen. I've got a big kitchen with a lovely view of the garden. We haven't got any children but we have got three cats.

NARRATOR: Sarah
SARAH: I live in an apartment in the city centre with my husband and two daughters. It's not very big but it has two bedrooms, a bathroom, a small kitchen, and a living room. We haven't got a garden but we've got a small terrace.

NARRATOR: Anton
ANTON: I live in a small house near the beach with my girlfriend. I love my house. It's so quiet. And I can swim in the sea every morning before I go to work.

NARRATOR: Muriel
MURIEL: My sister and I live in a house next to a big river. It's a very big house there are four bedrooms, two bathrooms, a living room, a dining room, a kitchen, a big hall and an enormous garden with lots of trees and a small lake. We even have a boat and I often go sailing along the river. It's lovely and quiet. I don't like living in noisy cities. That's why I moved to this house.

Writing

Ss own answers.

Key

TEST 3
Grammar

1 1 ours; 2 ones; 3 yours; 4 one; 5 them; 6 theirs

2 1 took; 2 had; 3 went; 4 gave; 5 told; 6 spent

3 1 I often wear a suit. 2 He sometimes goes to the gym. 3 She always drives to work. 4 It is often cold in Finland. 5 I never work at weekends. 6 They hardly ever go to the cinema.

4 1 She is looking for her book. 2 They are sleeping in the bedroom. 3 He isn't driving carefully. 4 Matthew is singing on the bath. 5 I am reading an interesting book. 6 Gloria is speaking on the phone.

5 1 drinks; 2 are doing/'re doing; 3 speak; 4 wears; 5 is wearing/'s wearing; 6 is raining/'s raining; 7 drive; 8 is playing/'s playing

6 Possible answers: 1 Italian food is better than English food. 2 Basketball is more exciting than tennis. 3 A car is faster than a bicycle. 4 Chinese is more difficult than English. 5 New York is bigger than my city. 6 Travelling by plane is more expensive than travelling by train.

7 1 b; 2 c; 3 b; 4 c; 5 a; 6 b

8 1 to; 2 Do; 3 playing; 4 prefer; 5 than; 6 going

Pronunciation

1

/θ/	/ð/
bathroom	brother
three	this
third	those
thirteen	there

2 1 prefer; 2 returned; 3 snowing; 4 exciting; 5 opera; 6 police; 7 carefully; 8 newspaper; 9 pullover; 10 sometimes 8 newspaper; 11 cartoon; 12 romantic

Vocabulary

1 1/8 the first of August; 8/5 the eighth of May; 12/10 the twelfth of October; 5/2 the fifth of February; 4/1 the fourth of January; 25/12 the twenty fifth of December; 15/6 the fifteenth of June; 23/4 the twenty-third of April

2 1 up; 2 in; 3 back; 4 at; 5 up; 6 together

3 Clothes: BELT, JACKET, SKIRT, TROUSERS, DRESS.
Weather: SUNNY, SNOWING, HOT, CLOUDY, FOGGY.

4

Types of film	Painting and art	Literature
horror	sculpture	novels
musical	impressionist	plays
cartoon	abstract	poetry

Reading

2 1 false; 2 true; 3 false; 4 false; 5 false; 6 false; 7 true; 8 true; 9 true; 10 false; 11 true; 12 true; 13 true; 14 false; 15 false; 16 true

3 1 Michelangelo; 2 Hemingway; 3 Van Gogh; 4 Van Gogh

Listening

1 1 true; 2 false; 3 false; 4 true; 5 false; 6 false; 7 false; 8 true; 9 false; 10 false

2 1 (about) once or twice a month; 2 blue; 3 (two words from:) nice, shy, friendly; 4 next week; 5 beautiful, green

Recording

My best friend is called John. He's about 45, and he's quite tall. He's bald and he's got brown eyes. In the past we played football together every week, but we're both a bit old for that now. But we still meet about once or twice a month and go out for a meal.

OK, let me tell you about my friend, Lucy. She studies with me at university. She's very pretty and slim and she's got …. erm…. fair hair and blue eyes – yes, that's right. She wears glasses. What else? Well, she's my best friend so of course I think she's nice. She's quite shy. But when you get to know her she's very friendly.

My friend David is 28 years old. Actually, it's his birthday next week. I met him at school. Now he works as a manager in a supermarket. He's got dark hair and he's tall. He's a bit fat, and he's got a big black beard. I think he's very handsome. He's a really nice man too, and he's always ready to help you when you have a problem.

My friend Lisa is 26 years old and she's a doctor. Erm … she's very slim. She's not very tall, and she's got long dark hair and beautiful green eyes. The last time I saw her was about three months ago, because she lives in Turkey. I really miss her.

Writing

Ss own answers.

TEST 4

Grammar

1 1 ever; 2 Has; 3 went; 4 been; 5 to; 6 I've

2 1 've/have had; 2 've/have seen; 3 've/have spent; 4 's/has arrived; 5 's/has played; 6 's/have been

3 1 can't; 2 don't have to; 3 can't; 4 can; 5 have to; 6 don't have to

4 1 When; 2 How many; 3 What; 4 Where; 5 How much; 6 How long

5 1 Peter and Mary are having dinner tomorrow evening. 2 I'm starting the course next month. 3 The president is opening the new museum on Sunday. 4 We are going to Paris in December. 5 What are you doing next weekend? 6 I'm going to the cinema with some/my friends on Saturday evening.

6 Possible answers: 1 I'm going to have a holiday in August. 2 I'm going to go to the beach with my parents. 3 I'm going to have cereal. 4 I'm going to go home. 5 I'm going to go home by car. 6 I'm going to have dinner. 7 I'm not going to do anything special. 8 Yes, I am. I'm going to buy a CD for my sister.

7 Possible answers: 1 Carrie went to the airport to meet her friends. 2 We're going to the stadium to watch a football match. 3 I'm studying English to get a good job. 4 Paula went to Egypt to see the Pyramids. 5 Tomorrow I'm going to the hospital to visit my grandfather. 6 Next year my daughter is going to university to study Psychology.

8 1 going; 2 to see/to watch; 3 playing ; 4 to speak/to learn/to study; 5 to have; 6 listening

Pronunciation

1

/iː/	/ɪ/
sleep	swim
these	this
green	slim
beach	visit

2 1 <u>Ch</u>emistry; 2 <u>H</u>istory; 3 poly<u>tech</u>nic; 4 <u>G</u>eography; 5 Mathe<u>mat</u>ics; 6 uni<u>ver</u>sity

3 1 You have to wait at the <u>light</u>. 2 I don't <u>like</u> to be late. 3 I often <u>drive</u> to the lake. 4 The blue one is <u>mine</u>. 5 It's faster to <u>fly</u> to Spain. 6 The chocolate cake is <u>nice</u>.

Vocabulary

1 1 suburbs; 2 rush; 3 return; 4 departure; 5 luxurious; 6 sightseeing

2 Possible answers: Subjects: Chemistry, Geography, History, Mathematics, Science, Languages. Places: kindergarten, secondary school, polytechnic, university. People: tutor, pupil, trainer, trainee, student.

3 1 BRIDGE; 2 CANYON; 3 MOUNTAIN; 4 RIVER; 5 HILLS; 6 COAST; 7 TUNNEL; 8 SEA

4 1 c; 2 a; 3 c; 4 b

Reading

2 1 true; 2 false; 3 true; 4 true; 5 true; 6 true; 7 false; 8 false; 9 true; 10 false; 11 false; 12 false

3 1 Money exchange, souvenirs and a safe; 2 The Castle; 3 At the swimming pool, or with a sauna, massage, or a visit to the solarium; 4 Tram and underground (or metro); 5 The Axa; 6 The Union; 7 The Axa; 8 The Axa

Listening

(points per answer in brackets. Total 20 points)

1 Yes (1); 2 Yes (1); 3 Because it was very traditional (1), she had to wear a uniform (1), and there were a lot of rules. (1); 4 Biology (1) and Chemistry (1); 5 Manchester University (1); 6 Chemistry (1); 7 A very nice lecturer (1); 8 He suggested she change to a different course. (2); 9 Information Technology (1); 10 part-time (1); 11 Italian (1) and German (1); 12 Russian (1); 13 It's an on-line course. (1); 14 Because it's hard to practise speaking. (2)

Recording

I = Interviewer
M = Martina

I: So, Martina, first of all, tell me something about your education.
M: Well, of course I went to primary school and secondary school. I really loved primary school. The teachers were fantastic and we all played a lot but at the same time we learnt a lot. When I went to secondary school it was completely different. My secondary school was very traditional. We had to wear a uniform, a blue skirt and jacket, and there were lots of rules. I didn't like it at all.
I: What were your favourite subjects at school?
M: Well, I always liked science, so I suppose my favourite subjects were Biology and Chemistry.
I: When you left school, what did you do?
M: I went to Manchester University to study Chemistry but I didn't enjoy it. Luckily I had a very nice lecturer called David and he helped me a lot. He suggested a different course, so after the end of the first year I started to study Information Technology. That was basically all about computers. And I enjoyed that a lot more.
I: Have you studied any courses since university?
M: Yes, well a couple of years ago I did a part-time course in new technologies. That was for work really. And I love languages so in the last few years I have studied Italian, German and I've just started a distance-learning course in Russian. It's difficult because you don't have normal classes. It's all on the Internet and it's hard to practise speaking. I don't really enjoy it but there are no places to study Russian in my town.

Writing

Ss own answers.

Pearson Education Limited
Edinburgh Gate, Harlow
Essex, CM20 2JE, England
and Associated Companies throughout the world

www.longman.com

© Pearson Education 2005

All rights reserved: no part of this publication may be reproduced, stored in a retrieval system, or transmitted in any form or by any means, electronic, mechanical, photocopying, recording or otherwise without the prior permission of the copyright holders.

The right of Fiona Gallagher, Robert Armitage, Robert Hastings and Rawdon Wyatt to be identified as authors of this work has been asserted by them in accordance with the Copyright, Designs and Patents Act 1988.

First published 2005

Designed by pentacor**big**

Illustrated by J. Luis Pardo, Pablo Torrecilla, and Pablo Velarde.

Set in Meta Plus Book 9.5pt
Printed in the UK by Ashford Colour Press Ltd.

ISBN 0582 84179 8